Freezer Cookbook

Marika Hanbury Tenison was born i[...] been interested in cooking and experimenting with recipes [...] as long as she can remember. She never had a domestic science training but learnt the hard way, by trial and error, and is still learning.

Married to the explorer and farmer Robin Hanbury Tenison, she now travels with him to little-known areas of the world. They have two children and live in a fourteenth-century farmhouse high up on Bodmin Moor. She finds her deep freeze invaluable as the family often entertain up to twenty people at weekends. She says, 'Without it, my food bills would soar and I would spend my entire time in the kitchen instead of being able to be with my family and friends.'

She has written twenty-eight cookery books including *Eat Well and Be Slim*, *Soups and Hors d'Oeuvres* and *Left Over for Tomorrow*. She has also written two travel books and is cookery editor for the *Sunday Telegraph*.

Other cookery books available in Pan

Batia Asher and Carole Robson	**Canny Cooking**
Kathy Barnes	**The Infra-Red Cook Book**
Mrs Beeton	**All About Cookery**
Carol Bowen	**The Microwave Cook Book**
Kathleen Broughton	**Pressure Cooking Day by Day**
Lousene Rousseau Brunner	**New Casserole Treasury**
Savitri Chowdhary	**Indian Cooking**
Huguette Couffignal	**The People's Cookbook**
Gail Duff	**Fresh All The Year** **Gail Duff's Vegetarian Cookbook**
Gay Firth and Jane Donald	**What's for Lunch, Mum?**
Theodora Fitzgibbon	**Crockery Pot Cooking** **A Taste of . . . series**
Michel Guérard	**Michel Guérard's Cuisine Minceur**
Anthony and Araminta Hippisley Coxe	**The Book of the Sausage**
Robin Howe	**Soups**
Rosemary Hume and Muriel Downes	**The Cordon Bleu Book of Jams, Preserves and Pickles**
Patricia Jacobs	**The Best Bread Book**
Enrica and Vernon Jarratt	**The Complete Book of Pasta**
Mary Laver and Margaret Smith	**Diet for Life**
Kenneth Lo	**Cheap Chow** **Quick and Easy Chinese Cooking**
Claire Loewenfeld and Philippa Back	**Herbs for Health and Cookery**
edited by R. J. Minney	**The George Bernard Shaw Vegetarian Cook Book**
edited by Bee Nilson	**The WI Diamond Jubilee Cookbook**
Elisabeth Orsini	**The Book of Pies**
Marguerite Patten	**Learning to Cook**
Jennie Reekie	**Traditional French Cooking**
Gwen Robyns	**The Potato Cookbook**
Evelyn Rose	**The Complete International Jewish Cookbook**
Rita G. Springer	**Caribbean Cookbook**
Constance Spry and Rosemary Hume	**The Constance Spry Cookery Book**
Katie Stewart	**The Shortcut Cookbook** **The Times Cookery Book** **The Times Calendar Cookbook**
Paula Wolfert	**Mediterranean Cooking**

Marika Hanbury Tenison's

Freezer Cookbook

Pan Original
Pan Books London and Sydney

First published 1976 as *Deep-Freeze Sense* by Pan Books Ltd,
Cavaye Place, London SW10 9PG
Revised and updated 1981

ISBN 0 330 26622 5
Printed and bound in Great Britain by
Richard Clay (The Chaucer Press) Ltd, Bungay, Suffolk

for Lucy, with my love
and to Winefride Jackson with thanks
for all her encouragement

Contents

Part 2

Acknowledgements

My thanks and acknowledgements go to the following, for whose help and cooperation I am grateful:

Adrienne Yelland, who helped to check and type the recipes

Julie and Vee, who helped to cook the food and clear up afterwards

Geoff, who grows the fruit and vegetables I freeze

Beekay Bauknecht Freezers

Suttons Seeds of Reading

Divertimenti of 68 Marylebone Lane, London W1

The Electricity Council, Trafalgar Buildings, 1 Charing Cross, London SW1A 2DS

Lakeland Plastics (Windermere) Ltd

Measurements and metrication

The weights and measures used throughout this book are based on British Imperial standards and the nearest workable metric units to keep the recipes in the right proportions.

International measures

Measure	UK	Australia	New Zealand	Canada
1 pint	20 fl oz	20 fl oz	20 fl oz	20 fl oz
1 cup	10 fl oz	8 fl oz	8 fl oz	8 fl oz
1 tablespoon	$\frac{5}{8}$ fl oz	$\frac{1}{2}$ fl oz	$\frac{1}{2}$ fl oz	$\frac{1}{2}$ fl oz
1 dessertspoon	$\frac{2}{5}$ fl oz	no official measure		
1 teaspoon	$\frac{1}{5}$ fl oz	$\frac{1}{8}$ fl oz	$\frac{1}{6}$ fl oz	$\frac{1}{6}$ fl oz

Conversion of fluid ounces to metric

4 tablespoons (2$\frac{1}{2}$ fl oz) = 70 ml (0·7 dl)
2 tablespoons (1$\frac{1}{4}$ fl oz) = 35 ml
1 tablespoon ($\frac{5}{8}$ fl oz) = 18 ml
1 dessertspoon ($\frac{2}{5}$ fl oz) = 12 ml
1 teaspoon ($\frac{1}{5}$ fl oz) = 6 ml
(all the above metric equivalents are approximate)

Equivalents

1 UK (old BST standard) cup equals 1$\frac{1}{4}$ cups in Commonwealth countries
4 UK tablespoons equal 5 Commonwealth tablespoons
5 UK teaspoons equal 6 New Zealand or 6 Canadian or 8 Australian teaspoons
1 UK dessertspoon equals $\frac{2}{3}$ UK tablespoon or 2 UK teaspoons

In British cookery books, a gill is usually 5 fl oz (¼ pint), but in a few localities in the UK it can mean 10 fl oz (½ pint)

Other non-standard measures include:
Breakfast cup = approx 10 fl oz
Tea cup = 5 fl oz
Coffee cup = 3 fl oz

Deep-freeze sizes

The capacity of a deep freeze is now measured in cubic feet and the metric equivalent given in litres. Hence a 4·8-cubic-foot deep freeze is also labelled as having a 136-litre capacity. For easy reference, the measurements relating to freezers in this book have been left in cubic feet.

Foreword

The deep freeze has become an accepted feature in the home of the 1980s. No longer is it a converted ice-cream container in which one hung upside down trying to find an unidentified package covered in ice; now it has become an extension of the refrigerator and a piece of kitchen equipment which, like the food mixer or electric liquidizer, is part and parcel of the 1980s. These days freezers come in all shapes and sizes and many of them are conveniently tucked on top of the conventional refrigerator. There are ways and methods of using the freezer that will lead to success and give satisfactory results and yet other approaches that can lead to disaster and disappointment.

Treated properly, it can be one of the most useful, time-saving and economical pieces of equipment in the modern kitchen. When I had my first deep freeze they were the exception and not considered essential as they are now. Since then I have learnt to use my freezer to its best advantage, not to take liberties with it, and to gear my cooking to make the most of its facility for saving time, money and waste, as well as its function as an extension to my larder, my refrigerator and my vegetable storage space. It serves me well and I certainly wouldn't be without it. In this book I wanted to try and get across all those valuable lessons I have learnt. I have also tried to overcome the still widespread notion that anything you *throw* into the freezer will come out better or at least as good as when you put it in, and to make people wary of the idea that by buying vast quantities of frozen convenience foods in bulk or a whole cow or pig you can save money and do right by your family. Also common, in my view, is the mistaken idea that dishes can be completely pre-cooked, frozen, and can then emerge exactly as they were first made to be reheated and served in perfect condition – there are, in fact, few dishes which respond well to this process and those that do have to be produced, cooked and frozen very carefully to ensure good results.

After years of experience I have increasingly become an advocate of using the freezer as a kind of holding bank, so that you have ingredients ready-prepared for recipes but the end result is a quick put-together of frozen and fresh ingredients, resulting in a fresh-tasting dish which may have taken only a short time to produce but which will have the authentic taste of home cooking.

I have also tried to produce sensible ideas on what is and what is not worth while buying in bulk for the average family. If you buy a pig and freeze it you will find, within quite a short time, that the family get bored with eating pork and that there is much more of the pig than you thought that is only suitable for stewing, boiling or mincing for sausage meat. Nothing can be *improved* by deep-freezing, a lot of things have a far shorter freezer-life than people realize, and unless the ingredients for the freezer are processed, wrapped, labelled and frozen properly they won't begin to live up to expectations. These are the processes that I hope to make clear in this new edition, that I hope to clarify in order to make your kitchen life less arduous, less boring and much more successful. I hope to offer a comprehensive guide to all aspects of successful freezing, whether you own a small- or large-capacity freezer, whether you have a kitchen garden or allotment and have excess vegetables, or whether you live in a city house or apartment and can buy vegetables in bulk from a greengrocer or market.

I shall point out all the pitfalls of freezing so that mistakes and disappointments (which may be expensive) are cut to a minimum and I hope to prove that by following my rules for using your deep freeze to its fullest advantage you can save time and expense. Both domestic and commercial freezing have taken enormous steps forward in the last few years and although the principles still remain the same as in the last edition of this book, there are plenty of new ideas on buying, packaging and preparation of produce for freezing which must now be added.

Marika Hanbury Tenison
Maidenwell
January 1981

Part 1

A background to deep-freezing

Chilling food is not just a science of the twentieth century. Frozen mammoth meat, for instance, has been dug up after centuries and been found to be perfectly edible, and there is no reason to suppose that primitive people living near frozen wastes did not make use of this natural larder. It isn't only the Americans who like their drinks clinking with ice; Nero, too, used to insist on it and kept stores of ice in deep cellars below his palace. The Romans also discovered that they could transport Colchester oysters to Italy in a perfect state by packing them in layers of ice and snow.

In Elizabethan times, almost every great house had its ice-house, an underground chamber where ice would keep almost right through the summer months. In winter, blocks were cut from frozen ponds or lakes; they were packed neatly around the walls of the circular ice-house and then the room was used for keeping meat, poultry and game fresh for some considerable time. In some cases, instead of underground chambers, deep pits were cut in the ground and lined with bricks; then, when the ice had been packed in, they were covered with thick layers of turf to give insulation. At that time, too, there were experiments going a step further into the actual preservation of food by freezing: for example, Sir Francis Bacon packed chickens in snow to try and find how long they would keep fresh.

In the mid-nineteenth century, experiments in freezing food began seriously. A big breakthrough in the fishing industry occurred when it was discovered that long-distance trawlers could keep their catch fresh by taking quantities of ice along with them on their expeditions. In 1880 the first refrigerated ship brought over a cargo of frozen beef from Australia to England. Clarence Birdseye, founder of the now immense frozen-food company, was one of the real pioneers of deep-freezing. It was he who discovered the advantages of quick-freezing and he developed a system of freezing packs of food between refrigerated plates to give the maximum, evenly spread freezing-power.

Experiments are still going on. Now most commercial vegetables are 'free-flowing'–individually frozen so that they do not stick in a lump, making it impossible to extract small amounts from large packs. Free-flow freezing is now being done by shooting the vegetables along a tunnel freezer where they bounce on a cushion of freezing air. Research has found that you, the purchaser, may be put off by packs of small cuts of meat, such as chops or steaks, that stick together, so most quality freezing companies now wrap such cuts individually, making it possible to use a small number at a time.

Shopping patterns, too, have changed as people become aware of the advantages offered by 'bulk' freezing buys which enable them to go to a freezer-market and buy frozen food in quantity at a budget price. The rising price of food has forced one to look more and more closely at the family budget and since the deep freeze can be more than just a convenience, many people are now buying produce when it is cheap in order to freeze it for use at a later date. Deep-freeze manufacturers are on our side; the early ice-cream type of cold-storage unit has been replaced first by cabinet freezers, and now by upright freezers and freezer cabinets attached to refrigerators which can be used for the storage of frozen food. Most deep freezes now have a 'quick-freezing unit' for initial speedy freezing, and many of the more expensive models also have a self-defrosting element.

One of the major problems of deep-freezing produce is the formation of ice crystals in the fibres of the food to be frozen. This crystallization takes place at between 31°F/−0·5°C and 24°F/−4°C, so that the faster food is frozen the better. Once produce has reached a temperature of 0°F/−18°C or below, crystals can no longer form, so it is essential that frozen food is brought down to this level and then stored below it. Once crystals have formed, although the food will not be damaged in any way from a health point of view (and in the case of meat will in fact be more tender), they tend to break up the fibres, causing a loss of juice and a considerable deterioration in quality when the food is brought to the table. A lot of research is being done on the fast-freezing of food, especially of large cuts of boned meat (bone through the centre of a joint acts as a good conductor of cold and helps to speed the process), but there are still problems to overcome.

Food, especially meat, can in theory be kept frozen for an indefinite period – like the mammoth meat. This, however, only works when it is frozen at an exceptionally low temperature. Home freezers are not equipped for this kind of intense low freezing and at the temperatures we depend on, the stored food has limited freezer-life. Although the guidelines usually given for this storage-life tend to be on the cautious side, the food does begin to deteriorate after that time and it becomes susceptible to rancidity, freezer burn (dehydration) and lack of flavour.

Advantages

Can you imagine what life in the kitchen would be like without hot water, or what it must have been like to cook on wood fires before the days of electricity and gas? These comforts are now considered an essential part of our everyday lives, and so too, I believe, is the deep freeze.

Britain, more than almost any other country, produces an astonishing wealth of all-the-year-round fresh food so that it is always perfectly possible to eat fresh produce. Even so there are the rather leaner winter months, while everything we grow has a season where it reaches the peak of its cheapness and availability. Our ancestors coped with this problem by curing, salting, bottling and, finally, canning food. Drying and, more recently, freeze-drying, have had their moments, but all these methods for prolonging the storage-life of food have one outstanding disadvantage – they change, in some degree, the basic nature of the food. Undoubtedly deep-freezing is by far the most successful way of preserving food ever to be discovered; it arrests the quality of food at the moment when it is frozen and, provided the freezing and thawing processes are correctly carried out, it is possible to enjoy frozen food that is as fresh and delicious as the day it was put into the deep freeze.

Don't, however, forget all the practices of old-fashioned husbandry; salting and curing give many cheaper cuts of meat a real lift, and deep-freezing cuts that have been treated in this way adds variety to the produce you store in your freezer.

A deep freeze is a convenience in the home, especially if one has a family and entertains. It is a boon to the present-day wife who goes out to work but also has to provide her family with nourishing meals. Used properly, the deep freeze can help cut down on shopping time, enabling one to shop once a week or even once a month instead of every day; a large store of produce is available and one can plan ahead to cook meals in bulk when time is not at a premium.

Sensible use of the deep freeze can also help to cut the cost of running a home. The initial price of the machine and its running costs obviously have to be taken into consideration, but the saving on petrol consumption, buying in bulk from freezer-centres or when commodities are at their cheapest, and the invaluable use that can be made of all leftovers can easily sway the balance – making the deep freeze a first-rate budget-beater.

For those interested in cuisine, too, the deep freeze can add a new dimension to their repertoire. For one thing, you have a whole wealth of stored goods from which to choose; you also have a ready-made storeroom for exotic dishes that can be made in season and eaten out of season, and you can easily experiment with exciting and often complicated dishes with the minimum of labour. I make large batches of pancakes, for instance, in one session, then freeze them and have at my fingertips ready-made pancakes which take little time to defrost and which can be filled with an infinite variety of exciting ingredients.

Pitfalls

It is not enough just to own a deep freeze. You have to understand it and treat it with respect. For many deep-freeze buyers, entering a whole new field of culinary art and disciplines can be alarming. It shouldn't be; the process is simple and pitfalls can usually be avoided by straight common sense.

The main problems likely to crop up in the day-to-day running of a household freezer are:

Deterioration of food Usually caused by the freezer's being kept at an inadequately low temperature, or by food's being stored for too long a period.

Deterioration of texture and flavour Nine times out of ten this is due to inadequate packaging. Everything stored in the deep freeze has to be well wrapped with all air excluded. Packages or containers that are not properly sealed, have holes, or enable air to get to the produce in any way, will result in the food's deteriorating after a short length of time. The deterioration may be only infinitesimal, but nevertheless a discerning gourmet will be able to tell the difference.

Odours or change of flavour Some things have an extra-strong smell and if they are not very carefully wrapped, this odour will spread to other items, especially if their wrapping is pierced or damaged in any way. Garlic is a typical example of this. In fact, most strong-smelling herbs and spices should be added to food *after* it has been thawed whenever possible, as dishes containing garlic do tend to develop an 'off' flavour if they are stored in the freezer for too long.

Some smells may inhabit the deep freeze. If the sides of the freezer are heavily frosted they will capture these odours and sometimes intensify them. All freezers should be regularly defrosted to avoid this.

Inadequate labelling (a common fault of the new freezer-owner) When you freeze something (a joint of beef, for example), it *looks* like a joint of beef and you can usually see clearly through the plastic wrapping what it is. Leave it in the freezer for a week or two, however, and you may as well have a chocolate cake inside the package. Ice crystals will have formed on the inside of the bag, and without actually opening the package it will be impossible to discover exactly what is there.

Wildcat buying for the freezer One might think this was something anyone experienced would automatically avoid, yet it happens to the best of us. Buying for the freezer can be rather like going to the sales and it is easy to be led into overbuying of commodities which seem like a fantastic saving at the time, but which become a liability even after a short period. Freezer-markets and butchers who sell meat in bulk have contributed to this particular problem in a big way, and even the veterans are not immune to it.

Some time ago I was offered a side of beef for an average of 30p per pound all over. Whoopee! I thought; fillet and rump steak for 30p a pound! What I hadn't taken into consideration was that the animal was a young one and therefore had only a small proportion of those luxury cuts; that by the time much of the bone had been cut out, I was actually paying around 40p for the meat itself; that a high percentage of the cuts were of the slow-cooking, cheaper variety (a good many of which I had never seen before and wasn't sure I wanted to see again) and that we were going to be living on beef (although it was a small bullock) for an awfully long time.

The same thing can happen in the freezer-market. Buying something like fish-fingers in bulk may seem like an economy, especially if they are on special offer, but beware of unknown brand-names, or packs that bear no brand-name at all. Their quality can be poor and you may well be saddled with a second-rate product that you will throw away in the end, or have to spend time masking with complicated and expensive sauces.

Even if you have your own garden and grow your own produce for freezing, you can still make mistakes. Early in my freezing days my husband impressed on me that he loved broad beans, picked when they were still small and crisp. Being one of those old-fashioned housewives who believe in quaint frills like pampering one's man and 'the best way' etc . . . I grew, podded and froze masses of small broad beans, staining my hands to the wrists with brown juice. After a month of having broad beans at almost every meal, he announced that he never wanted to see them again, and I was left with the vegetable compartment of my freezer packed with a commodity no one wanted.

Unbalanced stocking of the deep freeze If you have only a very small freezer, then you might well wish to use it only for storing luxuries you might otherwise not be able to afford. If, on the other hand, you have a large household and a big freezer and wish to take advantage of it in order to save on housekeeping bills, you should spread the load carefully so that you cover a comprehensive range of foods which will vary from luxury to mundane items.

Inefficient running of the deep freeze This is the age of fuel shortages and, since your deep freeze runs on electricity, you will want to do everything you can to make it run as economically as possible. If you find your freezer is using up more electricity than it should do, then the cause is probably one of the following: (a) The freezer is in a warm situation and therefore having to use extra power to keep it to the required temperature. (b) The freezer needs defrosting; a thick layer of ice on the inside of the freezer will result in the motor having to work overtime. (c) The freezer is understocked. Ideally the freezer should be kept at least three-quarters full to ensure maximum efficiency.

Deterioration of food after it has been thawed (a) All food has bacteria in it. The process of freezing arrests the growth of bacteria but it doesn't completely kill them. If dirt and germs are allowed to get near the food when it is being prepared for freezing, they will still be there when the product is thawed and the bacteria will get to work again – fast. Because the process of freezing does, to some extent, break up the fibres, food is more susceptible to the development of bacteria after it has been thawed. It is therefore essential that once food is removed from the freezer, it should be eaten as soon as possible. (b) The food was not of the highest quality in the first place. The freezing process can never *improve* food, but at best merely suspends it in the condition it is in prior to being frozen.

Buying a deep freeze

I know countless deep-freeze owners who have found that the freezer they first chose turned out to be inadequate for their requirements, especially in the autumn when the freezer is packed with fruit and vegetables. I have found this myself. The more I learn about freezing, the more space I require. There is therefore a very valid argument for choosing one that is bigger than you imagine you will need, although obviously this argument can be carried too far. One friend of mine jumped in with both feet and bought a 22-cubic-foot freezer as her first experiment. As there were only her and her husband in the family, and they did not do a great deal of entertaining, she soon found the freezer more of a liability than an asset; because it was nearly empty it used up a fair amount of electricity, and the sight of a few beefburgers and joints of meat in that vast space was depressing.

But before you decide the ideal size of freezer you require, you also need to find a home for it. It is often recommended that large freezers can be kept in an outhouse. I do this myself, but cannot honestly say it is the ideal situation. Mine is in our garage, just too far away for us to hear the emergency buzzer which means that if anything should go wrong, it might not be discovered for some time. As I use my freezer as an extended storeroom, keeping in it invaluable bits and pieces like grated lemon peel, fresh herbs and chopped green or red peppers, having to go outside the house whenever I need a pinch of this or that can be quite a problem, particularly with our joyous Cornish climate and the mists that swirl around Bodmin Moor in the winter.

The ideal situation for your freezer is in a cool scullery or larder next to the kitchen where it will be close at hand and use a minimum of electricity. Sadly, they don't make many houses that way any more; but at least they do now make a wide range of freezers so that you can usually find one to fit the position you have in mind.

When siting your freezer, remember that the cooler the situation, the cheaper it will be to run the machine; one in a warm kitchen, for instance, can cost a substantial amount more in running costs.

Commercial chest freezers are cheaper than the upright models, cubic foot for cubic foot, and they tend to be cheaper to run. Although chest freezers take up more ground space than the upright models, their capacity is more flexible and therefore more suitable for storing bulky, irregular packages of meat, poultry, etc.

Chest freezers of more than 12-cubic-foot capacity are most common in British households, although the number of small, upright freezers for flat-owners is steadily increasing. A 14-cubic-foot capacity freezer seems to be the most popular size for an average family. Now there are also slim models and freezers that partner a household refrigerator. Don't buy the first model you see. Most firms that make refrigerators make deep freezes and although the basic style is the same, they all vary in one way or another. Often, when space is at a premium, an inch or two can make all the difference.

Choose a freezer to fit the most suitable space you have available for it, that looks attractive in its surroundings, and that is slightly larger than you expect to be requiring. Bear in mind the use you are planning to make of it so that you will be able to count on a capacity large enough to take meat bought wholesale, home-grown produce if you have it and a quantity of precooked dishes for everyday or entertainment consumption as well as a basic store of fruit, vegetables, fish, poultry and bread.

Ensure that you have a model with a quick-freezing compartment or a switch for quick-freezing, and beware of second-hand models unless you know their history. The average freezer has a fifteen-year lifespan at least, provided that it is treated with respect. After this time the motor tends to wear out, trouble starts and it is usually advisable to buy a new freezer rather than to try to patch up the old one, especially as manufacturers are still improving on the design and efficiency of their machines. Although I think it can be dangerous to buy a second-hand model, it is worth shopping around for a shop-soiled or demonstration machine that is as good as new but may be sold for a greatly reduced price.

If you are exchanging an old machine for a new one, it is again worth sounding out more than one firm to see what trade-in price they will offer you. The price you might hope for when selling a second-hand deep freeze is dependent on the fifteen-year lifespan, and often it is more economical to advertise in a local newspaper than to take a trade-in price for it.

Locks are not a standard feature on all household freezers, but if you plan to keep yours in an outhouse or garage it might be as well to choose a model that can be locked when necessary. An automatic light on the inside of a freezer is an advantage, especially if the freezer is to be kept in a badly lit place.

Also check that the model you buy has a battery warning system which will set off a buzzer when the motor fails to run for one reason or another. Most models now have either a light or a sound warning system incorporated into the machine and I would strongly recommend the second, as a light may easily go unnoticed. A battery warning system can be added to a machine if one is not already installed as part of the working mechanism.

All deep freezes should be defrosted when necessary. A chest freezer will probably need to be defrosted about twice a year; an upright model will need more frequent defrosting, probably about four times a year.

Some freezers now have automatic defrosting systems and although these are obviously desirable, the advantage, at the moment, is reflected in the price of the machine. Automatic defrosting is, however, becoming a very much more common feature of deep freezes.

In Cornwall I have both a chest and an upright deep freeze and despite the initial extra price of the machine and the slightly higher running costs, I prefer the upright model. Storage is infinitely easier; it is much easier pulling out a basket from a shelf than leaning into the depths of a heavily stocked chest freezer, and although defrosting has to take place more often than in a chest freezer, it can be done quite quickly. One disadvantage is losing the working top of a chest model which can be useful if space is short, but as my chest freezer is kept in the garage, this doesn't really comc into the pros and cons of my argument.

Don't be confused by refrigerators that have an ice-making compartment on top of them with a star rating for storing frozen food. These compartments are not at a low enough temperature for the successful freezing of fresh produce. They can only be used for the storage of ready-frozen goods as indicated on the outside of most commercially frozen products.

Beware, too, of deep-freeze offers that include free frozen food with the purchase. They might sound like a good deal, but I know people who have been landed with a whole load of free food which was of such a low standard it was almost worthless.

Another danger zone is in buying a machine from redundant or superseded stock; you may have trouble getting repairs carried out.

Costs

A 14-cubic-foot capacity freezer will cost in the region of £180. It will have a storage capacity of about 11 kg (24 lb) per cubic foot – that is, 150 kg (336 lb) of food (think of 1-kg [2·2-lb] sugar bags) – and will use about 14 units of electricity a week if it is kept in a cool place – about 60p a week at the moment.

An upright model of the same capacity should cost around

£270, have the same storage capacity and cost about an extra 13p a week to run.

Despite the fact that these figures may look high on paper, you must remember that with efficient use of your deep freeze, it is possible to save around 10 per cent on your family food bills a year.

Insurance

Some companies will include a year's insurance in the price of a new deep freeze, or your own household policy may be increased to cover the contents of your freezer (this costs in the region of £6 per annum for freezer contents to the value of £250). Although all new freezers are guaranteed for a year following their purchase, you might consider taking out a maintenance contract after the guarantee has expired and this can usually be arranged through the retailer from whom you purchased the freezer.

Touching wood, I can say that in twenty-five years, although I have had scares, I have never had a deep freeze break down completely on me – but 'better safe than sorry', as they say.

Care and maintenance

Machinery of all kinds is sensitive: if it isn't properly maintained and looked after it cannot be expected to work properly. The deep freeze is no exception.

Keep the outside of the deep freeze clean by wiping it down with a soft, damp cloth and a liquid detergent. Do not use harsh abrasives or powders which might scratch the surface. Cover the working top of a chest freezer with stick-on vinyl to protect it from marks.

Check the battery warning system regularly to make sure the system is working and the batteries do not need replacing.

Do spot-checks with a freezer thermometer to make sure the temperature of your freezer is being kept at a low enough level for efficient freezing or storage (0°F/−18°C).

For top performance and minimum electricity bills a deep freeze should be kept three-quarters full whenever possible. In hot weather deep freezes that are kept in an outhouse should be covered with a blanket to give extra insulation. Ensure the door or lid of the freezer is kept tight shut at all times.

Defrosting Defrosting should be carried out when the freezer develops a slight smell inside or when there is frosting of 3 mm ($\frac{1}{8}$ in) or more over the inside walls of the freezer.

Have plenty of newspaper or freezer sacks and a blanket handy. Switch off the freezer at the mains, remove the frozen food, wrap it in newspapers or heavy-duty paper sacks and cover it with a blanket. Take out any removable baskets or partitions and place a bowl of very hot water in the freezer to speed up the defrosting process. Scrape off the ice with the plastic tool usually supplied with a new freezer, or with a wooden spatula – never use a metal instrument as this will damage the inside walls. Scoop or brush the ice and water into a plastic dustpan and mop up any water with a clean cloth or tea towel.

The frozen water from the inside of your deep freeze is distilled and can be used for filling a steam iron or the battery of a car.

Cleaning the inside of your deep freeze

Having removed every bit of ice and melted water, you must then wipe down the walls of the freezer to remove any trace of odour. The best way to do this is to wipe the inside with a cloth wrung out in a solution of clean water and vinegar, or water with some bicarbonate of soda added to it. Finally, wipe over with a dry cloth before switching on the mains again.

Turn the regulator up to high and the quick-freezing element on for a speedy lowering of the temperature.

Check the contents of your freezer as you replace them; replace any torn wrappings and put these packages on one side for consumption in the near future. Also check the dates of home-frozen produce so that your stock can be rotated.

If at all possible, keep the deep freeze closed for the next twelve hours so that the temperature will have time to build up before normal use is resumed.

Models incorporating a fan to help cool the condenser should have their back grill removed and the fan carefully dusted to remove fluff about once every six months. After the first year I would recommend having your freezer checked annually by a mechanic.

Power cuts and failures

Above all, my advice is *don't panic*. Even if the power does go off, your food will be quite safe in your deep freeze for at least twenty-four hours and in many cases even for up to three days, provided you always keep the lid firmly shut.

If your warning buzzer goes:

1 Check the electricity in the rest of the house to see if it is just the deep freeze that has cut out. If it has:

(a) Check to see whether the fuse has blown.

(b) Call a mechanic or service representative.

2 If the warning has sounded because of a power failure or cut to the house, telephone your electricity supplier to report the failure. Either someone will be sent to repair it, or you will be given the reason for the failure and told how long it is likely to last.

If you have advance notice of a power cut, switch on the fast-freeze mechanism four hours before the cut is due and do not open the deep freeze during this time.

The fuller your freezer is at the time of a cut, the longer the food inside it will keep frozen, so fill up any space in the freezer with crumpled newspaper or freezer sacks.

Cover the top of the freezer with heavy blankets to give maximum insulation.

Once the danger is over, switch on the fast-freezer for about four hours and keep the freezer tightly closed for six hours. If you are tempted to have a quick look inside and see that everything is all right, remember that in doing so you will allow a whole lot of hot air to rush into the freezer and that could cause some damage.

If the worst does happen and the food in the freezer does thaw out, here are a few pointers that will help to lessen that particular nightmare – as long as they are carried out as soon as the food has thawed but before the bacteria have had a chance to get working again. But first try to find a friend or a freezer-centre that will take the contents before they thaw. People are usually helpful in this kind of crisis and you may well be able to avoid the disaster.

If the food does thaw:

1 All vegetables must be cooked before being refrozen.

2 All meat, poultry and fish must be cooked before being refrozen.

3 All ice-cream or puddings made with fresh cream must be thrown away.

4 All precooked dishes must be eaten within 24 hours or must be thrown away.

5 Most fruit can be refrozen, although it will have lost flavour, juice and often colour as well.

6 Breads and cakes can be refrozen without harm.

Equipment and packaging materials

Keeping track of the contents and making sure they are properly packaged are the two factors which, above all others, contribute to the art of successful freezing. Food can never be improved by being frozen, but it can deteriorate due to being kept too long or to being carelessly packaged.

Keeping track of the contents is quite simple in the upright models. Decide which shelves you are going to use for meat, poultry, fish, vegetables, fruit and precooked dishes, and always follow that pattern. In most upright freezers the contents can be listed with a Chinagraph pencil on the inside of the door.

It is less easy to keep everything in the right place in the chest freezer. Upright metal wire partitions can be bought to divide the lower half of the freezer, and metal baskets to divide the top; in the case of a large chest freezer I find it useful to provide additional compartments by using freezer sacks or plastic carrier bags to divide up the contents. Packs of the same kind of fruit or vegetables can be put inside the carriers with those that are to be used first at the top and a description of the contents marked on the outside of the bag with a Chinagraph pencil.

Successful packaging means packages which are completely sealed, free of air inside the pack and tough enough to withstand knocking about inside the freezer. Although it should be tough (sharp bones may have to be double-wrapped to prevent their piercing the outer wrappings), packing material should not be *too* thick or it will insulate the food and result in its being frozen more slowly than is desirable.

Badly packed food will frost up quickly, making it almost impossible to see what is inside a pack. On the other hand, if all the air is excluded from a package, it will hardly frost up at all, so a transparent wrapping is an advantage.

Once food is frozen it becomes as hard as cement. Every time you remove something from the freezer, especially if it is from one of the lower levels, you are knocking one hard object against another. If the packages are going to stand up to such rough treatment, the packaging material must be of tough, heavy-duty standards. Over the years I have found it does not pay to buy inexpensive plastic bags or those sold in cheap offers. In the long run you are better off buying top-quality packaging material from a wholesaler specializing in this kind of goods, material that will not puncture easily and which can be used over and over again after careful washing and drying.

Packaging materials

Buying all packaging materials from a frozen-packaging wholesaler in large quantities will save money and disappointing results in the long run.

Polythene bags These come in all shapes and sizes and in varying thicknesses. Choose good-quality bags and pick as near to the right size as you can for any individual item that is to be frozen. Special gusseted bags can be bought for poultry; these make neat parcels. A new line of plastic bags has now come out with a self-sealing grip system. Although the small ones are useful for things like herbs, they are expensive and I wouldn't like to rely on the self-seal for long periods.

Test bags for holes before washing and discard any that are punctured or torn in any way. Wash polythene bags by turning them inside out and washing in warm water and a household detergent. Rinse them well and peg them upside down on a washing line to dry.

Plastic bagging by the yard A continuous bag that is cut as required. It has the advantage of making it possible to get the bags just the size you want, but you will also need a special heat-sealing machine to seal the bags effectively, otherwise you end up with a rather clumsy cracker effect.

Boilable plastic bags Made from strong polythene: must be heat-sealed and can be used for cooking and freezing small quantities of stews, sauces, etc.

Polythene containers with snap-on lids Expensive, but with a long lifespan and useful for ice-cream, many items of precooked food, vegetables and fruits. They should be well sealed with freezer tape and after use washed carefully in warm water with a household detergent. Rinse well and dry carefully before storing. They come in a variety of sizes.

Waxed cartons and containers Cheaper than polythene, and can be washed out and used again if they are treated carefully and have not been stained during freezer storage. Good for packing liquids, fruit and vegetables. Many have self-sealing lids of one kind or another but when in doubt always give a second wrapping of a polythene bag. Hot liquids or ingredients should never be put into these containers.

Kitchen foil Not usually strong enough to withstand the rigours of one parcel banging against another, but useful to divide individual portions inside a larger pack. For short-term freezing use double layers of kitchen foil or special heavy-duty freezer foil; fold over the edges of the parcel and crimp firmly together. (*Note* Foil is such a good conductor of cold that food stored in foil bags or trays freezes more quickly. Do not store foods containing vinegar, lemon juice or acid of any kind in foil.)

Foil bags Stronger than foil by the yard and useful for freezing home-grown vegetables and fruits that have been free-frozen before packing. Heavy-duty bags for putting straight from the freezer into boiling water are now available.

Aluminium foil trays with lids Made in an assortment of sizes, and ideal for freezing precooked stews or made-up dishes. The lids should be double-sealed with freezer tape for long storage.

These cannot usually be cleaned for re-use but they can be put straight from the freezer into the oven.

Fancy foil containers Good deep-freeze accessory suppliers now have an attractive selection of durable foil containers which are suitable for freezing and presenting to the table. I find the best supplier for these is Lakeland Plastics Ltd (see address at the beginning of the book under 'Acknowledgements'). Alcanfoil also make very versatile heavy-duty foil plates for freezing and displaying food which are especially useful for buffets and parties.

Vinyl-coated foil basins Ideal for individual pies of all sorts and for precooked individual puddings. Handled carefully, they can be washed out and re-used in some cases.

Insulated tubs Can be used for small quantities of fruit and liquid, and are perfect for ice-cream. On the whole they do not respond well to washing, as smells tend to pervade the substance of the containers; the usual carton size is about 2 dl (just over ¼ pint).

Cotton stockinette Useful for wrapping the sharp bones of meat to prevent perforation of plastic bags in the freezer.

Waxed freezer paper Can be used for separating items in a larger pack. Freezer paper can also be used for packaging if it is well sealed with freezer tape, but the paper is obviously not as tough as plastic.

Heavy-duty glass dishes and bottles Made from toughened glass for using straight from freezer to oven. An attractive new range of this glassware has been brought out by a subsidiary of Pyrex. All glass or other toughened dishes *must* be packed in polythene before being stored. Bottles can be used for storing liquids provided plenty of space is left at the top of the bottle for expansion.

Fireproof dishes I find it useful to have a number of dishes for freezing precooked meals for short-length storage. Obviously these dishes must be reasonably durable so that they don't crack, and as a rough guide I find that anything which will withstand oven heat will be perfectly happy in the deep freeze. Some precooked recipes really pack most easily in the dish they are to be served from (things like stuffed pancakes served in a sauce), and some (like cold mousses or soufflés) really cannot be packed and later transferred to a serving dish. Obviously you don't want to tie up your best serving dishes in this way for too long a time, so it is as well to keep them in a prominent position so that they will not be overlooked.

Sealing materials

Pumps Small pumps for extracting the air from packages to be frozen can be helpful to ensure that all the air is removed from polythene bags before sealing.

Self-sealing Sellotape or freezer tape Ordinary tape is not strong enough to stand the moisture in a deep freeze so it is better to buy tape made specially for this purpose.

Heat-sealing machines or irons for plastic bags A good investment *and* especially useful for sealing bags of fresh vegetables and small packets holding ingredients like herbs, lemon peel, etc. Easy to work once you get the hang of them and giving a far more effective seal than wire or plastic-coated tags. The machines must be kept free of dust or they will not function properly.

Wire ties Paper- and plastic-coated lengths of wire can be bought in bulk for tying plastic bags. Plastic-coated wires are better than paper-coated, and can be used over and over again. Some paper-covered wire ties have a label attached. The paper tags can also be used for sealing foil bags. Place the wire along the top and fold the top of the bag over a few times, then fold the ends of the wire inwards to secure it.

Rubber bands Tough rubber bands can be used instead of metal closures and can, of course, be re-used.

Labelling materials

Sticky-backed labels Sheets of different-coloured and different-shaped sticky-backed labels can be bought by the sheet. These are fine for short-term freezing but I find they do not last longer than about three months. For longer periods alternative labelling should be used.

Paper-covered metal sealing tags with labels attached Useful for short storage but I find they tend to disintegrate over a longer period.

Indelible marking pencils An extremely useful part of freezer equipment. A Chinagraph pencil will mark almost anything and is water-resistant.

Waterproof felt pens Probably easier to use than a Chinagraph pencil and will mark any package including plastic bags. (Ordinary felt pens run when they come into contact with moisture.) They come in about twelve colours so they can also be used for categorizing packages.

Miscellaneous equipment

Extra wire partitions can be bought for chest freezers.

If your freezer is not equipped with a battery-operated warning buzzer, one can usually be bought separately to attach to the freezer in case of failure.

Plastic carrier bags can be used to divide food in a chest freezer.

Air-extracting pump: small pump for extracting all air from packages.

A special deep-freeze knife with a serrated edge is useful for cutting up frozen produce into convenient quantities.

Most freezer-centres sell insulated or heavy-duty paper bags for taking frozen food home, and these can be used for dividing food in a chest freezer or for putting frozen food into when the freezer has to be cleaned and defrosted.

These days many foods are sold in plastic or waxed tubs and containers and these are useful for freezing small quantities. Ice-cream cartons are usually polythene and can be washed to use again. Ice-cube trays can be used for very small amounts of food that are to be frozen.

For those who find it difficult to keep track of the food in their freezer, it is now possible to buy freezer record books. There is also a freezer file with index cards on the market. My upright freezer is in my larder and I write a check-list on the outside, using a felt pen and wiping off all items as they are used up.

Note Most labelling is inclined to become damaged or faded during long-term freezing so I suggest double labelling to avoid confusion. Double-wrap ingredients for long-term freezing, labelling the produce on the inside as well as the outside covering.

A second larder and store cupboard

Trends in the kitchen and in cooking and household management seem to change year by year although, like fashions in clothes, cycles repeat themselves. The Victorians had huge larders, cold-rooms and storage-rooms; the first Elizabethans had ice-rooms and still-rooms. In the twentieth century, kitchens began to shrink and went on shrinking as houses got smaller and flats became more popular. As the kitchens shrank so too did the larder and any storage space, until shopping had to be done almost every day. Now the trend seems to be reversing itself again. Kitchens are getting larger, there is a movement back to those lovely farmhouse rooms with plenty of space and stripped pine tables, and to kitchens that double as dining-rooms. With scare after scare about shortages of one food or another, you may be tempted to stockpile foods. And, with inflation and the ever-rising cost of living, there is the need to buy in bulk in order to save money. In the 1980s, space in the kitchen area of the house has become an all-important consideration.

Today the deep freeze has become an almost essential provider of space for storing food. It can go a long way towards replacing the cool larders there once were in every house, with their shelves of marble and slate, and in some cases continuous running cold water channelled along the slabs to keep the temperature low. The deep freeze has the advantage over old-fashioned storage because food can be kept for months instead of days, and the chance of spoilage is almost nil. Almost any food, provided it is properly prepared and packaged, can be stored in the deep freeze, so your machine automatically becomes an extension of the household refrigerator and the larder.

Bulk-buying leads to cheaper food – and this applies not only to buying ready-frozen food in bulk from a freezer-market, but also to buying food in bulk from greengrocers, for example. When fruit or vegetables are at the peak of their season it is usually possible to buy them by the tray or basket rather than just by the kilo or pound and to make a considerable saving on the normal price. In this way you can stock up on meat, fish, vegetables and fruit when they are at their cheapest and store them in the deep freeze. If you plan a big bake-up, buy flour and other ingredients from a wholesaler rather than from a small shop.

Using your deep freeze to its fullest advantage can mean a far more efficient utilization of time. If you are making one stew, for instance, double the quantities: make two and freeze one of them to eat later. If you have a free day, freeze some of the basic recipes at the end of this book so that you will always have a speedily prepared meal at your fingertips. For those who make their own bread, cakes, buns, etc, the same thing applies: make really large batches at a time and freeze those you do not plan to eat at once. Bread and cakes keep really beautifully in the freezer and come out tasting every bit as good as when they were first made.

Those who like to make their own jams and marmalades but find they have no time when the fruit is at its peak can store it in the freezer to cook when they have plenty of time. Dinner or buffet-party food can be cooked in advance, leaving little to do before the guests arrive. So many meals are skimped on because of lack of time, but for the deep-freeze owner this pressure is eased by preparing the major part of a meal in advance so that only the finishing touch of sophistication need be added at the last minute.

The short cuts utilizing the deep freeze are numerous and can provide endless time-savers. If you are squeezing lemons, for instance, grate off the peel first, and pack it in small quantities to freeze. Frozen parsley tops can be taken straight from the freezer and crumbled to sprinkle over casseroles, soups and stews; other herbs can be treated in the same way. Vegetables can be chopped, blanched and frozen to add to casseroles and stews, or more finely chopped to provide a base for soups. Stocks can be made when there are bones, trimmings or poultry carcases around, then frozen as they are or boiled to concentrate the liquid and then frozen in ice-cube trays to make soup or to add to sauces and gravy.

The deep freeze can also be a money-spinner where leftovers are concerned. No more living on the remains of a joint or a turkey for days on end. The leftovers can be prepared and stored in the deep freeze for future use.

If one of the family needs a packed lunch, then the deep freeze again comes into its own. Small pies, sandwiches and snacks can be made in advance and frozen to take out the night before they are needed (or, in the case of sandwiches, on the morning itself). Commercial precooked snacks can be bought in bulk and stored until required.

Unless your larder is really cool and dry, some foods tend to go off if they are stored too long, and I have friends who swear by freezing pasta, rice and even nuts if they buy them in large quantities.

When planning parties, use your deep freeze as an extra aid to success. Apart from the basic cooking, you can also use it to provide those extra touches which can make a party something special. Ice-cubes, for instance, can be removed from the refrigerator, splashed with a little soda water to prevent the cubes from sticking together, packed in polythene bags and stockpiled before the party. Ice-cubes can also be made with a small leaf of mint, a little twist of lemon peel or even an olive in the middle to make drinks look extra-exciting. Many canapés can be made in advance and frozen to be reheated just before the guests arrive. White wine can be chilled quickly *provided it is not kept in the deep freeze for longer than 30 minutes – if it is kept for longer than this the chill will affect the wine and in the end the bottle will burst.* Cocktails, pre-mixed, without having ice added, can be stored in the deep freeze.

Cooking for the deep freeze

One of the greatest assets of a deep freeze is that you can to a large extent cook when you have the time and inclination.

If the correct procedures are followed, precooked food freezes most successfully and there is no reason why it should not be every bit as good as food that is prepared just before it is eaten. Like any other form of cooking, there is a certain art to cooking for the freezer and inevitably the cook improves with practice. As with fresh food, the packaging of precooked dishes is of paramount importance. It is also necessary to remember that most precooked food will have to be thawed and reheated, so it is always better to undercook rather than overcook dishes that you plan to freeze. The food will continue to cook whilst it is being reheated.

Many basic stews and casseroles can be partially made in bulk, frozen and used later as the basis of a large variety of different dishes. Fresh, good-quality mince, for instance, cooked with a basic sauce, can form the nucleus of dishes as varied as chilli con carne and shepherd's pie; a basic lamb stew can be turned, with a minimum of trouble, into a Lancashire hotpot or an exotic Eastern speciality rich in herbs and spices.

I myself prefer, on the whole, to cook the basic ingredients for dishes to be made up later rather than a quantity of the same finished dish which the family soon gets tired of. I once made 12×4 servings of savoury pancakes filled with a Bolognaise mixture and covered with a rich cheese sauce – delicious for one or two meals, but oh how bored my family got after the twelfth meal!

Unless you are freezing a completed dish such as a pie, which cannot be added to during the reheating process, I strongly recommend keeping seasoning to a minimum in precooked recipes which are to be frozen. Heavy seasoning, and especially the taste of garlic, tends to alter after a period in the deep freeze, and herbs, spices and seasoning can always be added before the dish is to be served. Those dishes that are designed to go straight from the freezer, via the oven, to the table and which do contain elaborate seasoning should be stored for only a short time.

As with any other food, precooked dishes will only taste as good after freezing as they did in the first place, so please do not fall into the trap of making something rather second-rate and keeping your fingers crossed that it will taste better after a stretch in the deep freeze – I can assure you it won't.

The best fully precooked dishes which need only putting into the oven to reheat before being served are almost always those encased in some kind of covering, or cooked in a rich sauce: things like stuffed pancakes, sweet and savoury pies, and stews and casseroles which incorporate a substantial sauce or gravy. Great care should be taken, however, with any food cooked in a white sauce that has been enriched with egg yolks, cream or lemon juice, as these are inclined to separate after freezing.

Do remember, when freezing leftovers, that food's becoming dessicated during its deep-freeze life is one of the greatest problems facing the home freezer. Sliced cooked meat, which has no protection, does not therefore respond well to freezing, and is apt to become flaccid and tasteless. It is far better to incorporate leftovers in a sauce, thereby giving some kind of lubrication to meat and poultry.

This is the age of the 'snack' (such a horrid word) and here again, with your deep freeze, you can produce such things as pizzas, quickly cooked items which can be fried straight from the frozen state, and a multitude of savoury appetite-satisfiers, at less than half an hour's notice. Many of these can, of course, be bought ready-made and ready-frozen, but, as always, those you make yourself will taste better, be of a superior quality and, in the long run, work out less expensive; the manufacturer, after all, has to cut costs and corners, but you know exactly where you are with home-made food.

Many precooked dishes, especially such things as pies and flans, are extremely fragile. Open-freeze such items before packing to prevent their being damaged in the freezer.

The do's and don'ts of freezing precooked dishes

Do make the best possible use of leftovers and take to buying large joints which can be utilized to make many off-shoot precooked dishes and save you money in the long run. A large joint may seem like an excessive outlay of money in the first place but the old song about beef, 'hot on Sunday, cold on Monday' etc really can pay dividends. Sunday's roast really can be stretched into a week of meals.

Do freeze in small rather than large quantities. A small precooked dish can always be added to, but a large one can be a liability.

Do cook double the quantity of stew and other dishes you require, cutting down on fuel bills and freezing half for a later date.

Do reduce leftover sauces, gravy, stock, etc and freeze it in small containers to add to other made-up dishes later.

Do use transparent film to separate precooked foods and snacks in individual portions that might otherwise stick together.

Do label precooked dishes with care so that you know all about them when you take the food from the freezer. Write down how many servings the dish is for, whether it will need additional seasoning when being reheated, and especially the date at which it was put into the freezer.

Do garnish precooked dishes when (or after) reheating rather than before freezing, to give the food a fresh, attractive appearance.

Do cook batches of 'starter meals' (see pages 176–203) so that you have a good stock of basic beef, lamb, pork and poultry dishes at your fingertips to turn into delicious and successful meals when you need them.

Don't keep precooked dishes in the freezer for too long. Precooked dishes, especially those that are highly flavoured, have a shorter freezer-life than basic fresh foods and they will deteriorate in flavour and texture after the suggested storage time.

Don't freeze dishes incorporating chunks of potato as these will go hard and often discolour during the dish's freezer-life.

Don't freeze dishes incorporating hard-boiled eggs, as freezing has an adverse effect on the eggs, making them hard and leathery.

Don't be too lavish with the use of garlic or herbs as these tend to develop an 'off' taste when frozen for any length of time. Instead add the flavourings when reheating the food whenever possible.

Don't overcook dishes that are to be prepared in advance and then frozen. Remember they will continue to cook whilst being reheated.

Freezing terms

Like so many things these days, freezing has its own language and special terms of reference. Usually they are fairly straightforward, but this quick guide may help if you get confused in any way.

Ascorbic acid Vitamin C in synthetic form; it is used to prevent various fruit and vegetables from discolouring during the freezing process. Ascorbic acid is in crystal form and can be bought from most chemists. If it is not available, lemon juice can be used instead.

Blanching Most vegetables need blanching for long-term storage in a deep freeze. Plunging vegetables into boiling water halts the action of enzymes in the fibres of the vegetables. If the vegetables are not blanched, the enzymes continue to work and the result is a lack of flavour, colour and nutritional value after a short period of storage in the deep freeze.

Blanch vegetables in a very large pan of fast-boiling water. Do not salt the water. It helps to use a special wire basket for containing the vegetables.

Time the blanching process from the moment the water returns to the boil after the vegetables have been added. Remove them as soon as the time is up (refer to blanching chart, pages 86–8) and plunge them immediately into iced water to cool them as quickly as possible.

Deep-freeze odours Food prepared for the freezer has to be extremely carefully wrapped or odours from one package will penetrate other ingredients. This is especially important with strongly aromatic foods such as smoked fish, onions, garlic, and highly spiced dishes like curry. Your deep freeze should always smell fresh and clean. If it does have a suspicion of a smell, defrost and clean the deep freeze (see page 30).

Defrosting The better your deep freeze, the less often it will need to be defrosted. Defrost the deep freeze *at least* once a year or when ice has formed on the inside of the cabinet.

Dehydration If frozen food is not properly wrapped, it will dry out in the deep freeze. Protect against dehydration by careful wrapping of all food and by excluding as much air as possible from the package.

Drip-loss Foods that are thawed too quickly (especially fish and meat) will suffer from a loss of their natural juices. Avoid this by planning ahead and by thawing when possible in the refrigerator rather than at room temperature (see thawing chart, pages 105–7).

Dry pack Fruit that is packed raw without sugar.

Dry sugar pack Fruit that is packed raw with granulated sugar.

Enzymes Substances present in all fresh foodstuffs. Their action is halted by blanching. If vegetables were not blanched, the enzymes would continue to work and after a period of freezing would cause damage to their flavour, colour and texture.

Fast-freezing The faster food is frozen, the better will be the end result. Most deep freezes now have fast-freeze switches for freezing food at home. Switch the fast-freezer on an hour or two before you plan to freeze produce. Keep the fast-freezer on until the food is frozen through.

Freezer burn Caused by dehydration, and an indication of bad packaging. Avoid any commercially frozen food that shows these signs. Freezer burn can be detected by dry white patches on produce.

Freezer-life If domestic freezers could reduce to a low enough temperature, there would be no reason why properly prepared and packed produce should not stay frozen for ever. Since this is not practical (at least not yet) all produce has a recommended freezer-life. Usually this is only a recommended storage-time but, on the other hand, the efficient freezer is the one where the turnover is relatively fast.

Free-flow 'Free-flow-packed' peas, beans, etc are frozen before being packed, and therefore remain separate in the pack instead of becoming a solid lump. This is obviously an advantage when packing in large quantities, as any amount of the food can be shuffled from the pack as required. In the home, free-flow freezing is done by spreading the prepared ingredients on a tray and open-freezing them before packaging.

Headspace Liquids expand when frozen and there is liquid in most fruit as well as in the more obvious things. If headspace is not left in the package either the package will burst or the contents will be damaged. Allow a headspace of about 1·25 cm (½ in) in most containers.

Individual packaging If chops, steaks, hamburgers, etc are frozen in one package, they will stick together. Avoid this by packing with waxed paper or polythene film between each layer of the food, or by individually wrapping the items in polythene film.

Moisture/vapour-proof wrapping Wrappings especially produced for deep-freeze packaging. Wrappings must be 100 per cent airtight and it is a false economy to try to get away with something less substantial.

Open-freezing Food that is frozen before packaging and then packed when hard. Spread food that is to be treated in this way on trays, fast-freeze, and package as soon as it is solid. Do not allow the food to thaw once it has been frozen.

Oxidation The absorption of oxygen into the fat cells of food, mainly meat. This occurs in badly packaged food and leads to a deterioration of texture and an 'off' smell in the food.

Perforation Avoid any commercially frozen packaged food that has a perforated package.

Syrup pack Fruit that is packed with a sugar syrup.

Temperature For fast-freezing the temperature of your deep freeze should be below −9°F/−23°C. For storage the temperature should be below 0°F/−18°C.

Thawing Thawing times and procedures vary for different produce. Meat, poultry and large fish should be thawed as slowly as possible; vegetables should be cooked from the frozen state. The refrigerator is the best place to thaw food slowly and meat thawed in this way will suffer the minimum of drip-loss.

Vacuum packs Food specially prepared for commercial freezing is often vacuum-packed ensuring that all air is excluded from the package. When buying cured meat or bacon, etc for the home freezer it is as well to buy it in such a pack. It is now possible to get a gadget for home packaging which gives a fair imitation of a vacuum pack.

Choosing food to freeze

The preparation of food for freezing is of paramount importance, and this first stage should be carried out with the greatest care. Above all, food for the freezer must be meticulously clean. Freezing will keep germs dormant, but if they are in the food in the first place, they will almost certainly increase if the food is allowed to thaw and then to stand around in a warm temperature.

All food that is to be frozen must be in prime condition. A disappointing casserole, for instance, will in no way be improved by being in the freezer; and a tough piece of meat will not be tenderized by being frozen for a few months.

Meat

If you plan to buy a lot of meat wholesale for freezing, do check first and see that you have plenty of room in the freezer to accommodate it all, and that you will not be denying yourself space for other items like home-grown vegetables or produce with a short season that you are looking forward to stockpiling. Remember also that meat should be fast-frozen before being stored. In most deep freezes only a limited amount can be frozen at one time; if you cannot accommodate everything at once, the remainder must be kept at a cool temperature (i.e. in a refrigerator) until it can be fast-frozen. The packages should be circulated as soon as they are solid so that a new batch can be put into the fast-freezing area of the deep freeze.

Buying from a butcher

There are, let's face it, butchers and butchers, and you tend to have to pay more for meat from one who cuts well and sells top-quality produce. If you buy from a good butcher, you should be able to rely on properly hung meat and on neatly and economically cut and trimmed joints. In general, less expensive butchers and chains of butchers' shops will often provide inadequately hung meat and joints that are prepared with too large a percentage of fat and with the tough tendons or gristle remaining in the joint. In the long run, more expensively priced meat can turn out to be an economy.

In the end, you have to tread a tightrope between the quality and standard of butchering and the price you are prepared to pay. A point I would like to make here is that all too many of us are prepared to accept what we are given without complaint. Tell your butcher if you are displeased with the meat purchased, and he will probably be glad to take the trouble to produce better-quality meat next time.

Beef

Buying from deep-freeze wholesalers

Many large firms now specialize in deep-freezing and deep-freeze supermarkets are springing up all over the place. Like every other type of shop, they vary, as does the quality of their goods. It is impossible to tell from the outside what frozen produce is really like, so, in a way, you have to rely more on the wholesaler himself. Good packaging is an indication – never, never buy any goods whose packaging is damaged in any way; check the date stamp and don't buy any meat that shows obvious signs of freezer burn or a lot of ice formation inside the wrappings.

The quality of meat and its tenderness can vary so much that it is usually worth trying a sample of the goods before making a big financial outlay on it (this, of course, applies especially to the more expensive cuts).

Watch the newspapers for news of price trends. If beef is going to be short for some time and therefore at a premium, there is usually some kind of advance warning. If you do think the price is likely to shoot up, buy in bulk before it does.

Beware of buying imported frozen beef. It may be cheaper, but remember it has travelled a long way and during that time it may have thawed and been frozen again more than once. Here again, it is usually worth trying a small joint before buying in large quantities.

When buying bulk packs of small cuts (i.e. steaks, etc), make sure they have been individually frozen or individually packed so that you can separate them.

Buying fresh beef wholesale

One often hears the most wonderful stories about people who have bought whole carcases of meat and saved an enormous amount of money, but I wonder how satisfied they would honestly claim to have been with the results of their purchases.

Soon after my experience of buying half a bullock (described earlier in 'pitfalls') I took a short course in butchering – some councils and some deep-freeze centres run this kind of course – and this has helped me to identify the different cuts of meat I am presented with. Now, if I want to get a large quantity of beef for freezing, I make arrangements with a butcher whom I know well. In this way I know the meat is of good quality and pay a reasonable sum to have it butchered professionally.

A quarter of a carcase is the most an average family can deal with at one time, and it is well worth spending some time preparing the meat before freezing it. Stewing beef, for instance, should be cut into cubes before freezing and packed in fairly small quantities. Trimmings can be minced (after any gristle has been removed). The bones make good, rich stock and any excess fat can be rendered down to make dripping by putting it in a roasting tin in a slow oven for a few hours. Joints for roasting should be trimmed and tied, if necessary, ready for the oven.

Buying half a bullock

Forequarter weighs 45–70 kg (100–160 lb) and consists of back, top rib, fore rib, 'leg of mutton' or shoulder cut, flank, brisket, clod, sticking, shin, bladebone, chuck.

Hindquarter weighs 67–80 kg (150–180 lb) and consists of sirloin with fillet, rump, topside, silverside, top rump, leg, skirt, flank, ox kidney.

Some guidelines for choosing beef

Smell: good-quality beef has a fresh but rich smell.
Looks: the lean meat should be a rich, bright red with a slightly brownish tinge to it – avoid dry-looking meat that has a very dark colouring. Even lean meat should have flecks of fat in it (these provide tenderness). The fat should be creamy yellow and in prime cuts there should be almost no gristle discernible.
Touch: prime meat should be firm and almost springy to the touch.

Prime cuts

Sirloin: roast on the bone, or bone and roll with the fillet removed. The larger the joint, the better the meat will be.

Porterhouse and entrecôte steaks: steaks cut from the upper part of the sirloin.

Fillet steak: cut from the bottom of the sirloin.

Wing rib: the sirloin without the fillet.

Medium cuts

Top rib, fore rib and back rib: roast on the bone or rolled with the bone removed.

Topside: medium- or slow-roast with frequent basting. Braise, pot-roast or boil with vegetables.

Coarse cuts

Silverside: boil or braise or salt and then boil. Use for stews.

Brisket: slow-roast, braise, pot-roast or boil. Ideal for salting.

Flank: thick flank can be slow-roasted. Thin cuts can be braised, pot-roasted or stewed.

Blade and chuck: stew or braise.

'Leg of mutton' cut: stew or braise.

Leg and shin: slow-stewing.

Skirt: stewing.

Offal

Oxtail: stewing.

Ox heart: stuff and slow-roast or braise.

Ox tongue: boil fresh or salt then boil.

Ox liver: stew or braise.

Ox kidneys: stewing, puddings and pies. Use surrounding fat for suet.

Ox cheek: slow-stewing.

Cow heel: boiling or stewing.

Tripe: boiling, stewing or frying.

Ox sweetbreads: slow simmering or stewing.

Lamb

Most of the points which apply to buying beef also apply to buying lamb.

For those who like the taste of mutton it is unfortunate that lamb gives the farmer a quicker turnover and that trends in eating have made lamb generally more popular. When you can find it, however, mutton is cheaper than lamb; its colour is darker and its smell richer.

Buying from a butcher

You always have to choose between a home-killed animal and one imported from Australia or New Zealand, home-killed usually being more expensive. Our own lamb is often better both in flavour and in texture, with larger joints and a sweeter, richer taste.

The price of lamb varies according to the season, usually

coming down after Easter, when it is relatively inexpensive. As with beef, good butchering leads to more economical cuts, so look for a butcher who really knows his business, and avoid joints that have too high a percentage of fat.

Buying from deep-freeze wholesalers

Most deep-freeze wholesalers deal almost entirely in imported lamb and prices are usually much lower than for fresh meat. The only way to know whether the meat you are buying is of good quality is to test it by cooking and eating it; so, whenever possible, try out a small quantity first before going ahead and buying large quantities.

Before buying any frozen meat check carefully that its packaging is no way damaged, that there is no air inside the package, no obvious freezer burn or excessive ice crystals inside the packing. Also check the date stamp.

Buy your lamb from deep-freeze wholesalers when the price of fresh lamb is at its highest.

When buying packs that contain more than one joint (some wholesalers sell bags with two or three legs or shoulders, for instance, especially when the joints are on the small side), make sure the joints are all individually wrapped inside the package.

When buying packs of small cuts (i.e. cutlets, chops, etc), make sure the cuts have been individually wrapped or frozen and are not sticking together.

Avoid joints which have brittle white fat as this is an indication that they have been frozen for too long.

Buying fresh lamb wholesale

Buying half or a whole lamb for deep-freezing is a far better bet for most average families than buying half a bullock; the size is easier to cope with and there is far less waste with a better ratio of prime to coarse cuts.

Buy the lamb when the season is at its height and, if you want a really sensational joint for a special occasion, ask to have the saddle kept in one piece.

Do ask the butcher to make sure the lamb is properly hung, as this will improve both the taste and texture of the meat.

Keep the best end of neck cut whole (unless you decide to freeze the whole saddle), as this is delicious roasted in one piece.

Trim off excess fat from joints for stewing (breast, scrag and neck) and divide into pieces before freezing.

A lamb will probably weigh about 13 kg (30 lb). It will take up about 2 cubic feet of room when prepared and packed for the freezer, and give two of each of the following joints: leg, loin, shoulder, best end neck, breast, middle neck, scrag, kidney.

Some guidelines for choosing lamb

Smell: lamb should smell fresh and slightly sweet.
Appearance: the flesh should be a light, clear pink, and the fat creamy-white. Legs and shoulders should be plump with a good layer of white fat. Yellow fat is an indication of age.
Touch: the flesh and fat should feel firm and moist.

Prime cuts

Leg: roast, or bone and roll and pot-roast. Cut pieces from the fillet at the top of the leg for kebabs, or cube a boned leg for kebabs or shashliks. Can also be boiled or salted and boiled.

Saddle: the back of lamb starting from the best end of neck to the end of the loin. Roast whole.

Shoulder: roast whole on the bone, or bone and roll for roasting. Can also be cubed and used for superior stews, kebabs or shashliks. Bone and roll for pot-roasting or braising.

Loin: roast whole or divide into chops and grill or fry.

Chump: divide into chops and grill or fry.

Medium cuts

Breast: bone and roll and roast, pot-roast, or braise. Stew or casserole.

Scrag end: cut into pieces and pot-roast, stew, braise or casserole.

Neck: cut into pieces and pot-roast, stew, braise or casserole.

Offal

Lamb's tail: a single lamb's tail will obviously not be very useful, but you may find a butcher who will be prepared to sell you about six; chopped and stewed, these make a most delicious, old-fashioned country dish.

Lamb's liver: fry, grill or braise cut into thin slices. Take care not to overcook as this will toughen the liver. Use minced for pâtés or terrines (it cannot be cut too thin).

Lamb's kidneys: grill or fry, but stop cooking immediately droplets of blood begin oozing from the kidney. The fat surrounding the kidneys can be rendered down to use as dripping.

Lamb's heart: a heart makes only one portion. Stuff and then roast or braise.

Lamb's tongue: a tongue makes only one portion. Boil or braise (or salt and boil) and serve hot or cold.

Sweetbreads: only one serving per pair of sweetbreads. Boil or stew until tender.

Brains: only one serving per set of brains. Poach and serve with a sauce.

Pork

Buying pork in bulk for freezing is not really as good as buying beef and lamb. The high percentage of fat means the meat cannot be stored for a long time and (to my mind, anyway) pork is such a rich meat that one does not want to eat too much of it. Unlike beef and lamb, pork has to be eaten fresh; therefore great care must be taken to see that it is frozen as quickly as possible after being killed.

Buying from a butcher

Some butchers specialize in pork and these are usually the best ones to go to if you want to buy top-quality pork for freezing. If possible buy pork straight from a cold-storage room rather than from the shop window.

Do not overlook some of the less expensive joints which can be made into excellent meals.

When buying roasting joints, score through the skin before freezing. Unless you are planning to store a boned and stuffed joint for a short time only, it is advisable to stuff the joint after thawing. Unstuffed joints should be prepared for roasting before being frozen.

Buying from deep-freeze wholesalers

Make sure the packaging surrounding the cuts of meat is not in any way perforated or damaged. Look out for freezer burn or excessive ice crystallization in the package.

When buying small cuts like chops, make sure they are individually frozen or wrapped so that they do not stick together.

Buying fresh pork wholesale

This is not something I would recommend for the average family unless you happen to be particularly fond of pork and are prepared to vary the cuts by salting some of them. If you do buy a whole side of pork, make sure you buy it from a butcher who will cut it into neat, not too large, joints for you, and that the animal is absolutely fresh when you freeze it. As it is not possible to freeze more than a certain quantity of meat at one time, it may be as well to collect the meat from your butcher's cold room at intervals.

A side of pork will probably weigh in the region of 22 kg (50 lb) and will consist of leg, belly, loin, neck end or spare rib, hand and head, two trotters, a kidney and possibly the liver.

Prime cuts

Leg: roast on the bone, or bone and stuff before roasting. Can be boiled to eat cold, or salted and then boiled to eat hot or cold. Fillets from the top end of the leg can be grilled or fried.

Loin: can be roasted whole or rolled and stuffed. Cut into chops, it can be grilled or fried.

Blade: the top part of the foreleg which can be roasted whole, or boned and stuffed.

Belly: cut into thin slices and fried or grilled; stewed; breadcrumbed and roasted; or salted and boiled.

Medium cuts

Spare ribs: can be roasted, braised, barbecued or stewed. Can be cut into cutlets and grilled, fried or braised.

Offal

Pig's liver: a bit strong in taste and better for using in pâtés, terrines, stews, etc than for grilling or frying.

Kidneys: can be grilled or stewed.

Pig's head: boiled. The cheek can be boned, and salted to eat cold as Bath chap.

Pig's trotters: boil or stew. After boiling they can be boned, breadcrumbed and fried.

Bacon and gammon

Cured and salted meats do not have as long a freezer-life as fresh meat, so do not buy or take out of the freezer too much at one time – it has a tendency to go off quickly once it has been thawed.

Bacon rashers, in small quantities, should be really well packed as the smell from cured meat can pervade other packages. Commercially vacuum-packed bacon will keep for longer provided the pack is in perfect condition and is not punctured in any way.

When you buy bacon or gammon, make sure that it has a fresh smell and there is not a hint of sliminess about the surface of the meat.

Thin-cut rashers are far more economical than thick-cut ones and it is well worth finding a shop that cuts its own.

Some guidelines for choosing bacon and gammon

Smell: the joint or rashers must have an absolutely fresh smell that may be slightly salty or smoky according to the cure. Green bacon is dry-salted or brined but not smoked.
Appearance: the flesh should be deep pink to bright red and without any yellow or bronze streaks or stains. Avoid cuts of a very dark colour as this usually means the piece has been cut for some time and will be dry. The fat should be white, never yellow.
Touch: the flesh and fat should be firm and never have an oily or slimy feel to it. The rind should be smooth and elastic and not too thick.

Cuts of bacon

Forehock: butt, small hock and fore slipper. Butt can be boiled. Small hock should be boned and casseroled. Fore slipper can be boiled.

Top streaky: can be boned and boiled or cut into thin rashers for frying or grilling.

Prime streaky: can be boiled in one piece or cut into rashers for frying or grilling.

Oyster: the end of the long back; can be cut into rashers.

Flank: can be sliced and fried or grilled.

Long back: cut into thin slices for frying or grilling.

Short back: cut into thin rashers for frying or grilling.

Back and ribs: can be boiled or cut into rashers.

Top back: can be boiled, braised, or cut into thick slices and fried.

Prime collar: the best boiling joint of all.

End of collar: an inexpensive boiling joint. Can be skinned, pressed and served cold; or can be boiled for three-quarters of the cooking time and then skinned, breadcrumbed and roasted.

Gammon joints

Slipper: can be boiled, or parboiled and baked.

Hock: boil, or parboil and bake and eat cold.

Middle gammon: cut into thin rashers for grilling, or boil whole.

Corner gammon: can be boiled or cut into thin rashers for grilling.

Poultry

Poultry is one of the best bets for the deep freeze; it keeps well and can still make a reasonably economical meal. The price, especially of chickens and turkeys, can vary considerably and doesn't always bear relation to quality; so, if you plan to freeze a number of birds, shop around and learn by practice to tell a plump, tender bird from an old, tough one.

If you have a poultry market near you, buy your birds there, as this can lead to a considerable saving. If you go to the country see if you can buy some farm-fresh, free-range chickens on your last day there; the taste will be infinitely better than that of battery-reared birds and they are usually a very reasonable price. Country markets can also be a good source of poultry that really does still taste like it did in Grandmother's day.

Turkeys should never be bought at the height of their season (i.e. just before Christmas) when the price is artificially high. Now that they are becoming a popular Easter feature, think about buying your Christmas bird just after the Easter holiday – by which time the price should have fallen.

Do buy fresh, rather than frozen, birds when possible. You can see what you are buying and know that you can judge the freezer-life from the date you put it in your own freezer.

Always remove the giblets from the birds before freezing and pack them separately. The giblets can be used for stock or saved up and made into delicious and inexpensive stews.

Do not stuff birds before freezing as stuffing has a shorter freezer-life than poultry and it can give the flesh a tainted flavouring.

When buying ducks for freezing, establish that they are not too fatty as this will shorten their freezer-life.

Buying fresh poultry

Birds bought from a poulterer are often of a better quality than are those bought from an ordinary butcher or in a supermarket. He, after all, has a reputation to keep up and will be prepared to give you advice on the best birds to freeze. Don't ignore boiling fowls as these often have a better flavour than roasting birds and can be made into many delicious dishes.

If you are prepared to pay for top-quality birds, try freezing those that can be bought from Marks and Spencer's food departments; they are expensive, but their taste is first-rate, they are plump and full of meat, and guaranteed 'fresh not frozen'.

Buying from deep-freeze wholesalers

Buy whole birds rather than chicken pieces, which have a shorter freezer-life and are liable to freezer burn because of the amount of cut surface exposed; they also work out more expensive in the long run and you have no carcase or giblets to make stock from.

Check packaging to make sure it has not been damaged or perforated. If possible check to see that the flesh has no freezer burn and avoid packages with an excess of ice crystallization on the inside.

Check the date stamp.

If you are disappointed in the quality of a bird you have bought from a deep-freeze supermarket, learn by your mistakes and buy from another source next time.

Birds that are sold frozen in bulk are usually factory-bred and tend to be lacking in flavour. Make up this deficiency by adding herbs and spices when cooking.

Freezing your own birds

Pluck, draw and prepare the birds ready for cooking. Pack carefully and label clearly whether the bird is for roasting or boiling.

Remove the cocks' combs and the feet and freeze them separately – they will make a rich and nourishing stock.

If you live in the country it is usually possible to make a good bargain by buying a quantity of birds for freezing from a local poultry-keeper or through the local newspaper. If you are prepared to pluck and dress them yourself, they will, of course, be cheaper still.

Some guidelines for choosing poultry

Spring chicken, broiler, or poussin These should weigh about 450 gr (1 lb); anything smaller will be almost totally devoid of taste. One bird should give two portions. After thawing, they should be split down the backbone and breastbone and then flattened out with a meat mallet for even frying or grilling.

Roasting chicken The skin should be white and the body plump and firm. The feet should be smooth and the beak flexible. The weight can vary from as little as 900 gr (2 lb) to as much as 3 kg (7 lb) and you should allow 200 gr (½ lb) chicken per serving if the bird is to be served hot.

Capon Richer in flavour than an ordinary roasting chicken, with a large amount of flesh-to-bone ratio.

Boiling fowl Choose a large bird and avoid those that have a very yellow skin. If you do want to joint the birds before freezing, wipe the joints with a damp cloth and wrap each one separately, or open-freeze joints before packaging.

Ducks The beak and the feet of the bird should be bright yellow and flexible, the breastbone pliable. Choose birds that are not too fat. Freezing old birds is really rather a waste of time and it is preferable to joint and casserole them before freezing.

Geese A good eating bird should have a pliable underbill and not be too fat.

Turkeys Gone are the days when all turkeys were enormous; now you can buy them as small as 2·25 kg (5 lb). Old turkeys tend to be tough – a good way to judge their age is by their legs, which should be smooth rather than rough and scaly. On the whole the larger birds do have a better flavour, but smaller ones can be given additional flavouring during the cooking period.

Chicken or turkey joints If you buy these from a shop or supermarket they will almost inevitably have been frozen and then thawed before going on display; refreezing will lead to loss of taste and texture. This is something you want to check out carefully before buying joints. Choose joints that are firm, with white, not yellowish, skin.

Fish

Surprisingly, despite modern methods of refrigeration and transportation, it is far more difficult to buy fresh fish in this country than it was fifty years ago. Because of the problems of keeping fish fresh, the bulk of it is sold frozen rather than fresh; and even in coastal areas most of the fresh fish is sold by cooperatives and is deep-frozen before being transported to markets.

If you are a fisherman yourself, if you live on the coast and have friends amongst the fishing fleet or in the local fish market, or if you are within reach of a first-class fishmonger who will tell you truthfully which of his fish are fresh and which frozen and then defrosted, then you can have a source of fresh fish for your own deep freeze. If none of these sources is available, then the results of freezing bought fish are bound to be disappointing.

The alternative to buying fresh fish is to buy it in bulk ready-frozen, and transfer it to your own freezer. Buy in small quantities at first; sample the fish, and test your source before buying in bulk.

Buying fresh fish

Choose fish that has a fresh, shiny look. The scales should gleam and the eyes still be bright. Avoid any fish that is limp and flabby. The fish should have a fresh, salty smell. Make sure the tails of fresh lobsters, shrimps, prawns and crayfish are tightly curled and will spring back into place if you straighten them out.

The colours of all fresh fish should be bright and clear.

Prepare fresh fish for freezing as soon as you get it home (having got it there in the shortest possible time). Freeze the fish whole; or gut, scale and fillet it ready for cooking. Separate packs of fillets or cutlets by wrapping each piece individually in cling-wrap, or open-freeze individually before packing.

Rub large fish with olive oil to prevent their drying out. Alternatively, seal them by dipping into cold water before open-freezing and then packing – a thin layer of ice will form around the fish, excluding all air.

If you have any doubt about the freshness of fish you are about to freeze, take no chances by cooking it in some acceptable dish before freezing the precooked dish.

Buying from deep-freeze wholesalers

Although this may be by far the most inexpensive way of buying fish, it may well not be the most satisfactory. The wholesaler should have taken just as much trouble freezing the fish as you would have done at home; although his equipment may be far more sophisticated, the end-product will still depend on the state the fish was in when he froze it and on how rapidly it was frozen.

Avoid like the plague any packages that are damaged or perforated in any way. Check the date stamps and look out for freezer burn or excessive ice formation on the inside of the packaging.

Try to buy untreated fillets of fish rather than fish that has already been breadcrumbed – the reason for breadcrumbing is often the poor quality of the fish.

Remember that the price of fish fluctuates enormously according to the season and weather conditions; there are times when you might find that frozen fish is actually more expensive than fish that is fresh.

Once you have bought frozen fish, get it home as quickly as you possibly can and put it straight into your own freezer. Fish usually thaws more quickly than meat and if it has been allowed to thaw on the way home there will be an inevitable deterioration of quality after it has been refrozen.

With small fish like prawns, or with fillets or cutlets, make sure they have been individually packed or open-frozen before being packed. A solid lump of fish in a package is not only impossible to deal with, but will also have suffered in the freezing process.

Freezing your own caught fish

Those who have fishing rights on a salmon, sea-trout or trout river are lucky; they have access to a wealth of good produce for the freezer. Remember, however, that the faster it goes from the river to the deep freeze, the better the results will be. It is not necessary to gut salmon or sea-trout before freezing (I feel the results are better if you don't) but in that case the thawing process must take place at the lowest possible temperature (in a refrigerator). Large fish other than salmon or sea-trout should be gutted and cut into fillets or cutlets before being open-frozen and carefully packed.

Speed in freezing is also important for sea fish that have been caught by the home fisherman. At sea they have ice containers for keeping the fish; for the amateur fisherman who wants to make a day of it, the best thing to do is to invest in a special insulated container with ice-bags. If this is not available, you can wrap the fish, as soon as it is caught, in thick layers of newspaper and keep it out of direct sunlight until you can get it home.

Vegetables and fruit

Nothing beats home-grown vegetables. I get my seeds from Suttons of Reading who have one of the most comprehensive lists and I have always found them most satisfactory. They send the seeds quickly and have a first-rate catalogue that offers advice to the home gardener on aspects of growing and freezing. There are certain varieties of the vegetables that freeze well that are better than others for the home grower and freezer, and each year these varieties are recommended in Suttons' catalogue.

For herbs and some rather more unusual vegetables I find the seed merchants Thompson and Morgan of Ipswich, Suffolk, have a good list. If you have even a small greenhouse it is worth having a try at growing things like chillis, green peppers and aubergines.

With fruit, I recommend growing the varieties that suit your own garden. When growing soft fruit like raspberries, bear in mind that it is usually the smaller, more compact fruit rather than the more showy, larger ones that make good material for the freezer.

Vegetables for freezing

Vegetables are among the best produce to freeze, but I personally feel that they should be used occasionally as an economy or as a time-saver rather than all the time. If you are without a garden, you can buy vegetables at the peak of their season when they are cheapest and in prime condition, and freeze them for later use. It is very convenient to have a store of frozen vegetables at your fingertips, needing only a few minutes' cooking and no preparation when time is at a premium. On the other hand, I am sure that everyone gets heartily sick of frozen peas with everything month in and month out, so I would suggest that you buy your favourite vegetables when they are cheap and freeze them to enjoy later, use frozen vegetables when you are pressed for time, but that you take advantage of the best of our wide range of fresh vegetables when they are in season.

Growing fresh vegetables

If you do have a garden, then freezing vegetables is more than just an economy – it is a rule of life. However well you plan your rotation of crops, there will nearly always be more fresh vegetables than you can eat at any one time and the rest should be frozen to last you through the lean months.

In gardening, I find, almost more than anywhere else, one learns all the time. Grow small rather than large rows of vegetables at a time, with frequent re-seedings. A long row of peas, for example, may look satisfying, but unless you are going to let some of them grow past their peak or are prepared to spend all night long podding and blanching, your life will become a nightmare of trying to beat the clock in order to harvest and freeze produce at the right time.

The best frozen vegetables of all are those which spend as little time as possible between being picked and being frozen. If you grow your own vegetables, only pick as many as you can cope with at one time. Pick them early in the morning before the sun has had time to get to them, but after the dew has risen, and prepare them in a cool place out of the sun. It may seem more pleasant to sit in the garden tanning yourself whilst shelling peas or topping and tailing beans, but their quality will be impaired by the ultra-violet rays.

Pick your vegetables when you know you have time to prepare them for the deep freeze. If you do pick more than you can cope with at any one time, store the remainder in a cool, dark place or in the bottom of a refrigerator.

Do grow vegetables your family really like. You may, for instance, be justifiably proud of the pounds of spinach you packed away in your freezer last year, but it won't do you much good if the family groan every time you serve it up.

The best thing about having your own garden is being able to choose vegetables when they are just as you like them – in my case, this is very much on the young side. I pick a lot of my broad beans, for instance, when they are only a few inches long and still have a bit of the dead flower-head sticking to them. At this stage the beans need not be shelled. (When you have to shell beans you throw away a lot of the goodness in the pods.) With your own garden you don't need to wait until the vegetables are commercially valuable, but can pick them when they are crisp, tender and succulent.

The vegetables should be of an even size and texture; they should be picked through carefully and anything discoloured, bruised or tainted in any way should be discarded. And don't be misled by those who say you can freeze vegetables successfully without blanching them. This does apply to a few items, but most will have a very short freezer-life if they are not blanched before freezing.

Try to grade vegetables as you pick them so that each batch you freeze will be roughly the same size, shape and length.

Above all, use your common sense when planning your garden. Freshly picked peas are delicious and it really isn't worth freezing them in vast quantities: commercially frozen peas are cheaper in the long run and, if you buy a good brand, better than anything you can produce yourself. Instead, concentrate on the more expensive varieties, or on those vegetables you cannot buy out of season.

Buying fresh vegetables

If you decide to buy vegetables in bulk for freezing, make sure you are getting good value for money. If you shop around you will notice that the price of fresh produce in the greengrocer's varies considerably from day to day and from shop to shop. Wholesalers will often be happy to sell a commodity to a private individual who is prepared to buy the whole tray or box. At peak periods you can often get a good bargain from a greengrocer by offering to buy up what is left of his produce just before he closes.

Choose vegetables that are ripe but not over-ripe. If you buy them in bulk, check that the vegetables at the bottom of a box are in the same condition as those on top. If you plan to buy a box of vegetables, don't be afraid of taking one out to test it for tenderness and quality.

Pick vegetables that are of a good colour and even in size and thickness. Test them to see they are absolutely fresh and crisp. Avoid any vegetables that have gone limp and flabby.

Vegetables that have been picked when the weather is either extremely wet or extremely dry will not be at their top quality. Those picked when damp will often have a rather musty smell or some indication of mould, and those picked in a drought will tend to be either limp or dehydrated.

Buying frozen vegetables wholesale

Here the deep-freeze supermarkets have really come into their own. Small quantities of frozen vegetables tend to be expensive but large packs can be very economical. Buy vegetables that have been 'open-frozen' before packaging so that they are not stuck together and will flow smoothly from the pack.

Avoid any package that has been perforated or damaged in any way. Avoid any signs of freezer burn or of excessive ice crystallization inside the pack. Check the date stamp.

When buying peas or beans check on the quality. You will usually find that there is a system of grading and the more expensive packs will mean smaller but sweeter and more tender vegetables.

Many deep-freeze wholesalers now sell packs of onions – peeled, chopped and ready for use – and these can be a boon if you cook a lot with onions. No more tears – but remember no more onion peelings, either, to give stocks that valuable extra flavouring and rich colour. Items like these are time-savers, but they are seldom economies in the long run.

Vegetables and fruit usually thaw more quickly than large pieces of meat, so they should be well wrapped in an insulated bag or sack before leaving the supermarket, and put into your own freezer immediately you get home. Always make the deep-freeze supermarket your last call before going home and, if possible, try to shop at a time when the supermarket will be relatively empty.

If you live a long way from the supermarket and do your bulk buying only once every few months, you may well find it worth investing in a large, specially insulated box or bag for transporting your frozen goods in.

Fruit for freezing

Sweet fruit like strawberries, raspberries, peaches and nectarines is most delicious eaten fresh; if you have to preserve it, then by far the best method is by freezing. If you grow your own fruit, do eat as much fresh as you can, and freeze the rest – don't get carried away to the extent that you freeze everything and deny your family the joy of eating it fresh from the garden. On the other hand, fruit that has to be cooked before being eaten is every bit as good from the freezer as when it is cooked from the fresh state.

One of the mistakes people seem to make when deep-freezing fruit is that they get mean and hoard it, so that they finish the year with pounds of leftover fruit in the deep freeze just as the new season's crop is coming in. Avoid this by prolonging the various fruit seasons, using the fruit from your freezer as soon as the season is over.

All fruit to be frozen should be at its prime, fully ripe but never bruised or damaged in any way. Second-quality fruit can be puréed to use in pies, puddings and sauces.

Remember that, on the whole, the smaller, more compact varieties of the soft fruits make better freezers than the larger ones.

Growing fresh fruit

Pick the fruit for freezing when it is at the height of its ripeness and quality, and grade it as you go. The fruit can be hulled as you pick it. All soft fruit should be open-frozen before being packed to preserve its shape and to prevent its sticking together in the packaging. Pack home-picked fruit in solid containers to prevent damage.

Pick the fruit early in the morning, after the dew has evaporated but before the sun has reached its maximum power. Freeze the fruit as quickly as possible after picking.

Use damaged or second-quality fruit to make fruit purées or pie fillings.

I personally feel that strawberries, unlike raspberries, are not totally successful in home freezing and I would suggest that it is better to eat as many as you can fresh and then to purée the rest raw to freeze and use in delicious pudding recipes.

Buying fresh fruit

In a good year, many fruit farmers sell their strawberries, raspberries, apples, etc on the plant, so that you pick your own and pay for what you pick. This is the best way of buying top-quality fresh fruit for your freezer; you can grade it as you go along and check it for any blemishes. Pick it carefully, straight into containers for freezing or into baskets, being careful not to damage the fruit as you pick. Get the fruit home and into the freezer with the greatest possible speed.

When home-produced fruit is at its peak, you can usually buy it in bulk from a greengrocer or, better still, from a wholesaler or market. Check the bottom of the container to make sure the fruit below is of as good a quality as the fruit on top. When you get it home, check through and discard any blemished fruit before freezing. You may be able to use this with other cheap, second-quality fruit to cook or purée before freezing for later use in pies and puddings.

Fruit that is imported (for instance, those delicious little seedless green grapes) is usually extremely seasonal, but can vary in price. Buy imported fruit when it is at the height of its season and freeze the quantity you think your family can cope with.

Buy Seville oranges when they are in season; if you cannot cope with marmalade-making straight away, freeze the oranges whole or cut into slices, and then cook them later (see page 272).

Imported fruit is always picked and brought into this country in an underripe state. In order to freeze it when it is fully ripe and mature, you may find you have to keep the fruit in a warm, dry place for a day or two before freezing: this applies particularly to tomatoes, peaches and other soft fruit.

Buying frozen fruit wholesale

The best buys I have found in the commercial fruit section are raspberries, gooseberries and apricots, but you can, nowadays, find almost any fruit in frozen form.

Check to see that the packaging around the fruit is in no way damaged or perforated. Check, if possible, to see that the fruit has not been affected by freezer burn and that there is not excessive ice crystallization inside the packaging.

Fruit packaged in bulk should have been open-frozen before packaging so that the fruit will flow freely from the bag.

Compare the prices of fresh frozen fruit packed raw against that frozen in sugar or in a syrup.

Herbs

A few herbs go a long way and I find it sad how little we English use them in our cooking these days, although a lot of people are beginning to grow herbs in pots or tubs and it is easy to have a good supply of the basic herbs on your kitchen windowsill. They don't take up a lot of room, can be grown in (and will grace) a herbaceous border, or can make a pretty corner of the garden in their own right. In the reign of Elizabeth I, a good herb garden was an important feature of the estate and the flavour of herbs was considered vital to most meat, fish and poultry dishes. Then, often, herbs were necessary to flavour salted or somewhat 'high' meat. Now they are just as necessary, for with modern methods of farming and preserving food, so many things have lost their own individual flavour. The subtle use of herbs in cooking is, to my way of thinking, one of the essentials of top-class twentieth-century cuisine.

Freezing is the ideal way to preserve herbs and enable you to have a supply of as-fresh-as-when-picked flavours all the year round.

Pick herbs in the morning after the dew has dried, but before the sun has reached its full strength. Choose herbs that are at their peak but not tough, and remove any tough stalks before freezing. (Small-leaved herbs like tarragon and thyme can be left on their stalks; the leaves can be quickly stripped off whilst the sprigs are still frozen.)

Pack the herbs in small quantities; seal packages of herbs with great care, as their smell is usually strong and can pervade other produce in the freezer.

Divide the herbs into bouquets garnis for using with various types of meat, fish and poultry, and for adding to stocks.

To use frozen herbs

Strip frozen herbs off stalks if necessary. If finely chopped herbs are required, crush them in the packet whilst still frozen to get a chopped texture. Add the frozen herbs to any recipes, salad dressings, etc.

For a dish that calls for a garnish of raw herbs, crush them whilst still frozen and thaw in a refrigerator until required.

The following is a list of herbs which I find grow well in my own garden, high up on windswept Bodmin Moor:

Easy-to-grow herbs

Basil Marvellous with any raw or cooked tomato dish.

Bay leaves Essential to almost any bouquet garni. Evergreen, so does not need to be frozen.

Chervil Used more widely on the Continent than parsley, and with a more subtle flavour.

Chives Delicious with soups and salad dishes of all kinds.

Coriander A very aromatic herb which gives Eastern overtones to chicken, lamb and vegetable dishes.

Dill Grows well, looks pretty and is delicious with fish.

Marjoram Good with any meat dish.

Mint Forget about the normal, prolific spearmint and grow apple, pineapple, orange and peppermint varieties.

Parsley One of the most invaluable flavourings.

Rosemary Another pretty garden plant that goes well with chicken and lamb. An evergreen, so not necessary to freeze.

Sage A little goes a long way, but it is delicious with pork, with any sausage dish and with tomato dishes.

Savory The traditional accompaniment to broad beans, but also good with other vegetables.

Tarragon A classic herb for chicken, fish and salad dishes. Use sparingly.

Thyme One of the prettiest of herbs. Grow the golden, silver and lemon varieties as well as the common one.

Bouquet garni combinations Pick the herbs first thing in the morning. Tie them in small bunches, pack in polythene bags, seal, label and freeze.

Bouquet garni for chicken

sprig parsley
2 bay leaves
sprig rosemary
small sprig thyme
Or:

sprig lemon thyme
sprig chervil
sprig tarragon
bay leaf
Or:

sprig parsley
sprig marjoram
sprig sage
bay leaf

Bouquet garni for pork

2 bay leaves
small sprig rosemary
sprig sage
2 sprigs parsley

Bouquet garni for beef

2 bay leaves
sprig parsley
sprig chervil
sprig marjoram

Bouquet garni for fish

2 sprigs parsley
sprig dill
sprig tarragon
2 bay leaves

Bouquet garni for stockpots

3 sprigs parsley (or chervil, or both mixed)
sprig thyme
sprig marjoram
sprig sage
2 bay leaves

'Free' food

How nice it is to find something 'free' these days. If you live in the country there is a surprising variety of foodstuffs in the fields and hedgerows that is well worth picking and freezing.

Elderflowers and berries

Apart from making an excellent champagne-type wine, elderflowers make the most delicious fritters to serve as a pudding.

Pick the flowers early in the morning, but after the dew has risen, when they are in full bloom. Cut the flower-heads off at

the top of the stalk (so that the flower-head remains intact) shake well to remove any insects, and open-freeze until firm. Pack the flowers carefully into a rigid container.
To use the flowers: dip frozen flower-heads into a fritter batter, deep-fry until crisp, drain on kitchen paper and serve with a generous sprinkling of caster sugar and with quarters of lemon.

Elderberries can be stripped off their stalks, open-frozen and packed like blackcurrants to use as an alternative to currants.

Violets

Violets make the prettiest decoration imaginable for cold puddings. Pick the violets early in the morning, cut off the heads with a pair of scissors at the top of the stalk, spread the flowers on a tray and open-freeze until solid. Pack carefully in a rigid container to prevent damage in the deep freeze.
To use the flowers: place the frozen flowers as a decoration on any fruit mousse.

Nettles

Young nettles make an excellent vegetable or soup. To use as a vegetable, pick young nettle shoots, blanch them in boiling water for 2 minutes and freeze like spinach.

Combine the nettles with a good stock to make a soup that is delicious and rich in iron. For a substantial dish, serve the soup with a light seasoning of nutmeg and a poached egg floating in each serving.

Dandelions

Dandelions are widely used on the Continent as a vegetable as well as a salad ingredient. Pick over young dandelion leaves and wash them well. Prepare for the freezer and use them as a vegetable exactly as you would use lettuce leaves.

Sorrel

Wild sorrel, which is to be found in most fields in this country, can be used in a surprising number of ways. Fresh, it makes a marvellous piquant addition to salads; frozen, it can be made into a subtle soup (see page 157), used as a spinach-type vegetable or as the base of an excellent sauce. A purée of sorrel (see page 168) makes a first-rate accompaniment to a rich, fatty roasted dish such as pork, duck or goose.

Hazelnuts

If you manage to get there before the squirrels do, you can often gather a good harvest of nuts from just one hazel bush. The fresh nuts can be stored in a warm dry place, but they tend to dry out and if you manage to gather quite a respectable amount it is well worth shelling and freezing them to use chopped in fruit salads or chopped and lightly roasted as a topping for a number of sweet and savoury dishes.

Bilberries (whortleberries, blueberries, herts, worts, etc)

Hard work to pick, but worth the effort as they make an excellent filling for pies. Hull the berries as you pick them, and open-freeze as soon as possible. Pack, label and freeze, and use them as you would blackcurrants.

Blackberries

About the most prolific of summer fruits and worth picking in large quantities. Pick when the sun is not full on the fruit and never when they are damp or soggy. Check over carefully before freezing to make sure they have no insects or maggots. Open-freeze and pack in the same way as any other soft fruit.

Blackberries can also be stewed with sugar and puréed through a sieve or food mill before freezing.

Hips, haws and rowan berries

These can be made into a good jelly to serve with game. Pick the fruit when it is fully ripe, wash well and freeze until you wish to make the jelly.

Preparation for freezing

Meat

Unless you are dealing with specific joints of meat, wrap cuts in small rather than large pieces.

Choose meat for the freezer as carefully as you would for any other purpose.

Bones take up a lot of unnecessary room in the freezer and as many as possible should be cut out and used to make stock. Sharp bones also cause damage to wrapping materials.

Meat is especially susceptible to freezer burn and the most successful packaging of all is the vacuum packs used commercially. For home freezing all air in the packaging that can be expelled should be squeezed out.

Large joints Wipe meat with a clean, damp cloth and prepare for the oven. Joints with awkward bones should be lightly wrapped in cotton stockinette before packaging to prevent perforation of the covering. Do not cover too thickly, however, as thick layers of wrapping can act as an insulator, slowing down the freezing process. Pack in heavy-duty polythene bags; press out all air; seal, label and freeze.

Large joints can also be wrapped in heavy-duty foil and sealed with freezer tape, but as foil tends to tear, it is best to overwrap the packages with polythene.

Small cuts Wipe meat with a clean, damp cloth, prepare for cooking. Pack in heavy-duty polythene bags; press out all air; seal, label and freeze.

Meat for stewing or casseroling Prepare meat for cooking before freezing. Pack in small quantities. Pack in heavy-duty polythene

bags; press out all air; seal, label and freeze. For convenient stacking in the freezer and to save space, pack the diced meat firmly in a rectangular container, place the container in a polythene bag, seal and freeze. When the meat is frozen solid, turn it out of the container, place the block in a heavy-duty polythene bag; press out all air; seal, label and freeze.
Note Stewing meat that you feel might be extra-tough can, for short periods, be frozen in a marinade of oil and lemon juice to help tenderize the meat and shorten the cooking time.

Minced meat Mince meat before rather than after freezing for speedy use when a quick meal is required. Pack in heavy-duty polythene bags in small quantities, or follow the instructions for 'meat for stewing or casseroling' above.

Steak, chops, and other cuts for frying With these small cuts the meat is especially susceptible to freezer burn because so much of the surface of the meat is exposed. They must, therefore, be very carefully packaged with all the air removed, and their freezer-life is less than that of large cuts.

Prepare steaks and chops for cooking, trimming off excess fat, etc. Separate steaks or chops with a layer of foil or polythene film and press firmly together as tightly as possible. Wrap in heavy-duty polythene bags; exclude all air; seal, label and freeze.

Offal Make sure offal is absolutely fresh before freezing. Prepare the offal for cooking, i.e. remove any excess fat and tough fibres, cut out the hard core from kidneys, and dice or slice the offal as necessary. Pack in small quantities in heavy-duty polythene bags; seal, label and freeze.

Hamburgers, meat balls, rissoles etc Prepare for cooking and open-freeze. Pack in a rigid container with foil or polythene film between layers. Fill any spaces in the container with crumpled kitchen paper; seal, label and freeze. To ensure no air gets into the container, it should be sealed with freezer tape or overpacked in a polythene bag. Hamburgers containing raw bacon should only be frozen for short periods. Instead of the traditional circular hamburgers, make them square for easy packaging.

Sausages Pack in small quantities, separating layers with foil or polythene film. Pack in heavy-duty polythene bags; press out all air; seal, label and freeze.

Sausage meat Pack in small quantities; wrap in polythene film and pack in heavy-duty polythene bags. Press out all air; seal, label and freeze (or follow instructions for 'meat for stewing or casseroling', above.)

Salted or cured meat Do not soak before freezing. Wipe with a dry cloth; pack in heavy-duty polythene bags; press out all air; seal, label and freeze.

Bacon

Make sure bacon is absolutely fresh and never sticky or slimy. Smoked bacon has a longer freezer-life than green bacon. Do not freeze joints weighing over 2·25 kg (5 lb) as these cannot be frozen quickly enough to give good results.

Bacon joints Wipe over with a clean, damp cloth and wrap tightly with foil. Pack in heavy-duty polythene bags; press out all air; seal, label and freeze.

Bacon rashers, gammon steaks, etc Separate layers with foil or polythene film. Pack in heavy-duty polythene bags; press out all air; seal, label and freeze.

Commercial vacuum-packed rashers or joints Examine packs carefully to make sure they have not been damaged or perforated in any way. Relabel and freeze.

Poultry

Whole chickens, ducks, guinea fowl and turkeys Remove giblets and wipe the inside of the bird with a clean, damp cloth. Prepare for cooking and truss if necessary. Wrap foil around leg-ends and wing-tips to prevent perforation of wrapping in the freezer. Pack in heavy-duty polythene bags; press out all the air; seal, label and freeze.

If you wish to have the giblets with the bird, pack them in a small, separate polythene bag and place it with the bird in the main package, but remember that giblets can be stored for a shorter length of time than the bird itself.

Chicken or turkey portions Wrap portions in polythene film, pack in heavy-duty polythene bags or pack tightly in rigid containers; seal, label and freeze.

Giblets Giblets make excellent stew, stocks and gravy; chicken livers make excellent sauces and pâtés. Pack chicken livers in small quantities in rigid containers; seal, label and freeze. Pack gizzards and hearts for stewing in heavy-duty polythene bags. Pack necks for stock and gravy in heavy-duty polythene bags.

Game

Hang all game before freezing.

Pheasant, partridge, pigeon, grouse Hang birds head down in a cool, dry place, from 4 to 8 days depending on how high you like your game and on the weather conditions prevailing during the hanging time. Pluck the hung birds; remove the heads but leave on the feet; pick out any shot if possible, and clean out the insides of the birds. Wrap the feet and wing-tips of the birds in foil to prevent any perforation of the packaging material during freezing; pack in heavy-duty polythene bags; press out all the air; seal, label and freeze. The long tail-feathers of pheasants can be frozen with the bird for decoration, but they should be carefully wrapped in foil to prevent their being damaged. Tough, old birds can be jointed before freezing to use for casseroles and made-up dishes – pack as for chicken portions.

For pâtés and terrines, strip the flesh off the birds (use the bones to make a rich stock). Pack the flesh in heavy-duty polythene bags.

Woodcock and snipe Hang the birds head down for 4–8 days in a cool, dry place, depending on how high you like your game and on the weather conditions prevailing. Pluck carefully, leaving the head, feet and entrails intact. Twist the head back and use the long beak as a skewer to anchor the legs in a trussed position. Wrap the birds in two layers of foil to prevent perforation of packaging material by the sharp beaks, and pack in heavy-duty polythene bags. Press out all air; seal, label and freeze.

Venison Venison must be hung before freezing or the meat will be tough and stringy. It should be hung for 5–8 days, depending on weather conditions. The meat is usually sold in cuts similar to those of beef and should be packed in the same way. Any tough cuts can be cut up for casseroling and frozen with a marinade of oil and lemon juice to help tenderize the meat.

Hares Hang hares, head down, unpaunched, for 5–6 days in a cold, dry place. Attach a bowl to the head to catch any blood (this helps to make the rich gravy for jugged hare and other dishes). Skin and clean the hung hare, reserving the liver. Divide into joints (unless the hare is to be roasted whole) and wipe well with a clean, damp cloth. Wrap each joint in polythene film, pack with the liver in a heavy-duty polythene bag; press out all air; seal, label and freeze. The blood can be frozen in ice-cube moulds and packed with the joints.

If you have more than one hare the saddles can be packed and frozen separately for roasting, and the remaining joints packed for stewing or jugging. The joints of a tough, old hare can be marinated in oil and lemon juice before freezing to help tenderize the meat.

Rabbits Should not be hung. Skin and clean and divide into joints. Wipe the joints with a clean, damp cloth, wrap in polythene film and pack in a heavy-duty polythene bag. Press out all air; seal, label and freeze.

Fish

Because of the strong aroma and the sensitive texture of fish, extra-special care should be taken when packing any fresh fish or shellfish.

Large fish to freeze whole Prepare for cooking or just wipe with a damp cloth. (Gutting a thawed fish is just one degree more unattractive than performing the same operation on a fresh one; but I personally find the taste of a large fish, such as a salmon, is even better if it is frozen with the guts still in.) Dip the fish into water and open-freeze until a solid skin of ice has formed. Wrap in plastic film and then in a polythene bag. Press out all air; seal, label and freeze.

Fillets or steaks Prepare for cooking (i.e. remove skin, etc); rub oily fish with lemon juice; dip white fish into water to which a handful of salt has been added. Wrap each piece of fish in waxed paper or plastic film and pack in a polythene bag (or open-freeze fish before packing); seal, label and freeze.

Lobster, crab and crayfish Cook and remove meat from the shell. Pack meat tightly in a rigid container or polythene bag; seal, label and freeze. The shells can be carefully washed out and frozen separately.

Prawns and shrimps Cook, cool quickly and peel or leave whole. Open-freeze and pack in polythene bags. Squeeze out all air; seal, label and freeze.

Oysters Remove from the shell, dip oysters into cold salted water, and pack with the liquid from the shells in rigid containers. Fill any headspace with crumpled foil; seal, label and freeze. (Always discard any oysters that are already open.)

Mussels Prepare for soup, stuff or make into sauce. Pack in rigid containers; seal, label and freeze. (Always discard any mussels that have opened of their own accord.) They can be repacked in their shells and frozen.

Small fish: sprats, whitebait, etc Open-freeze; pack in polythene bags; squeeze out all air; seal, label and freeze.

Vegetables

Fresh vegetables Grade and prepare for freezing; blanch if necessary (see chart below). Cool, dry and pack in polythene bags, polythene containers or special foil bags. Open-freeze small vegetables before packing. Seal, label and freeze.

Cooked vegetables and vegetable dishes Cook, cool quickly, pack in rigid containers, seal, label and freeze. Individual items like stuffed courgettes, tomatoes, aubergines, etc should be separated by waxed paper or plastic film. Pack fragile vegetables like asparagus in rigid containers.

Blanching vegetables

For long-term storage of most vegetables, blanching is essential. There are a few exceptions to this rule, however (some should be completely cooked and a few can be frozen raw), and these are listed in the vegetable freezer-life guide (see page 92).

The blanching times given are for average-sized vegetables. If, like me, you like to pick your vegetables from your own garden when they are exceptionally young, tender and sweet, cut down a little on the blanching time. Vegetables that are finely chopped or thinly sliced will obviously need a shorter blanching time than coarsely chopped or sliced ones.

When blanching some people make the mistake of trying to cope with too large a quantity of vegetables at a time. Blanch in small quantities, using a large pan of water and a special blanching basket which enables the boiling water to flow freely between the vegetables.

Always wait until the water is boiling really fast before adding the vegetables, and time the blanching process from the moment the water returns to the boil after the vegetables have been added.

Remove the vegetables immediately the blanching time is up and plunge them straight into a bowl of ice-cold water (add ice-cubes or freezer bags to cool the vegetables as quickly as possible).

As soon as the vegetables are cold, spread them on kitchen towels to dry. Make sure they are really well dried before freezing. Spread vegetables that are to be open-frozen (peas, beans, carrots, etc) on trays and fast-freeze until solid. Pack at once, as quickly as possible, and return to the freezer.

Vegetables that discolour when cut or trimmed should have lemon juice added to the blanching water.

The same water can be used for blanching successive vegetables unless they have a strong odour (e.g. cauliflowers) or are bitter (e.g. chicory).

Blanching chart

Vegetables and their preparation	Blanching time (minutes)
Artichokes (globe) whole: Remove outer leaves, trim tops with scissors. Rub stalks with lemon. Blanch in boiling water with 1 tablespoon lemon juice. Invert artichokes and leave to drain well	6–8
Artichokes (globe) hearts: Blanch in water with 1 tablespoon lemon juice added	3
Asparagus: Wash, trim to even lengths. Blanch in water with 1 tablespoon lemon juice added	1–2
Aubergines/egg plant: Slice or dice. Blanch in water with 1 tablespoon lemon juice added. Pack with polythene film or waxed paper between layers	2
Broad beans: Pod large beans; slice very young beans and pods, or leave whole	1

Vegetables and their preparation	Blanching time (minutes)
French beans: Top and tail. Leave young beans whole	1
Runner beans: Top, tail and slice	1
Beet tops: Trim off tough stalks and wash well	1
Broccoli: Divide into sprigs	2
Brussels sprouts: Trim off outer leaves. Blanch sprouts of uniform size. Drain well	1–2
Cabbage: Wash and shred or cut small cabbage in quarters. Drain well	1–2
Chinese cabbage: Wash and shred. Drain well	1
Carrots: Leave young carrots whole. Slice or dice large carrots	2
Cauliflower: Remove all outside leaves. Divide into florets	1–2
Celery: Trim and scrape if necessary. Cut into short lengths	1–2
Chicory: Trim, removing outer leaves. Add 1 tablespoon lemon juice to blanching water	2
Corn on the cob: Trim off leaves and silk surrounds	8–10
Courgettes/zucchini: Wash and cut into thin slices or dice	1
Cucumber: Cut into thick slices or dice	1
Egg plant, see *Aubergines*	
Florentine fennel: Trim and cut into fairly thin slices. Add 1 tablespoon lemon juice to blanching water	1
Kale: Shred and drain well	1

Vegetables and their preparation	Blanching time (minutes)
Leeks: Trim. Leave small leeks whole. Cut large leeks into thick slices	2
Mange-tout peas: Trim ends. Drain well	1
Marrow: Peel, cut into thick slices and remove seeds	1
Mushrooms: Slice firm mushrooms. Add 1 tablespoon lemon juice to water	1
Onions: Peel and chop or slice thinly. Leave very small onions or shallots whole	1–2
Parsnips: Trim, peel and cut into slices or small dice. Add 1 tablespoon lemon juice to blanching water	1–2
Peas: Pod and grade	1
Peppers: Remove core and seeds. Halve, cut into thin strips, or chop finely	1–2
Spinach: Wash carefully and drain well	1
Turnips: Trim, peel and cut into thin slices or small dice	1–2
Zucchini, see *Courgettes*	

Fruit

There are several ways of preparing and packing raw fruit for the deep freeze. The method you choose should be the most suitable one for the type and condition of the fruit that is to be frozen.

Open-freezing

Ideal for soft fruit – strawberries, raspberries, loganberries, currants, blackberries etc.

Pick over the fruit, removing any stalks or hulls. Make sure it is clean but do not wash unless this is absolutely necessary, as water is inclined to make the fruit soggy. If you do have to wash the fruit, make sure it is well dried before being frozen.

Spread the prepared fruit on a tray and freeze at the lowest possible temperature until solid – 30–60 minutes. As soon as the fruit is hard, transfer it to rigid containers. Fill up any gaps with crumpled kitchen paper, seal, label, and return to the freezer.

Note Red- and blackcurrants can be frozen on the stem. The frozen berries can easily be stripped off when you want to use them.

Freezing with sugar

Suitable for harder berries like gooseberries, and especially those with a skin, like cherries. Usually this method of freezing is used for fruit that is to be cooked. Also good for rhubarb, pineapple and citrus fruit.

Pick over the fruit, but do not wash unless this is absolutely necessary.

Pack the fruit in rigid containers with alternate layers of fruit and granulated sugar (the more bitter the fruit, the more sugar you will need to use). Leave 1·25-cm (½-in) headspace for the fruit to expand.

Freezing with sugar syrup

A sugar syrup helps to protect the texture of fruit during freezing. Fruit that discolours when peeled should be frozen in this way, and so should the ingredients for a fruit salad (except bananas).

The sweetness of the syrup depends on the tartness of the fruit, but as a general guide I would suggest using 250 gr (10 oz) sugar to 6 dl (1 pint) water.

Combine the sugar with the water, adding at least a tablespoon of lemon juice for fruit that discolours easily (e.g. apples and pears) or use ¼ teaspoon ascorbic acid crystals (these can be bought from a chemist) to every 6 dl (1 pint) syrup, stirring it into the hot syrup until the crystals have dissolved. Bring the sugar and water slowly to the boil, stirring occasionally. Simmer for 5 minutes and leave to get quite cold.

Prepare the fruit by peeling, chopping, slicing, etc. Add the fruit to the syrup and pack in rigid containers leaving at least 1·25-cm (½-in) headspace for the fruit to expand. Seal, label and freeze. As fruit is inclined to rise to the top of syrup you may need to put some crumpled greaseproof paper on top of the fruit in your package to keep it submerged.

Freezing fruit purée

Suitable for almost all fruit – in particular soft fruit like apples, pears, plums, damsons, apricots – and especially useful for fruit that is blemished or overripe. The fruit can be puréed raw or can be cooked and then puréed. It can be sweetened before freezing or when you come to use it. Fruit that discolours is best sweetened and cooked, and a tablespoon of lemon juice must be added to the fruit whilst it is cooking.

Raw purées: Mash or sieve the fruit or purée it through a food mill or in an electric liquidizer. Add sugar or leave the fruit as it is, but be careful to indicate on the label whether it has been sweetened or not. Pour the purée into rigid containers; leave at least 1·25-cm (½-in) headspace for the purée to expand. Seal, label and freeze.

Cooked purées: Pick over the fruit and combine it with as little water as possible (4 tablespoons is usually adequate for any quantity of fruit) in a heavy saucepan. Add sugar if a sweet purée is required and cook over a low heat until the fruit is soft. Purée through a sieve, through a food mill, or in an electric liquidizer, and leave to cool. Pack in rigid containers; leave at least 1·25-cm (½-in) headspace for the purée to expand. Seal, label (stating whethei it is sweetened or not) and freeze.

Freezing precooked fruit

It is often useful to have a stock of ready-stewed fruit which can be served by itself with cream or custard, or made into pies. Prepare and stew the fruit with sugar in the normal way. Leave to cool. Pack, leaving 1·25-cm (½-in) headspace for expansion. Seal, label, and freeze.

Preparation and freezing of fruit

Packing in dry syrup

Use on average 175 gr (6 oz) sugar for 2 lb (1 kg) fruit, increasing this quantity for very tart fruit and lessening it for fruit that is naturally very sweet.

Packing in sugar syrups

Syrup	Weight of sugar	Amount of water
Light	450 gr (1 lb)	1 litre (1¾ pints)
Medium	675 gr (1½ lb)	1 litre (1¾ pints)
Heavy	900 gr (2 lb)	1 litre (1¾ pints)
Very heavy	1·8 kg (4 lb)	1 litre (1¾ pints)

For all the syrups combine the water and sugar in a heavy saucepan and bring to the boil, stirring every now and then until the sugar has melted. Leave to cool and then use as required.

Note I recommend adding at least 1 tablespoon of lemon juice per 600 ml (1 pint) of water.

Apples

Slices: peel, core and slice apples, dropping the slices into cold, slightly salted water as you do so. Rinse and pat dry with kitchen paper when ready to freeze.

Open-freeze: place dried apple slices on trays, open-freeze until solid, pack in polythene bags, seal, label and freeze.

In syrup: use a medium syrup with the addition of lemon juice to prevent browning.

With sugar: blanch in a light sugar syrup for 1 minute, dry and layer with a sprinkling of sugar.

Purée: peel and core apples and cook with a little lemon juice and a minimum of water to prevent sticking until soft. Mash to a purée, cool and pack, seal, label and freeze.
Note Do not add sugar, so that the apple purée can be used either as a sweet or as a savoury apple sauce.

Apricots

Fresh apricots are only on the market at certain times of the year. When they are available it is well worth while making a deal with a greengrocer or taking a visit to your local market to buy a reasonably priced tray of the fruit.

Halved: halve the fruit and remove the cores. Pack with a covering of medium syrup, seal, label and freeze.

With sugar: halve the apricots and remove the stones. Blanch the halves in a medium syrup, drain well, cool and pack with a sprinkling of sugar between each layer.

Puréed: apricot purée is ideal for making mousses, fools and many other sweets. Halve the apricots, remove the stones. Add 1 cm (½ in) water to the saucepan together with about 225 gr (8 oz) sugar to each 450 gr (1 lb) apricots. Bring slowly to the boil and simmer gently until the apricots are really soft. Purée them through a food mill, an electric liquidizer or a food processer. Cool, pack, seal, label and freeze.

Bilberries, blackberries, cranberries, raspberries, currants, etc.

I find all these berry fruits are most successfully frozen open on trays (do not wash unless absolutely necessary), then packed when they are solid, sealed, labelled and frozen.

All these fruits should be hulled before being frozen and the more slowly you can defrost them the better.

Cherries

Choose fully ripened and unblemished fruit. Remove the stalks and stones (a useful tool can be bought for doing this surprisingly easily).

In syrup: use a medium syrup for sweet fruit and a heavy syrup for tart or cooking cherries.

Damsons, plums, greengages, etc.

Halve and remove stones.

In syrup: use a heavy syrup and be sure to add lemon juice to prevent browning.

Gooseberries

For long-term freezing: top and tail firm, ripe berries and blanch them in a light syrup for ½ minute to soften the skins. Drain well and cool.

In syrup: use a heavy syrup, pack, seal, label and freeze.

Open-freeze: freeze on trays, pack, seal, label and return to the freezer.

For short-term freezing: top and tail the fruit, open-freeze on trays, pack, seal, label and return to the freezer.

Grapefruit

Buy grapefruit when they are inexpensive and really good quality. Use them for quick breakfast starters and as part of a fruit salad or as the basis of some unusual desserts.

Using a sharp knife, cut the skin and membrane from the grapefruit. Cut out the segments from the membrane so that they remain whole if possible. Cover the segments with a medium-strength syrup, pack, seal, label and freeze.

Grapes

Grapes in one variety or another are available all year round now and since they do not freeze well and need, for real success, to be both peeled and de-pipped I suggest it is not worth the effort of freezing them.

Melons

Again, I do not feel the flesh of melons freezes well enough to be worth the trouble. Better by far to buy and enjoy them when they are in season and a reasonable price.

Mangoes

Mangoes can be found in the better greengrocers and markets and they are delicious. If you find them selling reasonably it is worth buying and freezing some to add an exotic taste to your fruit salads. Make sure the mangoes are ripe (they are usually sold unripe so put them in a brown paper bag, on a sunny windowsill, and leave them until they have a strong, sweet, smell and have light brown patches on the flesh). Thinly peel the mangoes and cut the flesh off the stones in thick slices. Pack in heavy syrup, seal, label and freeze.

I also like to purée the fruit raw with a little lemon juice and sugar and freeze the purée as a base for mousses, fools and ice-cream.

Peaches and nectarines

Choose firm, ripe fruit that is unblemished. Peel the skin (preferably with a silver knife) and slice the flesh off the stone into a heavy syrup with the addition of some lemon juice. Pack, seal, label and freeze. Defrost, still packed, in a refrigerator.

Pineapple

Pineapple can be bought cheaply at certain times of the year and can be a good bargain. Peel, core and cut into slices, fingers or dice and pack in heavy syrup. Do not freeze for longer than three months.

Rhubarb

Young rhubarb freezes well and makes a good freezer standby if you have a glut in your garden or can buy it cheaply in season. Trim the stems, cut into 3-cm (1-inch) lengths and blanch in light syrup for 1 minute. Drain and cool.

In syrup: cover with a medium syrup, pack, seal, label and freeze.

With sugar: put the rhubarb into a plastic bag with some sugar, toss well so that the pieces are coated with sugar, pack, seal, label and freeze.

Open-freeze: place the well-drained rhubarb on a tray and open-freeze until solid. Pack, seal, label and return to the freezer.

Strawberries

Quite frankly, I have never found strawberries to be worth freezing whole unless the berries are slightly underripe and very firm or are the small, firm, woodland variety. If they are firm they can be open-frozen, packed, sealed and labelled and they should be very slowly defrosted in a refrigerator.

Soft fruit is best frozen in purée form with a little lemon juice and some sugar.

Herbs

Remove any tough stalks (small-leaved varieties like thyme and tarragon can be left whole as the leaves are easily stripped off while the sprigs are still frozen). Pack in small quantities in small polythene bags. Seal, label and freeze. Because of the strong aromas of most herbs, great attention should be paid to careful packaging.

Dairy foods

Eggs Separate whites and yolks and pack in small or individual quantities in ice-cube trays or in small polythene tubs. Leave headspace for expansion. Seal, label and freeze.

Butter, margarine and lard Leave in its wrapping but overwrap, four to eight packets at a time, in a polythene bag. Seal, label and freeze.

Cheese Wrap in plastic film and overwrap in heavy-duty polythene bag. Squeeze out all air; seal, label and freeze. Cheese has a strong odour and therefore special attention should be paid to careful packaging.

Double or clotted cream Freeze in original containers but overwrap with a polythene bag. Seal, label and freeze.

Bread and cakes

Bread Pack in polythene bags; squeeze out all air; seal, label and freeze. Overwrap sliced and wrapped bread as well as whole loaves.

Cakes (*iced*) Pack in cardboard boxes; fill up spaces with crumpled kitchen paper or foil; seal, label and freeze. Open-freeze cakes with fancy icing before freezing.

Cakes (*not iced*) Open-freeze and pack frozen cakes in polythene bags. Squeeze out all the air; seal, label and freeze.

Small iced cakes Open-freeze before packing in rigid containers. Fill empty spaces with crumpled paper or foil; seal, label and freeze.

Buns, small cakes, baps, etc Pack in polythene bags; seal, label and freeze.

Pastry

Cooked pastry Pack fragile pastry (i.e. cases baked blind, etc) in rigid containers. Fill up spaces with crumpled kitchen paper or foil; seal, label and freeze.

Uncooked pastry Form pastry into a neat block, wrap in plastic film and overwrap in a polythene bag. Seal, label and freeze.

Sandwiches

Lightly wrap sandwiches with plastic film and pack in a polythene bag. Seal, label and freeze.

Batter

Pack batter in a polythene container, leaving headspace for expansion. Seal, label and freeze.

Precooked dishes

Pancakes, unfilled Separate each pancake with a layer of waxed paper or plastic film; pack in a polythene bag; seal, label and freeze.

Pancakes, filled Pack in a rigid container; seal, label and freeze.

Boiled puddings, sweet and savoury Pack in their bowls inside a polythene bag; seal, label and freeze.

Casseroles, stews, ragouts, etc Open-freeze in their cooking vessels and transfer to a polythene bag when frozen solid; seal, label and freeze. Or transfer the cooled food to a rigid container; seal, label and freeze.

Deep-fried food in batter or breadcrumbs Open-freeze and pack in a polythene bag when solid. Exclude all air; seal, label and freeze. Or pack in rigid containers with a sheet of waxed paper or plastic film between each layer.

Ice-cream Press down firmly into a polythene container; seal, label and freeze.

Soups and stocks Pour into rigid containers; seal, label and freeze; or reduce stock to one-third and store in ice-cube trays.

Sauces Pour cooled sauces into rigid containers; seal, label and freeze.

Pizzas, pies, etc To prevent damage in the frozen state, pack pizzas and pies between two cardboard picnic plates. Overwrap with a polythene bag; seal, label and freeze.

Freezer-life guide

Everyone has their own ideas about the length of time various fresh and cooked foods can be stored in a domestic deep freeze. Given 100-per-cent efficient wrapping, with the package totally sealed and all air excluded, a large joint of beef, for instance, can be frozen for an almost indefinite period, provided it has been taken to a low temperature in the shortest possible time. These conditions, however, can only really be produced commercially when food is vacuum-packed and speedily frozen by modern methods such as blast-freezing.

When using a home deep freeze it is always better to be on the safe side than to be disappointed with the end-product, so this guide is a conservative one.

It is most efficient to keep the deep freeze over half filled and to have a quick turnover of the contents. There may be occasions when one might wish to buy a commodity in bulk in order to bank it against rising prices, but, on the whole, it is more realistic and more economical in the long run to keep frozen produce rotating.

Foods with a high fat content will have a shorter storage life than those with most fat removed, as fat tends to take on a rancid flavour after a certain length of time.

Note The following table does not apply to commercially frozen products. Most commercially frozen food is marked with a conservative estimate of storage time.

Fresh foods

Meat

Beef	large joints	12 months
	small cuts	9 months
	steaks	5 months
	mince, hamburgers, etc	3 months
	cubed for stews	4 months
	salt beef	6 months
Lamb	large joints	8 months
	large joints, stuffed	2 months
	chops, noisettes, etc	6 months
	cubed for stews	4 months
Pork	large joints	6 months
	large joints, stuffed	2 months
	chops	4 months
	fat pork e.g. belly, etc	3 months
Veal	large joints	6 months
	large joints, stuffed	2 months
	escallops and chops	3 months
Smoked meats		2–3 months
Meat fat	for rendering, etc	2 months
Dripping		2 months
Offal	kidneys, hearts, etc	2 months
Tripe		2 months
Sausages	fresh	2 months
	smoked	3 months
Bacon	joints/rashers specially packed for deep-freezing	5 months
	ordinary vacuum-packed joints/rashers	2–3 months
	home-packed joints	
	(smoked)	2 months
	(unsmoked)	1½ months

Meat *continued*		
	home-packed rashers	
	(smoked)	$1\frac{1}{2}$ months
	(unsmoked)	1 month
Poultry		
Chicken	whole for roasting	9 months
	joints	6 months
	off the bone	4 months
	giblets	2 months
	whole stuffed	2 months
Duck	whole for roasting	8 months
	joints	6 months
	giblets	2 months
	whole stuffed	2 months
Goose	whole	6 months
Guinea fowl	whole	8 months
Turkey	whole	8 months
	joints	6 months
	off the bone	4 months
	giblets	4 months
Game		
Grouse	young and tender	8 months
	old, jointed	6 months
Hare	large joints	8 months
	small joints	6 months
Partridge	young and tender	8 months
	old, jointed	6 months
Pheasant	young and tender	8 months
	old, jointed	6 months
Pigeon		8 months
Rabbit	joints	6 months

Game *continued*		
Venison	large cuts	10 months
	small cuts	8 months
Woodcock and snipe	(do not draw)	4 months
Fish		
Smoked fish	whole	8 months
	sliced	4 months
Shellfish		2 months
Whole white fish	large	6 months
	small	4–5 months
Haddock	whole	6 months
	fillets	4 months
Herring	whole or filleted	4 months
Mackerel	whole or filleted	4 months
Salmon	whole	6 months
	cuts or steaks	4 months
Turbot	steaks	4 months
Fillets or steaks of other fish		3 months
Vegetables		
Artichokes, globe	whole or hearts	12 months
Artichokes, Jerusalem	purée or soup only	12 months
Asparagus		9 months
Aubergines/egg plant	blanched	12 months
	sautéed	6 months
Avocados	puréed with lemon juice	1 month
Beans, broad	shelled, blanched	12 months
	young, whole in pods, sliced, blanched	6 months
Beans, French	blanched	12 months
	unblanched, raw	2 months

Vegetables *continued*		
Beans, runner	blanched	12 months
Beetroot	cooked	12 months
Beet tops	blanched	6 months
Broccoli	blanched	12 months
Brussels sprouts	blanched	12 months
Cabbage	blanched	6 months
Cabbage, Chinese	blanched	6 months
Carrots	blanched	12 months
	whole, young, unblanched	3 months
Cauliflower (florets only)	blanched	12 months
Celeriac	cooked	2 months
Celery	blanched	4 months
Chicory	cooked	4 months
Corn on the cob	blanched	12 months
Courgettes/zucchini	blanched or sautéed	6 months
Cucumber	cooked	4 months
Egg plant, see *Aubergines*		
Florentine fennel	blanched or puréed	4 months
Kale	blanched	6 months
Leeks	blanched	6 months
Marrow	blanched	12 months
Mushrooms	blanched or sautéed	6 months
	button, raw, unblanched	3 months
Onions	raw	3 months
	cooked	4 months
Parsnips	blanched	12 months
Peas (large)	blanched	12 months
Peas (small)	blanched	12 months
	raw, unblanched	3 months

Vegetables *continued*		
Peas (*mange-tout*)	blanched	8 months
Peppers, green or red	blanched	12 months
	raw	3 months
Potatoes	chipped/part fried	8 months
	new/parboiled	8 months
	baked	6 months
	mashed	3 months
Spinach	blanched	12 months
	raw	3 months
Tomatoes	puréed	12 months
	skinned, whole	3 months
Turnips	blanched	12 months
Zucchini, see *Courgettes*		

Herbs	
trim leaves off stems or leave whole	6 months

Fruit		
Apples	blanched slices	8 months
	puréed	12 months
Apricots	whole or puréed	12 months
	halved	6 months
Bananas	puréed only with sugar and lemon juice	3 months
Bilberries	raw	12 months
Blackberries	raw	12 months
Cape gooseberries	peeled and sliced in syrup	6 months
Cherries	raw or in syrup	12 months
Cranberries	raw or puréed	12 months
Currants	raw or puréed	12 months
Damsons	whole or stewed	8 months

Fruit *continued*

Figs	whole	12 months
Gooseberries	whole or puréed	12 months
Grapefruit	segments	12 months
	whole for marmalade	6 months
Grapes	whole or halved in syrup	6 months
Greengages	whole or stewed	12 months
Lemons	sliced, whole or juice	12 months
	peel, grated in small quantities	12 months
Limes	as lemons	
Loganberries	whole or puréed	12 months
Melons	balled, raw or in syrup	8 months
Nectarines	skinned, packed in syrup	8 months
Oranges	whole, sliced or juice	12 months
	peel, grated, in small quantities	12 months
Peaches	skinned and packed in syrup	8 months
Pears	blanched, in syrup	12 months
Pineapples	packed with sugar or in syrup	4 months
Plums	raw or stewed	12 months
Raspberries	raw or puréed	12 months
Rhubarb	cooked in syrup	12 months
Strawberries	raw, puréed or in syrup	12 months
Fruit purée	raw	12 months
Fruit salad	in syrup (do not add bananas)	8 months
Glacé or crystallized fruit		12 months
Candied peel		12 months

Nuts		
Chestnuts	blanched	6 months
	puréed	6 months
Shelled nuts	raw, whole or chopped	12 months

Dairy foods		
Eggs	separated	8 months
(do not freeze hard-boiled eggs)		
Butter, salted		3 months
Butter, unsalted		6 months
Margarine		4 months
Lard		5 months
Cream cheese		3 months
Soft cheese		3 months
Hard cheese		6 months
Cream, whipped, double or clotted		2 months
(do not freeze single cream)		

Bread and cakes		
Bread, white and	baked	3 months
brown	unbaked	2–3 weeks
Cakes	not iced or filled	4 months
	iced	2 months
	yeast cakes, e.g. doughnuts	2 months
	meringues	12 months
	fruit	3 months
	unbaked	2 months
Scones	baked	2 months
	unbaked	2–3 weeks
Pastry	unbaked	6 months
	baked	4 months

Bread and cakes *continued*

Choux pastry	unbaked	4 months
	filled	2 months
	unfilled	4 months
Sandwiches		3 months
Batter	uncooked	3 months

Precooked foods

Boiled puddings		4 months
Casseroles, stews, ragouts, etc		4–6 months
Cooked fish dishes		2–4 months
Curries		3 months
Custard (not suitable for freezing)		
Deep-fried food in batter		1 month
Deep-fried food in breadcrumbs		1 month
Dips		1 month
Flan cases	unbaked	4 months
	baked blind	6 months
	filled	2 months
Galantine and brawn		4 months
Ice-cream		3 months
Mayonnaise (not suitable for freezing)		
Meringue puddings		6 months
Minced meat dishes: shepherd's pie, moussaka, etc		2 months
Mincemeat		4 months
Mince pies		2 months
Pancakes	unfilled	4 months
	filled	2 months
Pâtés and terrines	highly spiced	1 month
	not-too-spiced	2 months

Precooked foods *continued*		
Pies	game	3 months
	meat	4 months
	fruit	4 months
	sweet	3 months
Pizza		6 months
Potted fish		4 months
Potted meats		6–8 months
Sauces	white	4 months
	meat	6 months
	tomato	6 months
	with eggs	1 month
	with cream	1 month
(*Note* mayonnaise or mayonnaise-based sauces will not freeze)		
Soups	general	4 months
Stocks	vegetable	3 months
(Remove all fat)	meat and poultry	4 months
	cooked carcase	3 months
Stuffed vegetables: e.g. cabbage leaves or courgettes		4 months
Stuffing		2 months
Sweet or savoury mousses		2 months
Vegetables		4 months
Water ices and sorbets		4 months

Thawing guide

For all commercially frozen prepared products follow the instructions on the outside of the package.

Meat should be thawed as slowly as possible to prevent bleeding, preferably in a refrigerator.

Poultry and game should be thawed in the same way as meat.

Small fish, fish fillets and breadcrumbed fish fillets and fingers, etc can be cooked straight from the frozen state. Large fish should be thawed as slowly as possible, in the refrigerator.

Vegetables, with very few exceptions, should be cooked straight from the freezer.

Fruit that is to be served fresh should be thawed in the refrigerator as slowly as possible, to prevent juice leakage. Fruit that is to be cooked can be heated straight from the freezer. Most precooked dishes can be cooked straight from the freezer.

In emergencies thawing of some foods can be speeded up by placing sealed polythene bags in warm water, but this is not really advisable as it tends to result in loss of flavour and texture.

As all produce varies in size, packaging, etc the following is only a rough guide.

Food	Thawing time: hours per 450 gr/1 lb at room temperature	in the refrigerator
Meat		
Large joints*	2	5
Small cuts*	2	5
Steaks*	1½	4
Poultry (Whole birds must be thawed thoroughly before cooking; joints can be cooked from frozen state but will need longer time)		
Chicken*	3	10
Duck*	3	10
Turkey*	3	10
Goose*	3	10
Guinea fowl*	2	8
Game		
Small birds*	1	6
Large birds*	2	8
Venison*	3	10
Fish		
Large, whole*	thaw only in refrigerator	24
Flat*	thaw only in refrigerator	4
Fillets*	cook from frozen state, or thaw in refrigerator	4–6
Breadcrumbed fillets†	1	4
Battered fillets†	cook from frozen state	
Oysters, scallops* Crab* Lobster, crayfish*	thaw only in refrigerator	8
Prawns (unpeeled)*	thaw only in refrigerator	8

* Thaw in wrapping

† Remove wrapping before thawing

Food	Thawing time: hours per 450 gr/1 lb at room temperature	in the refrigerator
Prawns (peeled)*	thaw only in refrigerator	4

Vegetables Most vegetables are better cooked straight from the frozen state. Cauliflower and courgettes, however, benefit from thawing.

Food	at room temperature	in the refrigerator
Fruit		
Soft, to eat as fresh*	2–4	6–8
To be cooked	no need to thaw	
Purées	2½	6
(purées to serve hot do not need thawing)		
Dairy foods		
Eggs (separated or beaten)	2	4
Butter	5	9
Margarine	2	9
Lard	2	9
Cheese (hard)	2	9
Cheese (soft)	1	6
Cream (double)	5	9
Bread and cakes		
Unbaked cake mixture	2	5
Baked cakes	2–4	4–8
Unbaked dough	4	8
Baked bread	2	4
(Sliced bread can be put straight from freezer into toaster)		
Unbaked pastry	2	5
Baked pastry	2	4
Sandwiches	4	8
Batter	2	4

* Thaw in wrapping

Food	Thawing time; hours per 450 gr/1 lb at room temperature	in the refrigerator
Cooked meat dishes		
Casseroles, stews	4	8
(Not always necessary to thaw before reheating)		
Soups	no need to thaw	
Roast meat	4	8
Cooked vegetables	no need to thaw; heat through	

Roasting meat from the frozen state

Although some people recommend roasting meat taken straight out of the freezer, I myself do not find this satisfactory. I have a sneaking feeling commercial producers say this to make their product more attractive to the cook who hopes to cut down on time.

I would suggest whenever possible thawing all large joints slowly in the refrigerator before cooking. Obviously this means planning your meals in advance, but then most of us do that anyway if we are designing a meal around something as expensive as a roast.

If meat is cooked from the frozen state, it is extremely difficult (I would say almost impossible) to get it cooked just right – even with a meat thermometer. As the meat will thaw and cook from the outside, you tend to have the outside very overcooked and the centre undercooked. In spite of using foil or see-through roasting bags, I find the meat has a definite tendency to dry on the outside.

One of the arguments given for cooking meat straight from the freezer is that you conserve the natural juices which may be lost through the meat 'bleeding' during the thawing process. If the thawing is done slowly, there should be a minimal loss anyway.

Meat roasted from the frozen state will have to be cooked for far longer than meat that has been thawed, and will therefore cost more in fuel.

I recognize, however, that there are times when there will not be time to thaw joints so, although I am against this method of cooking in principle, here are roasting times for meat that is to be cooked straight from the freezer. Pushing one or two metal skewers through a large joint of meat will speed up the cooking process.

Beef (top-quality roasts, i.e. sirloin, topside, entrecôte, fillet, etc)
Preheat oven to moderately hot (400°F, 200°C, regulo 6). Weigh joint and calculate the cooking time to 1 hour per 450 gr or 1 lb. Place meat in a roasting tin and cook for 15 minutes to seal in the juices. Cover meat lightly with foil or wrap in a see-through roasting bag. Reduce heat to moderate (350°F, 180°C, regulo 4) and cook to within 30 minutes of the specified time. Test temperature with a meat thermometer plunged right into the centre of the meat at 10-minute intervals until the temperature reaches 140°F or 60°C for rare-cooked beef, and 155°F or 68°C for well-cooked beef.
(*Note* the cooking time will, of course, vary a little depending on whether the meat is on or off the bone.)

Lamb Follow the instructions for beef, testing with a thermometer until the temperature in the centre has reached 170°F or 76°C for slightly pink flesh and 180°F or 82°C for well-cooked meat.

Pork Cook for 20 minutes, uncovered, in a moderately hot oven (400°F, 200°C, regulo 6), then cover with foil, or place the meat in a see-through roasting bag, and continue as for beef. The internal temperature, when the meat is fully cooked, should be at least 190°F/87°C.

Slow-roasting joints Lightly cover joint with foil or put in a see-through roasting bag and place in a preheated moderate oven (350°F, 180°C, regulo 4). Cook as for top-quality joints but add on an extra 15–30 minutes to the roasting time.

Steaks and chops Here again I am very much of the 'thaw before cooking' train of thought and to me, steaks and chops are inclined to be less well flavoured and less tender if they are cooked straight from the freezer. It is also more difficult to judge the cooking time accurately and few things could be more unattractive than a fillet steak which is burnt on the outside with the centre not only rare but ice-cold. The freezer-to-fire method is rather more successful with very thin steaks, hamburgers, etc. Frozen steaks and chops should be fried or grilled over a lower heat than normal, with the heat raised at the end of the cooking time to brown the meat.

Reheating precooked dishes

This, to be honest, is a tricky question and although approximate reheating times are given for the recipes in this book the final judgement lies with you.

Timing for heating frozen dishes depends on a great many factors. The size and depth of the dish you are using, for instance, can make as much as 15 minutes' difference in cooking time for the same amount of ingredients. Thawing thoroughly will shorten the time needed to recook or reheat. Precooked foods packed in foil containers will obviously cook or reheat more quickly than those in an ordinary serving dish and, however careful one is, oven temperatures do vary from one oven to another.

In order to avoid disappointment, allow plenty of time for the recooking process, and always test a dish by pushing a skewer through the centre when you think it is cooked. If the skewer is piping hot then the centre – the most vulnerable part of the dish – should be thoroughly hot.

Pies and puddings with pastry tops should be watched with care to ensure that the top doesn't brown too much before the fillings are cooked. If the topping begins to brown too quickly, cover it with a sheet of greaseproof paper which you have dipped in cold water.

Seasonal foods to freeze

Obviously there are seasonal variations every year and supply is often regulated by market fluctuations; here nevertheless are some guidelines for buying produce when it is at the peak of both quality and cheapness.

January: home produce

Meat	beef, pork, bacon
Game	partridge, pheasant, hare, venison
Poultry	chicken, duck, turkey
Fish	bream, brill, coley, Dover and lemon sole, halibut, herring, mackerel, sprats, turbot
Vegetables	beetroot, broccoli, Brussels sprouts, cabbage, carrots, cauliflower, celery, leeks
Fruit	apples, pears, early rhubarb

January: imported produce

Fruit	oranges, lemons, grapefruit, dates, mandarins, clementines, satsumas, ortaniques, Seville oranges for marmalade, hazel and Brazil nuts, chestnuts

---

February: home produce

Game	hare
Fish	mackerel, oysters, salmon, scallops, sprats, turbot, whitebait, whiting

Vegetables	Brussels sprouts, cabbage, cauliflower, celeriac, celery, leeks, parsnips, seakale, spring greens, swedes
Fruit	early rhubarb

February: imported produce

Fruit	plums, oranges, lemons, grapefruit, dates, mandarins, clementines, satsumas, ortaniques, Seville oranges for marmalade

---

March: home produce

Fish	mackerel, oysters, salmon, scallops, whitebait
Vegetables	broccoli, Brussels sprouts, cabbage, cauliflower, celeriac, celery, leeks, parsnips, seakale, spring greens, swedes
Fruit	early rhubarb

March: imported produce

Vegetables	fennel, chicory
Fruit	pineapple, apricots

April: home produce

Meat	spring lamb
Fish	mackerel, red mullet, prawns, salmon, trout, whitebait
Vegetables	globe artichokes, broccoli, Brussels sprouts, celeriac, leeks, parsnips, spinach, spring greens, swedes
Fruit	rhubarb

April: imported produce

Vegetables	fennel, chicory
Fruit	grapes, pineapple, apricots

May: home produce

Meat	spring lamb
Fish	crab, herring, red mullet, plaice, prawns, salmon, trout, whitebait
Vegetables	globe artichokes, asparagus, aubergines, broccoli, cauliflower, courgettes, new carrots, peas, spinach, spring greens, swedes, tomatoes
Fruit	rhubarb

May: imported produce

Vegetables	fennel, chicory
Fruit	avocados, cherries, plums, pineapple, apricots

June: home produce

Fish	crab, hake, herring, lobster, red mullet, plaice, prawns, salmon, shrimps, trout, whitebait
Vegetables	globe artichokes, asparagus, aubergines, broad beans, French beans, cauliflower, courgettes, new carrots, new potatoes, peas, spinach, tomatoes
Fruit	cherries, gooseberries, loganberries, peaches, raspberries, rhubarb, strawberries

June: imported produce

Vegetables	globe artichokes, courgettes, asparagus, red and green peppers, Chinese cabbage, tomatoes, aubergines
Fruit	seedless grapes, fresh figs, white grapes, peaches, nectarines, melons, plums, bananas, pineapples

July: home produce

Fish	crab, haddock, hake, halibut, herring, lobster, grey mullet, red mullet, plaice, prawns, salmon, shrimps, sole, trout
Vegetables	globe artichokes, asparagus, aubergines, broad beans, French beans, runner beans, cabbage, cauliflower, corn on the cob, courgettes, leeks, new carrots, new potatoes, peas, spinach, tomatoes
Fruit	blackcurrants, cherries, gooseberries, loganberries, peaches, plums, raspberries, redcurrants, strawberries

July: imported produce

Vegetables	globe artichokes, courgettes, asparagus, red and green peppers, Chinese cabbage, tomatoes, aubergines
Fruit	seedless grapes, fresh figs, white grapes, peaches, nectarines, melons, plums, bananas, pineapples
Fish	scampi tails, squid

August: home produce

Game	blackcock, grouse, hare, ptarmigan, snipe
Fish	crab, haddock, hake, halibut, herring, lobster, grey mullet, red mullet, plaice, prawns, salmon, shrimps, sole, trout, turbot
Vegetables	globe artichokes, aubergines, French beans, runner beans, cabbage, cauliflower, celery, corn on the cob, courgettes, leeks, parsnips, peas, spinach, tomatoes
Fruit	apples, blackberries, blackcurrants, cherries, damsons, gooseberries, loganberries, peaches, pears, plums, raspberries, redcurrants, strawberries

August: imported produce

Vegetables	globe artichokes, courgettes, red and green peppers, Chinese cabbage, tomatoes, aubergines
Fruit	seedless grapes, fresh figs, white grapes, peaches, nectarines, melons, plums, bananas, pineapples

---

September: home produce

Game	blackcock, grouse, hare, partridge, plover, ptarmigan, snipe, wild duck and geese, woodcock (Scotland)
Poultry	goose, turkey
Fish	crab, haddock, hake, halibut, herring, lobster, grey mullet, red mullet, oysters, plaice, prawns, sole, turbot
Vegetables	globe artichokes, runner beans, Brussels sprouts, cabbage, cauliflower, celeriac, celery, courgettes, leeks, parsnips, peas, spinach, swedes
Fruit	apples, bilberries, blackberries, damsons, grapes, greengages, pears, plums

September: imported produce

Fruit	avocados, melons, apples, pears, pumpkins, cranberries

October: home produce

Game	blackcock, capercaillie, grouse, hare, partridge, pheasant, plover, ptarmigan, snipe, wild duck and geese, woodcock
Poultry	goose, turkey
Fish	cod, haddock, hake, herring, mackerel, grey mullet, oysters, plaice, scallops, sole, sprats, turbot

Vegetables	Brussels sprouts, cabbage, celeriac, celery, leeks, parsnips, spinach, swedes, turnips
Fruit	apples, blackberries, damsons, grapes, pears

October: imported produce

Fruit	avocados, melons, apples, pears, pumpkins, cranberries

November: home produce

Game	blackcock, capercaillie, grouse, hare, partridge, pheasant, ptarmigan, plover, snipe, wild duck and geese, woodcock
Poultry	goose, turkey
Fish	cod, haddock, hake, herring, mackerel, grey mullet, oysters, plaice, scallops, sole, sprats, turbot
Vegetables	Brussels sprouts, cabbage, celeriac, celery, leeks, parsnips, spinach, swedes, turnips
Fruit	apples, grapes

November: imported produce

Fruit	avocados, melons, apples, pears, pumpkins, cranberries, passion fruit, chestnuts

---

December: home produce

Game	capercaillie, hare, partridge, pheasant, plover, snipe, wild duck and geese, woodcock
Poultry	goose, turkey
Fish	cod, haddock, hake, herring, mackerel, grey mullet, oysters, plaice, scallops, sole, sprats, turbot, whiting

Vegetables	Brussels sprouts, cabbage, celeriac, celery, leeks, parsnips, seakale, swedes, turnips

December: imported produce

Fruit	avocados, melons, apples, pears, pumpkins, cranberries, passion fruit, lychees, oranges, lemons, grapefruit, satsumas, ortaniques, nuts and chestnuts

The frugal side of freezing

Up to now, we British have not been careful shoppers, but we should begin to take as much trouble as the traditional French housewife over our marketing: we are going to have to squeeze our tomatoes to make sure they are ripe and worth the money we are paying for them; pick out the best vegetables instead of leaving it to the greengrocer to give us what he likes; ask and keep an eye open for cheap cuts and trimmings of anything from smoked salmon to bacon pieces; and refuse – the louder the better – to buy anything that is of bad quality or overpriced.

Don't throw away anything that could be used to make a nutritious meal. Take pride in producing a meal that is appealing to the eye as well as to the palate at the lowest possible cost, instead of relying on the status symbol of a meal made of labour-saving but expensive materials.

Your deep freeze can help you save money on the housekeeping bills in a hundred different ways. You can buy when things are cheap and plentiful; you can also cut down on waste and make good use of all those bits and pieces you normally throw away. And remember, if you don't have time to use up those leftovers when they are available, they can always be frozen to use at a later date when you have time on your hands.

Here are a few ideas, but as you get used to making the most of your freezer, you will undoubtedly think up a lot more economical tips yourself.

Lemons Lemon rind is a great flavouring aid to cooking. When a recipe calls for lemon juice, don't ignore the rinds. Grate the rind of the lemon before squeezing out the juice; pack in small quantities in polythene bags; seal, label and freeze. Use from the frozen state to flavour puddings and savoury dishes.

Oranges Orange peel is another good source of flavour. Store orange peel in the same way as lemon peel and use it to flavour puddings, soups, stews and casseroles. Especially good with beef and pork and as a flavouring ingredient for tomato soup.

Vegetable peelings Much of the goodness of vegetables is in the skin. Use all vegetables (except cauliflower, cabbage and other strong-smelling vegetables) to give flavour to stocks for freezing. Mushroom, onion and tomato skins are particularly good flavouring ingredients.

Apple peel Apple peelings contain a lot of flavour and a high percentage of pectin. Blanch the peel in boiling water to which a tablespoon of lemon juice has been added, and freeze it to make apple jelly with later.

Stale cheese That old heel of Cheddar cheese in the refrigerator can be grated up and used in a hundred dishes - don't throw it away just because you have no call for cheese at that particular moment. Grate the cheese finely; pack in small quantities in polythene bags; seal, label and freeze to use as required. Grated cheese does not need thawing before use.

Pastry trimmings However carefully one follows a recipe, there always seems to be some pastry left over from the pie, tart or flan you have been making. Uncooked pastry freezes well.

Poultry giblets Poultry necks, hearts and gizzards make delicious stews and savoury dishes. When you have stockpiled a few sets of giblets use them to make a first-class nourishing meal. Freeze poultry livers separately to make into savouries or pâtés. When you buy a duck, use the neck skin and giblets to make the delicious pâté on page 169.

Poultry carcases Both cooked and raw poultry carcases make a good stock base. Never throw away any carcase; if you haven't time to make the stock immediately, freeze the carcase for use at a later date.

Stale bread White breadcrumbs can be used to make toppings or to add bulk to many dishes. Grate stale bread; pack in small quantities in polythene bags; seal, label and freeze. Breadcrumbs can be used from the frozen state.

Leftover soup The soup you made for last night's dinner may have been delicious but that does not mean you want to serve it again at once. Freeze leftover soups, labelling them carefully to show the ingredients, and use them later as a base for other soups.

Meat trimmings Gristle and tough fibres don't make good eating but they do contain a lot of flavour and goodness. Don't throw them away but use them to flavour and give additional strength to stocks. If you can't use them at once, pack the trimmings in a polythene bag, and freeze them to use later. I keep a large polythene bag labelled 'stock scraps' to accumulate smaller packages of bits and pieces that will make a good stock. When I have enough ingredients collected, I make the stock.

Bacon rinds Bacon rinds add flavour to stocks. They can also be rendered down in a low oven to produce good dripping for frying or basting a roast joint. Pack strained bacon fat in small containers; seal, label and freeze. Bacon fat can be used straight from the frozen state.

Smoked and green bacon bits and odd cuts These can often be found in shops that cut their own bacon. Use these pieces to flavour soups, and for pâtés, fillings and risottos. Keep pieces whole for stock or soup. Remove the skin and mince or finely chop the flesh of other pieces; pack in small quantities; seal, label and freeze to use at a later date.

Bones Butchers who bone and roll a joint for you often don't ask if you would like the bone – always insist on having it to use for soups, gravy and stocks.

Chutneys and preserves Good use can be made of much second-quality produce, for example green tomatoes, a glut of courgettes or cheap small or damp strawberries in making the most delicious chutneys, pickles and preserves; but there isn't always time to use the produce when it is available. Prepare for cooking, pack in polythene bags, seal, label and freeze to use later.

Cheap and special offers

Cheap and special offers are something to be treated with caution but with an eye to a good thing. You have to weigh up carefully whether the offer has been made simply to promote sales, or because the produce has not sold or is out of date, or whether it is due to a surplus of that particular commodity. If the offer is genuine and you can store it in the deep freeze and will enjoy using it, then grab the opportunity to buy something at a saving. Beware of cheap offers of minced meat or meat specially for the freezer. Minced meat often has a high proportion of fat and gristle and is merely the off-cuttings of a whole lot of different joints of varying qualities, and meat sold cheaply for the deep freeze may be cheap but it may also be of inferior quality.

Beware of cheap offers of chicken portions. These will almost always be from chickens that have already been frozen and defrosted and so are not suitable for deep-freezing. They can, on the other hand, make excellent stocks or be used for casseroles and stews (see pages 143 and 200) and then be frozen to make the basis of successful quick meals.

Leftovers

I have a feeling that the tendency to use only convenience foods and to rely on small cuts of meat, chicken quarters and expensively cooked meat such as steak and chops is coming to an end. If economy is the order of the day, then a large joint or chicken is a money-spinner providing one hot meal and a number of cheap 'stretcher' meals made with the cold leftovers. It may take you a little extra time to prepare these 'stretcher' meals, but it is amazing how much you can do with the basis of a little deliciously cooked cold meat or poultry. It is these meals that save on the housekeeping bills.

Using up leftovers, however, may not always be possible for someone who has a job as well as a home to run. Here again the deep freeze can make life easier. With careful planning the original hot meal can be served on the day before there is time to do a little bulk cooking with the leftovers and these, partially or completely cooked, can then be frozen to serve at a later date. This helps to break up the monotony of relying on the remains of the Sunday joint right through the week (shades of 'hot on Sunday, cold on Monday', etc).

I think it is time we all got over the feeling that leftovers are *infra dig* and accepted their invaluable role in keeping cost down. It doesn't cost you very much more to cook a large joint than it does a small one, and there is no doubt that cold meat can be carved more economically and stretched much further than a hot roast which often falls to pieces as it is cut. There is much to be said for cooking a piece of meat with the express purpose of using it for leftovers (especially if you cook it together with a joint that is to be served hot – doubling up and thereby reducing cooking expenses), particularly if you are prepared to take the trouble to do exciting things with the cold meat. With minced or diced cooked meat, some onions and a good rich stock, you have the basis of literally hundreds of different dishes at your fingertips.

I am a fanatic about leftovers. I use onion skins, tomato skins, mushroom stalks and even young carrot tops for stock; beetroot and turnip tops as a vegetable; leftover meat and poultry (however small the quantity) to make other dishes or sauces and leftover vegetables to make soup. Very, very, little is thrown away in my kitchen and my most recent discovery in the leftover repertoire is the use of leftover salad with salad dressing (however little salad I make there always seems to be some over and once it has dressing on it is useless for serving a second time). Liquidized to a fairly smooth purée the salad makes the most delicious basis for a cold summer soup or a light and hot winter *potage*.

Gluts

This is an ugly word, but a glut, too, can be a money-spinner where the deep freeze is concerned. Take advantage of freak crops of fruit and vegetables, of good fish catches or of meat bargains and freeze in bulk when produce is abnormally cheap. And don't be put off if the produce you get your hands on isn't of the very highest quality – as long as it is fresh and wholesome and you are prepared to take trouble to make it appetizing, these ugly sisters can make a big saving on the family budget.

The quality of the produce must not, however, fall below a certain level, or you will only be wasting money. Fruit, for instance, can be puréed and will still be delicious, even if it is slightly on the small side or a little overripe and squashy – but it shouldn't be bruised or damaged, or the taste will have deteriorated. Vegetables can be overlarge and slightly tough, but still make a good soup or purée, provided you trim off any tough parts; but they must be fresh and otherwise in good condition.

If you grow your own fruit and vegetables, you may also have your own glut in the garden. Inundated with cucumbers from the greenhouse? Make delicious soups or unusual old-fashioned vegetable dishes. Too many tomatoes? Then make them into a versatile tomato sauce which can be added to soups, or used as a sauce for many fish, meat and poultry dishes and with spaghetti and other pasta. Too much spinach? Make thin pancakes or cannelloni and stuff them with a traditional Italian filling of spinach mixed with cottage cheese to make an appetizing lunch or supper dish that freezes well.

Slightly blemished or bruised apples can be peeled, cored, chopped and stewed to use for puddings or sauces; overripe fruit can be stewed and the juice drained off and frozen to use as a fruit drink that is full of vitamin C (good as a natural base for milk shakes, too).

In the fish line, fresh sprats and whiting have a short season, but are often extremely plentiful and cheap when they are available. They freeze well and thaw quickly, providing some delicious dishes that really do taste of the sea. Mackerel and herrings, too, are often cheap and plentiful but do make sure they are absolutely fresh; if you have time, fillet them before open-freezing and packing. Try cutting some of the fish into thin strips before freezing, and using it to form the base of a Mediterranean fish soup to serve as a main course. Fish soups made with herbs and saffron used to form a large part of the diet of fishing communities around our coasts not too long ago, but they do need plenty of finely chopped parsley mixed in at the last minute before serving, so stock up on that when it is in season too.

Coping with a glut of soft fruit

In a good fruit year you may find you have more fruit on your hands than you can cope with at one time, especially when some of it may not be of good enough quality to freeze whole. This particularly applies to red- and blackcurrants – it takes time to strip them off their stalks and to top and tail them. There is, however, an easy way to cope with quantities of this sort; it takes little time to prepare and will provide you with the base of many puddings for the months to come.

Leave the currants on their stems and cook them gently with sugar until soft. Purée the fruit through a food mill or a sieve. (Do not use an electric liquidizer as this will mash up the stalks too – a Mouli food mill will separate out the pips and stalks.)

Cool the purée and pour it into a large, flat baking tin and open-freeze until solid.

Turn out the frozen purée and, working quickly, cut it into conveniently sized squares with a special deep-freeze knife that has a sharp, serrated edge. Wrap each square in polythene film; pack them neatly in a polythene bag, seal, label and freeze.

When you want to use the purée as a base for pies, mousses, fools or sauces, etc, turn one or more of the frozen squares into a saucepan and heat until melted over a low heat.

Freezing for parties

Dinner parties

Dinner parties are fun – or they can be. All too often, unfortunately, they turn out to be exhausting and nerve-racking for the person who produces them. Sometimes I look at the hostess and feel guilty. The guests argue lightheartedly and enjoy the food and drink, while the poor cook looks washed out, having made all this possible (with just a little help from her husband) and is probably longing to go to bed.

Planning a dinner party ahead and utilizing your deep freeze fully helps to turn the tables, however. You can organize yourself for a dinner-party by cooking the dishes in advance, when you have the time to give the food your complete attention.

Keeping precooked dishes for even as little as 48 hours in the deep freeze does them no harm provided they are treated in the right way. This can mean that when the day of the dinner party arrives, you have time to take things easy.

Choose dishes for precooking that you know will freeze well. Cook them almost completely and freeze them in the dishes they will be served from – or, better still, partly cook them and add seasoning and garnishes just before serving. This gives an authentic freshness to the dishes and also means that, should there be any mistake in the flavouring, this can be rectified before the food appears on the table.

Check through the recipes to see what will freeze well, and then work your favourite dinner-party recipes to fit in with a freezing plan.

Thawing is always something that needs care, so work out

exactly when each dish will need to be taken out of the freezer to be ready for the party itself. Leave a little extra time in case thawing takes longer than you expect – this can happen in cold weather or if the dish you have frozen is larger or deeper than normal.

Remember that however much care you take, it is possible for precooked frozen food to look a bit jaded even though the taste will be perfect – so never garnish before freezing, and on the night have handy garnishing material to give the food a garden-fresh appearance.

Above all, don't get in a flap. Nothing is more tiring than worrying and, although I know it is sometimes very hard to believe, an awful lot of people go to dinner parties to see the people that give them and not just for the food – and they would undoubtedly like to see you looking carefree. So – when in doubt – sit down, relax and have a drink to make everything seem less of a drama.

Buffet parties

You can cook ahead for buffet parties in the same way as for dinner parties (see above). Cook food that can easily be eaten with a fork whilst standing up. When multiplying recipe quantities, remember that the more people there are, the less they seem to eat – so for twenty people, multiply a recipe quantity to feed about sixteen.

French bread and rolls can be put straight from the freezer into a medium-hot oven and will take about 10–15 minutes to thaw and heat through to be delightfully crisp.

Plan out an operational list in advance. If your oven space is not very large, don't plan to have a lot of dishes that will need heating through at the same time and, if possible, plan everything so that it will be ready half an hour before the guests arrive, allowing time for emergencies.

Barbecue parties

Most food for barbecues needs to be marinated. Chops, steaks, chicken joints etc can be prepared in advance and frozen in the marinade. This also helps to tenderize the meat. Barbecueing can take a long time, especially if the fire is not scorching hot, and it is possible to part-cook the marinated meat before freezing it to quicken up the process of barbecueing. A nice fresh fruit salad makes a good ending and this too can be made in advance and frozen; but remember not to include bananas, which get soggy and discoloured.

Party perks

Ice-cubes One always needs plenty of ice at a party and with your deep freeze you can stockpile cubes for days in advance, ensuring that you have an adequate supply on the evening.

Remove the cubes from the tray, shovel them into a polythene bag, sprinkle with a little soda water to prevent the cubes from sticking, seal the bag and store them in the freezer.

More exciting ice-cubes can be made by adding a stuffed olive or a thin twist of lemon peel to each section of the ice-tray before freezing.

Lemon slices So that you don't have the messy business of cutting up lemon slices for drinks at the last minute, you can do this in advance and freeze the slices. Pack in a rigid container with waxed paper or polythene film between each layer of lemon slices. Seal, label and freeze. Unwrap and thaw the slices at room temperature for 1 hour, or use frozen.

Glasses If you are serving iced drinks on a hot day, there is nothing nicer than having an ice-frosted glass to drink from. If you have the space, put the glasses into the freezer for 10 minutes before serving the drinks.

Cocktails If you plan to serve a complicated cocktail mix, you can make it in advance and freeze it for up to 1 week.

If the liquid is frozen in a bottle, make sure there is plenty of room for the liquid to expand – or you will find a shattered bottle on your hands.

Any mixed cocktail left over from the party can also be frozen for a short period.

Summer drinks To give a frosted look to cold drinks, add a frozen strawberry or a frozen sprig of mint just before serving time.

Drinking companions Smoked salmon sandwiches go well with any drinks and have a luxury air without being too expensive. Remove the crusts from very thin slices of buttered brown bread, place a very thin layer of smoked salmon on each piece of bread and sprinkle with a little freshly ground black pepper. Roll up as neatly and tightly as you can. Wrap each roll tightly in foil and chill for 30 minutes in a refrigerator. Cut the roll into very thin slices.

Pack the cut slices in a rigid container with waxed paper or polythene film between each layer of sandwiches. Seal, label and freeze.

To thaw the sandwiches, leave them unwrapped at room temperature for about 2 hours. Other cocktail sandwiches can be made in the same way.

Quiches, which freeze well and can be made in a wide variety of flavours also make delicious accompaniments to drinks at informal get-togethers or cocktail parties. Cut hot quiches into finger-sized pieces. Try also making mini-pizzas in sizes which can be eaten in one's fingers. Pizzas can be put straight from the freezer into the oven and reheated.

Party puddings In the spring, collect violets from the hedgerows, remove their stalks and open-freeze the flowers. Pack in a rigid container, seal, label and freeze.

Sprinkle the frozen flowers on cold party puddings to give them a really exotic touch.

The super-freezers

In spite of everything that manufacturers of frozen food and deep freezes will tell you, there are certain made dishes and raw produce that freeze better than others. The home freezer would do well to concentrate on the following list of fresh and precooked produce.

Fresh foods

Meat

Beef, lamb, mutton and lean pork joints of all sizes; minced meat, composites, sausages, bacon, ham.

Fish

Plaice, trout, cod, kippers, salmon, monkfish – whole fish, cutlets or fillets, shellfish for short-term freezing.

Poultry and game

Chicken, duck, turkey, pheasants. All poultry and game freezes well – whole birds or joints.

Vegetables

Most vegetables except salad ingredients freeze well: especially beans (French, broad and runner), peas, spinach, broccoli.

Fruit

Top freezers are raspberries, gooseberries, all currants, melon and pineapple in sugar, rhubarb.

Pastry

It's very useful to be able to thaw some ready-made pastry in an emergency. Keep supplies of puff, short-crust and flaky pastry.

Herbs

All varieties.

Precooked foods

Bread and cakes

Rolls, buns, cut or uncut loaves (white and brown), large and small cakes, uncooked biscuits.

Meat

Stews, casseroles, meat loaves, meat sauces, stuffed vegetables, pâtés and terrines, meatballs, puddings and some pies.

Fish

Fish cakes, pies, mousses, soufflé bases, breadcrumbed and battered fish.

Pancakes

Unfilled, or filled with savoury and sweet fillings.

Pastry

Pies filled with savoury or sweet fillings, flan cases, jam tarts.

Stocks

Stocks freeze well if all the fat is removed from the surface. Chicken and beef stocks are essential.

Soups

Most soups freeze well: tomato, mushroom or consommé can be used as sauces in emergencies.

Puddings

Ice-cream, fruit sweets, mousses, iced soufflés, tarts, flans and pies.

Cooking your favourite recipes for the freezer

If you like cooking, then you will probably have a number of favourite recipes which you want to freeze in advance to use later. Perhaps you will not find these recipes in a book on deep-freezing.

A wide-range of precooked dishes can be frozen for short periods, but there are various do's and don'ts which need to be adhered to. Look at this list when you are planning to cook ahead and make sure that your recipe fulfils the following rules.

Don't freeze a dish that has hard-boiled eggs or cooked whole potatoes in it.

Don't choose dishes that need very strong seasoning or spicing before freezing. In most cases these can be added during the reheating process.

Don't freeze dishes with thin sauces that include cream as this may separate when the dish is reheated. Cream can usually be added later. Sauces with a flour base, however, can have cream added to them. Sauces that include egg yolks should not be frozen either, but the yolks may be added later.

Do make sure that you slightly *under*cook any dish that is to be frozen. It will continue to cook whilst being reheated.

Do give plenty of lubrication to cooked meat dishes by making sure the meat is well covered by a sauce or gravy. If, when the dish is reheated, you find you have too much juice, you can always spoon some off.

Having checked all these points, prepare your dish in the usual way, allowing time for reheating when you use the dish. Cool it as quickly as possible, pack, seal, label and freeze. Do not store for longer than 1 month and add extra seasoning and spices when reheating.

Slimming with the deep freeze

Here the deep freeze doesn't help *you* on your crash slimming course so much as your family – who can be fed without placing so much strain on your appetite and temper. The deep freeze saves you the agony of starving yourself while having to cook meals to feed other hungry people.

This is a plan for a quick slimming bash which I have used on many occasions and which I recommend to make life easier for you, the slimmer, and for your hungry family.

When you decide it is time to go on a diet, choose which day you intend to start (a week or fortnight when things are quiet and social life is at a minimum) and then plan out your campaign in great detail. Cook in advance for the rest of the family so that all you have to do is reheat their meals (with a clothes peg on your nose to avoid the temptation coming from those lovely aromas). While their fattening feasts are heating you can concentrate on making your own tempting little salads of low-calorie ingredients.

Avoid eating with them as this often provides you with unnecessary temptation and often you find them, just out of cussedness, wanting to pick at your diet foods as well as scoffing their own delicious dishes.

Fresh lemon juice is a great aid to the slimmer – so stock up when lemons are cheap, and have a lemon-and-boiling-water drink when you get hungry between meals.

Dog-food

Tinned dog meat is expensive and you will probably find you can make a considerable saving by preparing your own dog-food from the cheapest fresh meat trimmings.

You can buy frozen dog-food in bulk from most frozen-food wholesalers, but I have frequently found the quality to be so poor that my dogs just turn their noses up at it. I find a better bet is to make an arrangement with my local butcher to supply me with bones and cheap trimmings of meat once a month. These are not expensive, you know what you are getting, and you don't have the palaver of boiling up sheep's heads or other rather unsavoury ingredients.

Mince or chop the meat ready for eating and pack in one-portion bags; seal, label and freeze.

Wrap bones in foil and pack separately.

In emergencies the frozen meat can be unwrapped, combined with water and heated through until thawed.

Part 2

Stocks and soups

Few things make better eating and give more value for money than richly flavoured and nourishing home-made soups. They are cheaper and infinitely nicer than anything that comes out of a packet or tin, they don't need a lot of preparation and there are thousands of taste combinations to experiment with. Soups freeze well and can be reheated straight from the frozen state, providing a meal in minutes.

First you must have a good stock; although stock cubes are useful in an emergency, they have nowhere near the richness and flavour that is contained in a home-made stock. Make stock from raw or cooked bones or poultry carcases whenever you have the ingredients available, enrich them with vegetable trimmings and a bouquet garni, and freeze them for use as required. To save space in the freezer, strain the stock when it is cooked, return it to a clean pan and boil fast until the stock is reduced to about a third of its original volume. Cool the concentrated stock and pour it into ice-cube trays. Open-freeze the stock, then pop out the cubes and pack them in a polythene bag, seal, label and freeze. To use, combine frozen cubes with water and heat through, adding more stock cubes or water as necessary.

For cream soups, freeze the soup before adding the cream. Reheat the soup until it reaches boiling point, lower the heat and add the cream as required.

Pack soups and stock in rigid containers and always leave 1·25-cm (½-in) headspace for expansion in the container.

Make vegetable soups when vegetables are at their cheapest to provide economical dishes for the following months. If you grow your own peas, use the pods to make a delicious green soup after shelling the peas.

Use a light hand when adding seasoning and spices to soup for freezing. More flavour can always be added at a later date. For long-term freezing, garlic should be avoided. If a recipe requires the flavour of garlic, fry a finely chopped clove or two in a little bacon fat or olive oil until the garlic is transparent. Drain off excess oil or fat, add the frozen soup and reheat. Or rub the saucepan you intend to use for reheating the soup with a clove of garlic that has been crushed with a fork; by these methods you get the flavour of the garlic without having had to freeze the garlic in the soup.

Do not garnish soups until you reheat them. Add ingredients like chopped parsley, chives, etc when the soup is ready to serve.

Soup garnishes like finely chopped green peppers, croûtons of crisply fried bread (plain or flavoured with a little lemon juice or curry powder) can also be frozen to use at the last minute. Green peppers can be added in the frozen state; bread croûtons should be reheated in a moderately hot oven for a few minutes. Crescents or tiny circles of puff pastry also make a good garnish for soup; they can be cooked, frozen and reheated from the frozen state in a moderately hot oven for a few minutes before being added to the finished soup (see page 233).

Chicken stock from a raw carcase

Storage time: 4 months

1 chicken carcase and giblets
2 onions
2 carrots
2 sticks of celery with leaves
2 rashers fat bacon
water, salt, 8 peppercorns
bouquet garni

Break up the chicken carcase. Wash the onions, leave the skins on and roughly chop them. Clean and halve the carrots. Roughly chop the celery. Chop the bacon.

Cook the bacon in a large, heavy pan, without extra fat, over a low heat until plenty of fat has seeped into the pan. Add the chicken carcase, raise the heat, and cook until browned on all sides. Pour over enough water to cover, add the onions, carrots, celery, peppercorns and bouquet garni and season with salt. Bring to the boil, remove any scum from the surface, cover and simmer gently for 2½ hours.

To freeze: Strain the stock through a sieve lined with muslin; cool, and refrigerate until any fat has formed a solid layer on the top. Remove all the fat, pour the stock into plastic containers, leaving 1·25-cm (½-in) headspace for expansion. Seal, label and freeze.

To use: Turn the frozen stock into a saucepan and heat over a low flame until melted.

Game stock from a cooked carcase

Storage time: 3 months

1 pheasant carcase or 2 pigeon, grouse or partridge carcases
2–4 bacon rinds
2 onions
2 carrots
2 sticks celery
bouquet garni
2·5 litres (4 pints) water
salt and 6 peppercorns
2 chicken stock cubes

Break up the carcase and combine it with all the other ingredients in a large pan. Bring to the boil, skim off any scum from the surface, cover and simmer for 2–2½ hours. Cool, strain through a sieve lined with muslin, and leave in a refrigerator until the fat has formed a solid layer on the surface. Remove all fat.

To freeze: Transfer the stock to a polythene container, leaving 1·25-cm (½-in) headspace for expansion. Seal, label and freeze.

To use: Transfer the frozen stock to a saucepan and heat through until the stock has melted and comes to the boil. Use as a base for rich-tasting, nourishing soups.

Fish stock

If you are freezing fish you may well have some bones, trimmings and heads left over – don't throw them away. Use them to make a good fish stock which can add enormously to the flavour of sauces to serve with fish dishes or to the taste of fish that is to be poached.

Storage time: 3 months

900 gr (2 lb) fish bones, heads and trimmings
1 onion, peeled and roughly chopped
50 gr (2 oz) firm mushroom stalks
2 sprigs parsley
pinch thyme
bay leaf
1 tablespoon lemon juice
6 dl (1 pint) water
3 dl (½ pint) white wine
salt and pepper

Place all the ingredients in a large pan, season with salt and pepper, and bring to the boil. Remove any scum that forms on the surface, cover, and simmer gently for 1 hour. Leave to cool and strain through a fine sieve lined with muslin.

To freeze: Pour the stock into polythene containers, leaving 1·25-cm (½-in) headspace for expansion. Seal, label and freeze.

To use: Turn the frozen soup into a saucepan and heat gently until the stock is thawed. Use for soups, sauces or as a poaching liquid.

White stock

Use in place of chicken stock for cream soups or white-sauce recipes like ragouts, etc.

Storage time: 3 months

1 onion
2 carrots
2 sticks celery
900 gr (2 lb) mixed veal and lamb or mutton bones
juice 1 lemon
bouquet garni
salt and white pepper
2·5 litres (4 pints) water

Peel and roughly chop the onion and carrots. Roughly chop the celery. Combine all the ingredients in a large, heavy pan. Season with salt and pepper, cover with the cold water, and bring to the boil. Remove any scum from the surface, cover tightly, and simmer gently for 4 hours. Strain through a sieve lined with muslin. Cool and leave in the refrigerator until any fat forms a solid skin on the surface. Remove all fat.

To freeze: Pour the cold stock into polythene containers, leave 1·25-cm (½-in) headspace for expansion, seal, label and freeze.

To use: Put the frozen stock into a saucepan and heat through over a low heat until melted. Use as required.

Note: Stocks always vary in flavour and strength. If your stock isn't tasty enough, boil it after removing the fat until the flavour is enriched, or add a chicken stock cube to the basic stock.

Beef stock (brown)

Suitable for vegetable soups, meat soups, gravy, etc, but not for cream soups.

Storage time: 3 months

900 gr (2 lb) beef bones
2 onions
2 carrots
1 stick celery
1 leek
37 gr (1½ oz) lard or dripping
any leftover vegetable peelings, giblets, bacon rinds, etc
bouquet garni
water
12 peppercorns
salt

Chop the bones into roughly 12-cm (5-in) pieces. Quarter but do not peel the onions. Peel and coarsely chop the carrots. Roughly chop the celery and leek.

Heat the lard or dripping in a large, heavy pan. Add the bones and cook over a high heat until nicely browned on all sides. Add the onion (and bacon rinds, etc, if available) and cook for a further 3 minutes. Add the remaining vegetables, bouquet garni and enough water to cover the ingredients. Bring to the boil, add the peppercorns, season generously with salt, skim off any scum that rises to the surface, cover and simmer for 3–4 hours.

Remove the stock from the heat, strain through a sieve lined with muslin and leave to cool. Chill in a refrigerator until any fat forms a solid skin on the surface.

Lift off all fat with a spoon dipped in very hot water.

To freeze: Pour the cold stock into polythene containers, leaving 1·25-cm (½-in) headspace for expansion. Seal, label and freeze.

To use: Put the frozen stock into a saucepan and put over a low heat until melted and hot through. Use as required.

Note: Stocks always vary in flavour and strength. If your stock isn't tasty enough for your purpose, reduce it by boiling after removing the fat to intensify the flavour, or add a stock cube or some meat extract.

To clarify stock

Some recipes require a clear stock. A basic household stock can easily be clarified without going into the more complicated and expensive process of making a true consommé.

You can clarify most stocks by straining twice through a sieve lined with a double thickness of muslin. When they cool and settle they will become clear, depositing a small amount of sediment in the bottom of the bowl. By this time stock will usually have jellied and the clear jelly can be carefully spooned out, leaving behind the sediment. If the stock is not jellied, a further straining through muslin will usually rid the stock of any impurities.

Consommé

Storage time: 3 months

150 gr (6 oz) shin beef
1·5 dl (¼ pint) water
1 small onion
1 carrot
1·2 litres (2 pints) brown stock with the fat removed

bouquet garni
1 egg white
1 eggshell
salt and white pepper

Shred the meat finely with a sharp knife and leave it to soak in the water for 15 minutes. Peel and roughly chop the onion. Peel and roughly chop the carrot.

Combine the stock, meat and water, bouquet garni and vegetables in a heavy pan, bring to the boil, skim off any scum from the surface and simmer gently for 2 hours.

Strain through a sieve lined with muslin and return to a clean pan. Beat the egg white until fluffy. Add the egg white and the crushed eggshell to the stock and bring to the boil, whisking all the time. When the mixture boils, remove it from the heat and leave to settle. Repeat the boiling, whisking and settling process twice more, then strain through a sieve lined with muslin. By this time the consommé should be quite clear and sparkling. Season with salt, pepper and some lemon juice and sherry if required.

To freeze: Pour into polythene containers, leaving 1·25-cm (½-in) headspace for expansion. Seal, label and freeze.

To use: Hot – put frozen consommé into a heavy pan over a low heat, until melted and hot through.

Cold – thaw at room temperature or in a refrigerator until melted. Serve well chilled.

Note: The cooked shin beef can be combined with a vinaigrette dressing and chopped chives and capers to make an excellent salad. It can also be potted (see page 172).

Quick soups using frozen consommé

Add shredded cooked beetroot, lemon juice, chopped chives and a topping of sour cream to cold consommé for an attractive summer soup.

Add chopped avocado, lemon juice and a little Tabasco to consommé for a good hot dinner starter.

Add flaked tuna fish (and sherry and lemon juice if not already used) to hot consommé for a light first course.

Shred raw young carrots very finely and add them to consommé that has been brought just to the boil; cook the carrots for 5 minutes until just tender and serve hot or cold with a spiking of lemon juice and a little sherry.

Very thinly slice 50 gr (2 oz) firm button mushrooms, add to the hot consommé and cook for 2 minutes. Servc hot with a garnish of finely chopped parsley or chervil.

Oxtail soup

Good and nourishing as this soup is (cheap, too), it does take time to prepare. Ideally this is a recipe where you can double the quantities and cook them together – saving time and fuel – and freeze one serving for a later date.

Serves 2×6 portions Storage time: 2 months

2 oxtails
2 onions
2 carrots
2 leeks
$1\frac{1}{2}$ tablespoons dripping
1 small turnip
$1\frac{1}{2}$ tablespoons flour
4·2 litres (7 pints) boiling water
1 tablespoon tomato purée
bouquet garni
salt and freshly ground black pepper

Ask your butcher to joint the oxtails. Quarter but do not peel the onions. Peel and roughly chop the carrots. Peel and roughly chop the turnip, and thickly slice the leeks.

Melt the dripping in a large, heavy pan, add oxtails and cook over a high heat until lightly browned. Remove meat with a slotted spoon, add vegetables and cook over a medium heat until lightly browned. Add oxtails, sprinkle over the flour and mix well. Cook until oxtails are browned on all sides. Pour over boiling water, blend in tomato purée, add bouquet garni and season with salt and pepper. Bring to the boil, cover very tightly (put a layer of foil underneath the lid if necessary), and simmer for 2–3 hours until the meat is actually falling off the bones. Strain soup, leave stock to cool and then chill in the refrigerator until the fat forms a solid skin over the surface. Separate the meat from the vegetables and discard the vegetables. Shred the meat off the bones. Remove the fat from the stock and add the shredded meat.

To freeze: Pour the soup into polythene containers, leaving 1·25-cm (½-in) headspace for expansion. Seal, label and freeze.

Second-stage ingredients

- 1 glass Madeira or medium dry sherry
- 1 tablespoon cornflour
- 2 tablespoons finely chopped parsley
- seasoning

To use: Turn frozen soup into a heavy pan and heat through gently until boiling. Combine the sherry or Madeira with the cornflour and mix to a smooth paste. Add the mixture to the soup and cook for 5 minutes over a medium heat stirring continuously until the soup is thickened and smooth. Add the parsley, check seasoning and serve at once.

Soupe à l'oignon

This soup is supposed to have the magic properties of curing a hangover. Freeze it to give quick comfort at Sunday brunch after a Saturday-night party.

Serves 6 Storage time: 3 months

50 gr (2 oz) butter
3 tablespoons olive oil
900 gr (2 lb) onions
2 tablespoons flour
1·5 litres (2½ pints) beef stock
1 tablespoon meat extract
4·5 dl (¾ pint) dry white wine
salt and freshly ground black pepper

Peel and thinly slice the onions and divide into rings. Melt the butter with the oil in a heavy saucepan, add the onions and cook over a moderately high heat, stirring well, until the onions are well browned but not burnt. Sprinkle the flour over the onions and stir until well blended and lightly browned. Gradually add the stock, stirring all the time, over a moderate heat until the mixture comes to the boil. Add the wine, season with salt and pepper and mix in the meat extract. Cover and simmer gently for 30 minutes.

To freeze: Cool as quickly as possible, pour into polythene containers, leaving 1·25-cm (½-in) headspace for expansion. Seal, label and freeze.

Second-stage ingredients

6 thickish slices French bread
butter
100 gr (4 oz) Parmesan cheese

Turn the frozen soup into a saucepan and cook over a gentle heat until the soup has thawed and comes to the boil. Check seasoning, cover and simmer for 15 minutes.

Butter the slices of French bread and place each one in the bottom of a soup bowl, or, better still, a small earthenware pot. Pour over the hot soup and, when the bread slices rise to the surface, sprinkle them with the cheese. Brown under a hot grill until cheese has melted and is a light golden-brown.

Note: To give a more piquant taste, the bread can be spread with Dijon mustard instead of butter.

Jerusalem artichoke soup

Jerusalem artichokes are easy to grow but, unless puréed, they don't freeze well. They do, however, make an admirable soup which can be frozen and titivated when you require it. Some recipes recommend cooking the artichokes in the milk or stock, but I feel this makes the soup too rich and bland.

Serves 4 Storage time: 3 months

675 gr (1½ lb) Jerusalem artichokes
12 gr (½ oz) butter
1 litre (1¾ pints) chicken stock
1 teaspoon lemon juice
salt and white pepper

Peel artichokes (young ones can be peeled in a mechanical potato peeler, but the old ones just need patience, I'm afraid). Cook them in boiling, salted water until tender and then mash with the butter until absolutely smooth with a potato masher. (Or rub through a fine sieve, purée in an electric liquidizer or a food mill.)

Combine the purée in a clean pan with the stock and lemon juice. Bring to the boil, stirring all the time; season with a little salt and pepper and simmer for 10 minutes.

To freeze: Cool. Pour into polythene containers, leaving 1·25-cm (½-in) headspace for expansion. Seal, label and freeze.

Second-stage ingredients
4 tablespoons cream
1 egg yolk
pinch nutmeg

To use: Put frozen soup into a heavy pan and heat slowly until the soup comes to the boil. Lower the heat to just simmering.

Beat together the cream and egg yolk until absolutely smooth.

Add the egg mixture to the soup and cook for 2 minutes, stirring constantly and without allowing the soup to boil. Check the seasoning and stir in a pinch of nutmeg.

Serve with crisp croûtons of fried bread.

Potage St Michel

Watercress has a limited season and doesn't freeze well in the raw state, but you can use it to make a watercress butter for sandwiches and steaks (see page 171) or to make subtly flavoured green soups.

Serves 4 Storage time: 2 months

2 potatoes
1 onion
4 sticks celery
2 bunches watercress
37 gr (1½ oz) butter
1·2 litres (2 pints) chicken stock
1 teaspoon lemon juice
pinch mixed herbs (2 teaspoons mixed, finely chopped, chervil, tarragon and thyme)
salt and freshly ground black pepper

Peel and coarsely grate potatoes. Peel and finely chop the onion. Finely chop the celery, discarding the leaves. Remove tough stalks and chop watercress.

Heat the butter in a large, heavy pan. Add the potatoes, onion and celery and cook over a low heat for 5 minutes, stirring continuously with a wooden spoon to prevent browning. Add the watercress and cook for a further minute. Add the stock, lemon juice and herbs, season with salt and pepper, bring to the boil and simmer gently for 30 minutes.

Purée the soup through a fine sieve or a food mill, or in an electric liquidizer.

To freeze: Cool. Pour into a polythene container, leaving 1·25-cm (½-in) headspace for expansion. Seal, label and freeze.

Second-stage ingredients

2 rashers streaky bacon
2 tablespoons cream

To use: Turn the frozen soup into a heavy pan and heat over a low flame until hot through.

Remove the rinds and finely chop the bacon. Fry the bacon without extra fat, over a medium high heat, until crisp. Drain well on kitchen paper.

Bring the soup to the boil; check seasoning; lower the heat and stir in the cream.

Serve at once with a sprinkling of bacon on each serving.

Carrot and orange soup

Use old, tough carrots when they are at their cheapest. Can be served hot or cold.

Serves 4 Storage time: 3 months

450 gr (1 lb) carrots
1 onion
2 tablespoons olive oil
7·5 dl (1¼ pints) strong chicken stock
juice and finely grated rind 1 orange
2 bay leaves
bouquet garni
salt and freshly ground black pepper
1 tablespoon finely chopped parsley or chives
2 tablespoons sour cream

Peel and chop the carrots. Peel and chop the onion. Heat the oil in a saucepan, add the onion and carrot, and cook over a low heat until the onion is transparent and all the oil has been absorbed. Add the stock, orange juice, orange peel, bay leaves and bouquet garni and season with salt and pepper. Bring to the boil, cover, and simmer for 30 minutes or until the carrots are absolutely tender. Remove the bay leaves and bouquet garni and purée the soup to an absolutely smooth consistency through a fine sieve or a food mill, or in an electric liquidizer. Cool. Pack into a polythene container, leaving 1·25-cm (½-in) headspace for expansion. Seal, label and freeze.

To use hot: Turn the frozen soup into a saucepan and heat over a low flame until hot through. Taste for seasoning and serve at once with a teaspoon of sour cream and a sprinkling of finely chopped parsley or chives in each bowl.

To use cold: Leave the soup in the refrigerator to thaw overnight. Turn into a bowl and beat with a wire whisk to mix all the ingredients. Taste for seasoning. Pour into chilled soup bowls and garnish with a teaspoon of cream and a sprinkling of finely chopped chives or parsley in each bowl.

Lettuce soup

A good way to use up a glut of lettuces.

Serves 4   Storage time: 2 months

1 onion
2 heads lettuce
1 potato
50 gr (2 oz) butter or, better still, bacon fat
1 tablespoon flour
4·5 dl (¾ pint) strong chicken stock
4·5 dl (¾ pint) milk
4 tablespoons double cream
salt and white pepper
pinch nutmeg
2 tablespoons finely chopped chives

Peel and finely chop the onion. Wash and shred the lettuces. Peel and finely chop the potato. Melt the butter in a saucepan, add the onion, and cook over a low heat until the onion is transparent. Add the lettuce and potato and continue to cook over a low heat, stirring continuously to prevent sticking, for 3 minutes. Blend in the flour and mix well. Gradually add the stock, stirring constantly. Bring to the boil, add the milk, cover and simmer for 20 minutes. Purée the soup through a fine sieve or a food mill, or in an electric liquidizer. Cool. Pack in a suitable container, leaving 1·25-cm (½-in) headspace for expansion. Seal, label and freeze.

To use: Turn the frozen soup into a saucepan and heat over a low flame until hot through. Add the cream. Season with salt, pepper and a pinch of nutmeg, and serve at once with a garnish of finely chopped chives.

Tomato ice

One of the perfect deep-freeze first courses.

Serves 6   Storage time: 3 months

- 1·35 kg (3 lb) ripe tomatoes
- 1 shallot
- ½ teaspoon each oregano and sage, finely chopped
- 1 tablespoon tomato purée
- salt and freshly ground black pepper
- 1 teaspoon meat extract (e.g. Bovril)
- 1 teaspoon caster sugar
- juice 1 lemon
- 1 carton sour cream
- 1 teaspoon grated horseradish
- mint leaves

Roughly chop the tomatoes. Peel and chop the shallot. Combine the tomatoes and shallot in a heavy saucepan with the herbs and tomato purée. Season with salt and pepper, mix in the meat extract and cook over a low heat for 30 minutes, stirring occasionally to prevent sticking.

Purée the mixture through a food mill or a sieve. (Do not use a liquidizer as this emulsifies the seeds of the tomatoes.) Blend in the sugar and lemon juice. Pour into an ice-tray, leaving 1·25-cm (½-in) headspace for expansion; seal, label and freeze.

To use: Just before serving, turn into a bowl, break up the ice with a wooden spoon, and beat until just mushy but not thawed. Pile into glass bowls, put a dollop of sour cream mixed with horseradish on each one, and top with a small sprig of mint.

Green soup with sorrel

Wild sorrel can be found in almost any hedgerow.

Serves 4   Storage time: 2 months

- 1 medium onion
- 25 gr (1 oz) butter
- 6 dl (1 pint) picked-over spinach without stalks
- 6 dl (1 pint) picked-over sorrel without stalks
- 1½ tablespoons flour
- 9 dl (1½ pints) chicken stock
- salt and freshly ground black pepper
- pinch nutmeg
- 4 tablespoons sour cream
- 1 teaspoon grated horseradish

Peel and finely chop the onion. Melt the butter in a heavy pan, add the onion, and cook over a low heat until the onion is soft and transparent. Add the spinach and sorrel and cook over a low heat, stirring occasionally, for 5 minutes. Blend in the flour. Add the stock, season with salt, pepper and a pinch of nutmeg, bring to the boil and simmer gently for 10 minutes. Purée through a fine sieve or food mill, or in an electric liquidizer. Thin with a little extra stock if necessary. Cool. Pour into a suitable container, leaving 1·25-cm (½-in) headspace for expansion. Seal, label and freeze.

To use: Reheat the soup and pour into bowls. Combine the horseradish with the sour cream and float a spoonful of this cream in each bowl.

EEC soup with almonds

Can be served either hot or cold.

Serves 6 Storage time: 2 months

900 gr (2 lb) firm Brussels sprouts
2 potatoes
1 large onion
50 gr (2 oz) butter
9 dl (1½ pints) chicken or white stock
3 dl (½ pint) milk
salt, freshly ground black pepper
a little ground nutmeg
100 gr (4 oz) flaked, blanched almonds (these can now be bought in packets)
1·5 dl (¼ pint) cream

Peel and roughly chop the sprouts, removing any yellow leaves. Peel and chop the potatoes into small dice. Peel and finely chop the onion. Melt the butter in a heavy pan, add the onion, and cook over a low heat for about 5 minutes until soft and transparent. Add the sprouts and potatoes and cook for a further 3 minutes, stirring all the time, until all the butter in the pan has been absorbed. Add the stock and milk and mix well, scraping the bottom of the pan. Season with salt, pepper and nutmeg, bring to the boil, and simmer gently for 20 minutes. Purée the soup through a food mill or in an electric liquidizer.

To freeze: Cool. Pour into polythene containers, leaving 1·25-cm (½-in) headspace for expansion. Seal, label and freeze.

To use hot: Thaw the soup at room temperature for about 4 hours. Turn into a saucepan and heat through until hot. Roast almonds in a hot oven for about 2 minutes until crisp and golden. Check seasoning, add cream, and mix well. Add almonds just before serving.

To use cold: Thaw the soup at room temperature for about 4 hours. Mix with a wire whisk. Check seasoning, blend in cream, and chill in the refrigerator until absolutely cold. Mix in almonds just before serving.

Curried apple soup

This is another soup that can be served hot or cold.

Serves 6 Storage time: 3 months

1 small onion
3 teaspoons olive oil
2 teaspoons curry powder
450 gr (1 lb) cooking apples
1·2 litres (2 pints) chicken stock
salt and freshly ground black pepper
1 teaspoon lemon juice
4 tablespoons cream

Peel and finely chop the onion. Combine the oil and onion in a saucepan and cook over a low heat until the onion is soft. Add the curry powder and continue to cook, stirring all the time, for 3 minutes. Remove from the stove.

Peel, core and roughly chop the apples. Add the apples to the onion and curry powder and mix in the stock. Season with salt and pepper and mix in the lemon juice. Bring to the boil and simmer gently for about 20 minutes or until the apples are absolutely tender. Cool and purée the soup through a food mill or a sieve, or in an electric liquidizer.

To freeze: Cool the soup. Pour into polythene containers, leaving 1·25-cm (½-in) headspace for expansion. Seal, label and freeze.

To use: Thaw the soup at room temperature for about 3 hours and turn into a saucepan. Heat over a low flame until hot through; season with salt and pepper and mix in the cream. Serve hot, or pour into glass bowls and chill in the refrigerator until icy cold.

Sauces

Many basic sauces, provided they are not thickened entirely with cream or egg yolks, freeze well and make quickly heated standbys.

Pack sauces in polythene containers, leaving 1·25-cm (½-in) headspace for expansion. Use them straight from the frozen state. Do not over-season – spices can be added during the reheating process. Unless you plan to freeze a sauce for a short term only, add the garlic, too, when reheating.

Tomato sauce, sauce Bolognese, apple sauce, gooseberry sauce and Cumberland sauce are amongst those I find most invaluable.

Plum sauce

Make from windfalls or bruised fruit. An excellent sauce to serve with roast chicken, gammon, or cold meats.

Serves 4 Storage time: 6 months

225 gr (8 oz) onions
900 gr (2 lb) cooking plums
3 dl (½ pint) malt vinegar
225 gr (8 oz) sugar
salt and pepper

Peel and chop onions. Wash plums and remove stalks. Combine plums and onions in a saucepan with the vinegar and sugar. Season with salt and pepper, bring to the boil, and simmer until the fruit is tender. Rub through a fine sieve or purée through a food mill.

To freeze: Cool as quickly as possible. Pack in polythene containers, leaving 1·25-cm (½-in) headspace for expansion. Seal, label and freeze.

Second-stage ingredients

6 gr (¼ oz) ground ginger
6 gr (¼ oz) ground allspice
pinch nutmeg
½ teaspoon dry English mustard
37 gr (1½ oz) butter

Turn the frozen sauce into a heavy pan. Heat over a low flame until thawed but not hot through. Add remaining ingredients, bring to the boil, and simmer for 10 minutes, stirring to prevent sticking.

Gooseberry sauce

Well worth making when gooseberries are in season. It is traditionally served with mackerel, but I find it goes well with other fried oily fish and also with roast duck. You can find sorrel in fields and hedgerows.

Serves 4–6 Storage time: 4 months

450 gr (1 lb) gooseberries
4 tablespoons water
handful of sorrel leaves
25 gr (1 oz) butter
salt and white pepper
sugar

Top and tail gooseberries, combine with the water, and cook until absolutely tender. Add the picked-over sorrel leaves, mix well, and cook for a further 3 minutes. Purée through a fine sieve or a food mill, or in an electric liquidizer. Return to a clean pan, add the butter and season with salt and pepper. Add just enough sugar to take away the extreme tartness of the fruit but not enough to make the sauce sweet. Simmer for 2 minutes.

To freeze: Cool as quickly as possible. Pack in a polythene container, leaving 1·25-cm (½-in) headspace for expansion. Seal, label and freeze.

Second-stage ingredients

4 tablespoons water
generous pinch nutmeg

Combine the frozen sauce with the water in a heavy pan. Heat gently until the sauce is thawed. Add the nutmeg, check seasoning, and simmer for 3 minutes.

Cumberland sauce

Delicious hot or cold, with ham, brisket, tongue, duck or game.

Serves 6   Storage time: 1 month

juice and thinly pared rind 1 orange
juice and thinly pared rind 1 lemon
275 gr (10 oz) redcurrant jelly
1·5 dl (¼ pint) port
3 teaspoons Dijon mustard
¼ teaspoon cayenne pepper
pinch ground ginger
salt and white pepper

Cut any white membrane from the orange and lemon peel and cut the peel into the thinnest possible *julienne* strips. Melt the jelly in a saucepan, add the port, orange and lemon juice, orange and lemon peel, mustard and the spices. Season with salt and pepper and simmer gently for 10 minutes.

To freeze: Cool as quickly as possible. Pack into a polythene container, leaving 1·25-cm (½-in) headspace for expansion. Seal, label and freeze.

To use hot: Turn the frozen sauce into a heavy pan and place over a low flame until thawed and hot through.

To use cold: Thaw at room temperature for about 3 hours.

Misto sauce

To serve with plain boiled vegetables or roast meat or chicken. Buy cheap bacon trimmings to make the sauce when you can get them. Grocers who cut their own bacon will often sell you these very cheaply.

Serves 6 Storage time: 2 months

225 gr (8 oz) bacon trimmings
1 large onion
25 gr (1 oz) butter
2½ tablespoons flour
½ teaspoon Dijon mustard
4·5 dl (¾ pint) strong beef stock
1 tablespoon vinegar
1 teaspoon meat glaze or meat extract
salt and freshly ground black pepper

Remove the rind from the bacon and finely chop the flesh. Peel the onions, slice thinly and divide into rings. Melt the butter in a heavy pan, add the bacon and cook over a low heat for 5 minutes, stirring to prevent browning. Add the onion and continue to cook over a low heat until onion is soft and transparent. Add the flour and mustard, mix well and gradually blend in the stock, stirring continuously until the sauce comes to the boil and is thick and smooth. Mix in the vinegar and meat glaze or extract, season with salt and pepper and simmer for 8 minutes, stirring frequently.

To freeze: Cool as quickly as possible, pack in a polythene container, leaving 1·25-cm (½-in) headspace for expansion. Seal, label and freeze.

Second-stage ingredients

½ tablespoon olive oil
1 tablespoon finely chopped parsley
1·5 dl (¼ pint) dry white wine

Heat the oil in a heavy saucepan, add the frozen sauce and cook over a low heat until the sauce is thawed through. Bring to the boil, simmer for 2 minutes, check seasoning and stir in parsley and white wine. Serve at once.

Italian tomato sauce

Serve with pasta or as a sauce to accompany steaks, grilled meat and chops, roast chicken and lamb.

Serves 6 Storage time: 4 months

900 gr (2 lb) ripe tomatoes
2 large onions
3 tablespoons olive oil
1 tablespoon tomato purée
1 teaspoon sugar
1 teaspoon white wine vinegar
salt and freshly ground black pepper

Peel the tomatoes by dipping them into boiling water for 1 minute and then sliding off the skins. Remove the core and seeds and finely chop the flesh. Peel and very finely chop the onions.

Heat the oil in a heavy pan. Add the onions and cook over a low heat until the onions are soft and transparent. Add the tomatoes, tomato purée, sugar and vinegar, season with salt and pepper, cover and cook over a high heat for 10 minutes, stirring to prevent sticking.

To freeze: Cool the sauce as quickly as possible and pour into a polythene container, leaving 1·25-cm (½-in) headspace for expansion. Seal, label and freeze.

Second-stage ingredients

2 cloves garlic
1 tablespoon olive oil
pinch dried oregano
½ tablespoon fresh basil or ¼ teaspoon dried basil

Peel the garlic cloves and crush them through a garlic press. Heat the oil in a heavy saucepan, add the garlic and cook over a low heat until soft and transparent. Add the frozen sauce and cook over a low heat until thawed through but not hot. Add the herbs, bring to the boil, cover and simmer for 5 minutes.

Sauce Bolognese

Serve with all kinds of pasta, as a snack on toast, or as a filling for savoury pancakes

Serves 6 Storage time: 3 months

350 gr (12 oz) bacon
100 gr (4 oz) chicken livers
1 onion
1 stick celery
1 carrot
2 tablespoons olive oil
225 gr (8 oz) lean minced beef
1½ tablespoons tomato purée
1 teaspoon grated lemon rind
3 dl (½ pint) beef stock
4 tablespoons white wine
salt, freshly ground black pepper

Remove the rinds of the bacon and mince the rashers. Mince the chicken livers. Peel and very finely chop the onion. Very finely chop the celery. Peel and mince the carrot.

Heat the olive oil in a heavy pan, add the bacon and onion and cook over a low heat until the onion is soft and transparent. Add the carrot and celery and cook for 3 minutes. Add the beef, raise the heat and cook until meat is well browned. Add the chicken livers and cook for a further 2 minutes, stirring well. Blend in the tomato purée and mix in the lemon rind, stock and wine, and season with salt and pepper. Bring to the boil, cover, and cook over a low heat for 30 minutes.

To freeze: Cool as quickly as possible, pack in a polythene container, leaving 1·25-cm (½-in) headspace for expansion. Seal, label and freeze.

Second-stage ingredients

1 clove garlic
1 tablespoon olive oil
pinch nutmeg and ground cloves
pinch dried oregano
1·5 dl (¼ pint) double cream

Peel the garlic and crush it through a garlic press. Heat the oil in a heavy pan, add the garlic and cook over a low heat until the garlic is soft and transparent. Add the frozen sauce and continue to cook over a low heat until the sauce is thawed but not hot through. Add the nutmeg, cloves and oregano and continue to heat until the sauce comes to the boil. Cover and simmer for 5 minutes. Remove from the heat, blend in the cream and serve at once.

Chicken liver sauce

A useful sauce to make in bulk when you can find chicken livers. In towns these can usually be bought in large supermarkets and in the country they are often in evidence on poultry stalls at local markets. Remember that chicken livers will almost undoubtedly have been frozen before they go on sale, so do not refreeze before cooking as the flavour will deteriorate.

The sauce can be served with spaghetti or other pasta, or with rice. It goes well with vegetables: courgettes, broad beans or with Brussels sprouts. You can also use it for filling vegetables that are to be served stuffed, like marrows, courgettes, large onions, tomatoes and cabbage leaves.

Serves 6 Storage time: 3 months

4 thin rashers streaky bacon
1 large onion
1 large carrot
1 tablespoon vegetable or cooking oil
450 gr (1 lb) chicken livers
1 tablespoon tomato purée
1·5 dl (¼ pint) stock
1·5 dl (¼ pint) dry white wine
salt and freshly ground black pepper

Remove the rind and very finely chop the bacon. Peel and very finely chop the onion and the carrot. Heat the oil in a saucepan, add the bacon and cook over a low heat until the bacon begins to crisp and the fat has melted. Add the onion and continue to cook over a low heat until the onion is soft and transparent. Add the carrot and cook for a further 3 minutes, stirring to prevent sticking. Add the livers, stirring to prevent sticking, and cook over a high heat until the livers are browned.

Add the tomato purée, stock and wine, season with salt and pepper, mix well, cover, and simmer for 20 minutes.

To freeze: Cool. Pack in polythene containers, leaving 1·25-cm (½-in) headspace for expansion. Seal, label and freeze.

Second-stage ingredients

1 clove garlic
pinch oregano and sage
salt and freshly ground black pepper

Turn the frozen sauce into a heavy saucepan. Peel the garlic and put it through a garlic press. Add the garlic and herbs and place over a low heat until the sauce comes to boiling point. Season with additional salt and pepper, cover, and simmer for 10 minutes. Serve at once.

Note: As a quick snack (freezer-to-table in about 20 minutes) the sauce can be served with hot toast.

Sorrel purée

Serve with fish, chicken, pork, goose or duck.

Serves 4 Storage time: 2 months

450 gr (1 lb) sorrel
12 gr (½ oz) butter
1 tablespoon flour
1·5 dl (¼ pint) strong stock
½ teaspoon caster sugar
salt and freshly ground black pepper
pinch cayenne and nutmeg
2 tablespoons double cream

Pick over the sorrel and remove any tough stalks. Cook the sorrel in boiling salted water for a few minutes until it is tender. Purée the sorrel through a fine sieve or a fine food mill, or in an electric liquidizer.

Melt the butter in a saucepan, add the flour and mix well. Gradually blend in the stock, stirring continuously over a medium flame until thick and smooth. Add the sorrel and sugar, mix well, season with salt, pepper, cayenne and nutmeg.

To freeze: Cool. Pack into polythene containers leaving 1·25-cm (½-in) headspace for expansion. Seal, label and freeze.

To use: Turn the frozen purée into a heavy saucepan and place over a low heat until purée comes to boiling point. Remove from the heat, blend in the cream and serve at once.

Lemon compote

This tart, rather unusual accompaniment for poultry or game is a real winner and is especially good with a fatty bird like duck or goose. Make it when lemons are cheap and tarragon is in season.

Serves 4 Storage time: 3 months

6 thick-skinned lemons
6 sprays fresh tarragon
450 gr (1 lb) sugar
4·5 dl ($\frac{3}{4}$ pint) water

Use a potato peeler to thinly pare the rind from the lemons without removing any of the white membrane. Cut the rind into thin *julienne* strips and pour some boiling water over to cover. Drain off the water and leave to cool.

Cut off all the white skin and membrane from the lemons and remove pips. Cut lemons into thin slices. Cover tarragon with boiling water and drain at once. Place the lemon slices in a shallow dish and sprinkle over the tarragon leaves.

Combine the sugar and water, bring to the boil and boil for 5 minutes. Add the lemon peel, pour the syrup over the lemons and leave to cool.

To freeze: Pack in a polythene container. Seal, label and freeze.

To use: Thaw overnight in a refrigerator. Serve chilled in a glass dish.

Savoury butters

Savoury butters can add a sparkle to a great number of plain dishes, but they are fiddly to make. Prepare your savoury butters when you have a bit of time on hand and store them in the deep freeze. You will only need a few thin slices at a time and these can be cut straight from the frozen block; the rest can be returned to the freezer for use at a later date.

Storage time: 2 months

Serve in thin slices with beefburgers or hamburgers, steaks, fried or steamed fish, chicken, or combined with another ingredient for sandwiches.

Basic recipe:

100 gr (4oz) soft butter
flavouring ingredient
seasoning

Combine the flavouring ingredient and the seasoning with the butter and mix until well blended. Shape the butter into a sausage-shaped roll about 2·5 cm (1 in) in diameter. Wrap tightly in foil, pack in a polythene bag, seal, label and freeze.

To use: Cut slices of savoury butter 6 mm (¼ in) thick as required.

Parsley butter

Mix 2 tablespoons finely chopped parsley with the butter and season with a little salt, freshly ground black pepper and a tiny pinch nutmeg.

Garlic butter

Press 2 small cloves garlic through a garlic press and add to the butter with a little salt and freshly ground black pepper. (Do not store for longer than 1 month.)

Chive butter

Add 2 tablespoons finely chopped chives to the butter. Blend well and season with salt and freshly ground black pepper.

Stilton butter

Mash 2 tablespoons Stilton cheese with the butter until the mixture is smooth. Season with a little cayenne pepper.

Herb butter

Soften 1 teaspoon mixed dried herbs in a little hot water. Drain and mix with the butter and season with salt and freshly ground black pepper.

Horseradish butter

Add 2 teaspoons finely grated fresh horseradish to the butter, mix well and season with salt and freshly ground black pepper.

Watercress butter

Add 2 tablespoons very finely chopped watercress to the butter with ½ teaspoon lemon juice, salt and freshly ground black pepper. Mix well until blended.

Pâtés and terrines

Some of the best things in life (in the culinary sense) require time and patience to make, although they need not be in any way expensive. Pâtés and terrines fall in this class. The results are delicious but the making of them is often arduous and here, once again, your deep freeze comes into its own. Instead of making one quantity of the dish, you make two or more, freezing some to use at a later date. Because of their flavouring and spices, pâtés, terrines, and other foods that fall into this category should not be stored for too long in the freezer, but they will keep satisfactorily for at least a month, so that with the same amount of effort you can produce more than one superb dish at a time.

Pâtés should be smooth and extremely rich to taste; terrines are a coarser version of pâté with plenty of fat and liberal seasoning. Thaw pâtés and terrines, still in their wrappings, in the refrigerator for at least 12 hours or overnight. They can be coated with aspic after thawing and turning out, and garnished with parsley to give a fresh, newly made look.

Potted shin beef

Serves 4 Storage time: 2 months

150 gr (6 oz) cooked shin beef from the stockpot (see page 142)
100 gr (4 oz) butter
pinch mace
pinch cayenne
salt and freshly ground black pepper
1 tablespoon brandy or sherry

Pick out the shin beef from the vegetables used in the stock.

Melt the butter until just foaming but not turning brown. Add the beef, mace and cayenne and season with salt and freshly ground black pepper.

Mix well and stir in the brandy or sherry.

To freeze: Remove from the heat, cool and pack into a rigid container. Seal, label and freeze.

To use: Leave to thaw in a refrigerator for 6–8 hours. Spread on sandwiches or turn out, garnish with parsley and lemon quarters and serve with hot toast.

Potted ham or game

A useful way of making the most of a small amount of strong-tasting cooked meat or game. The result is a pâté-like mixture which can be served with toast as a first course, as a picnic ingredient or as a sandwich spread.

Serves 4–6 Storage time: 1 month

275 gr (10 oz) cooked ham, pigeon, hare, pheasant, wild duck, etc
100 gr (4 oz) unsalted butter
salt and freshly ground black pepper
1 tablespoon brandy or sherry
pinch dried marjoram, thyme and mace

Strip the meat off any bones and cut away any gristle or tough fibres. Mince the meat twice through the fine blades of a mincing machine or pound it to a paste with a pestle and mortar.

Melt the butter, add the meat and season with salt and plenty of freshly ground black pepper. Mix in the brandy or sherry and the herbs and mace. Cook over a low heat for 2 minutes and pack, whilst still warm, in an earthenware container.

To freeze: Cool; open-freeze until solid and then turn out the potted meat by running hot water over the container. Pack in a polythene bag, seal, label and freeze.

To thaw: Transfer the potted meat to its original earthenware container, cover with polythene film and thaw overnight in a refrigerator.

To use: Melt an extra 12 gr (½ oz) of butter, pour it over the potted meat and leave until set.

Potted crab

This makes a good starter and freezes well. Economize by buying a whole crab when shellfish is at its cheapest and extracting the flesh yourself. This is a boring job, but the reason crabmeat is usually so expensive is the time it takes to extract the meat from the body and claws.

Serves 4 Storage time: 2 months

75 gr (3 oz) butter
225 gr (8 oz) brown and white mixed crabmeat
3 egg yolks
3 tablespoons cream
salt, pepper and a pinch of mace and cayenne
1 tablespoon brandy
1 tablespoon freshly grated Parmesan cheese

Melt the butter in a heavy pan. Add the crab, egg yolks (well beaten) and cream, season with salt, freshly ground black pepper, mace and cayenne and cook, stirring continuously with a wooden spoon, over a very low heat until the mixture is smooth and well blended - do not boil. Cook for 3 minutes until thick, mix in the brandy and the Parmesan cheese, and cook for a further 2 minutes or until the cheese has melted.

To freeze: Cool and pack into suitable containers (small cream cartons are useful for this.) Seal, label and freeze.

To use: Thaw overnight in a refrigerator. Turn out and serve on a bed of lettuce leaves garnished with quarters of lemon. Accompany with hot toast or brown bread and butter.

Duck neck pâté

If you raise your own ducks or can buy them from a poulterer who will leave their necks on, use the neck skin to make this really first-rate pâté, stuffed and roasted inside the duck neck. (You can also make it from goose neck or from a large capon.)

Serves 4 Storage time: 1 month

2 ducks' necks with skins; gizzards, hearts and livers
1 clove garlic
1 tablespoon parsley
2 egg yolks
325 gr (12 oz) pork sausage meat
pinch mace and ground cloves
2 juniper berries, ground fine
salt and freshly ground black pepper

Cut the skin as near to the base of the neck and as near to the head as possible: the best way is to use kitchen scissors and then slip the skin off the neck, making sure you remove the windpipe.

Stretch the necks by running the back of a knife along them. Sew up one open end with a needle and strong cotton.

Cut off as much meat as possible from the neck bones. Mince the neck meat with the gizzards, livers, hearts and garlic. Finely chop the parsley. Beat the egg yolks. Combine the minced meats with the egg yolks, parsley and sausage meat, mix in the mace, ground cloves and juniper berries and season with salt and plenty of freshly ground black pepper.

Stuff the necks with the mixture, press it down firmly, and sew up the open ends. Cook with the bird, basting frequently, for about 1½ hours.

To freeze: Cool as quickly as possible; wrap in plastic film and then in a polythene bag. Seal, label and freeze.

To use: Thaw in wrapping, overnight in a refrigerator. Unwrap, cut into thin slices and serve as a first course with hot toast, or with salad as a summer dish.

Meat dishes

Starter beef stew or casserole recipe

Beef stews or casseroles almost always require the addition of onions and at least another vegetable. For my starter recipe I combine beef with onions, carrots and a rich stock. I keep the seasoning to a minimum and cook the meat for only three-quarters of the time it would normally need to become tender. (The cooking times given in the recipes are only a rough guide as these will, of course, vary depending on the quality of the meat.) Other vegetables, spices, herbs, wine and any additional ingredients are added to the basic recipe on the day it is to be served.

Make a batch of the starter recipe when beef prices are low or when you buy part of a carcase. In this way it is possible to double-up dishes, saving fuel costs and providing a bank of potential stews or casseroles that can be varied in any number of ways.

2×4 servings   Storage time: up to 3 months

1·35 kg (3 lb) lean beef	4 large onions
flour	450 gr (1 lb) carrots
salt and pepper	75 gr (3 oz) dripping
pinch allspice	1·2 litres (2 pints) rich beef stock

Trim off any fat or gristle from the meat and cut it into neat 2·5-cm (1-in) cubes. Season the flour with salt, pepper and just a little pinch of allspice. Roll the meat in the seasoned flour until well coated on all sides. Peel and chop the onions. Peel the carrots and cut them into small dice.

Heat the dripping in a heavy frying pan. Add the onions and cook over a low heat until the onions are soft and transparent. Remove the onions from the pan with a slotted spoon and add the meat to the fat. Cook over a high heat until the meat is well browned on all sides. Remove the meat from the pan and combine it with the onions and carrots in a casserole dish. Add the stock to the juices in the pan, stirring continuously until the liquid comes to the boil. Pour the gravy over the meat, cover tightly and cook in a moderate oven (350°F, 180°C, regulo 4) for 45 minutes.

To freeze: Cool, pack in a suitable container, seal, label and freeze.

To use: Thaw the stew at room temperature in its container (or turn the frozen stew into a heavy pan and heat slowly until thawed). Add the second-stage ingredients and seasoning, and continue cooking until the meat is tender.

Second-stage recipes

The following recipes are just a few ideas for using your 'starter' base. An enormous variety of alternative dishes can be made, depending on the ingredients you have to hand.

Quickies

Add chopped leftover vegetables to the thawed stew and simmer for 30–40 minutes or until meat is tender.

Add tomato purée, mushroom ketchup (see page 271) or Worcester sauce to the stew to give a richer flavour during the final cooking period.

Stir 2 tablespoons fresh, chopped parsley into the cooked stew just before serving.

Add frozen mixed chopped vegetables to the thawed stew and cook until the meat is tender.

Beef goulash

Serves 4

1 × 225-gr (8-oz) tin tomatoes
2 tinned red pimentos
4 potatoes
1 × 4 servings starter beef stew
1–2 teaspoons paprika pepper
1·5 dl (¼ pint) red wine
1 tablespoon tomato purée
2 bay leaves
salt and freshly ground black pepper

Roughly chop the tomatoes (I cut them in their tin with a pair of scissors). Chop the pimentos. Peel the potatoes and cut them into 2·5-cm (1-in) cubes.

Thaw the stew and turn into a heavy pan. Add the tomatoes, pimentos, paprika, wine, tomato purée and bay leaves and bring to the boil, stirring to prevent sticking. Add the potatoes, cover tightly and simmer over a low heat (or cook in a moderately hot oven – 350°F, 180°C, regulo 4) for 30 minutes or until the meat is tender and the potatoes are cooked. Check seasoning before serving.

Serve with a salad or green vegetable and with rice if you wish the dish to stretch further.

Beef stew with dumplings

Serves 4

1 × 4 servings starter beef stew
1 small cabbage
2 tablespoons vegetable oil
3 dl (½ pint) ale
pinch caraway seeds
1 tablespoon Dijon mustard
100 gr (4 oz) self-raising flour
50 gr (2 oz) shredded suet
1 tablespoon grated raw onion
½ teaspoon dried mixed herbs
salt and freshly ground black pepper

Thaw the stew. Roughly chop the cabbage. Heat the oil in a large, heavy pan, add the cabbage and cook over a low heat, without browning, for 3 minutes until soft. Add the stew, ale, caraway seeds and mustard. Mix well, bring to the boil, cover and simmer for 30 minutes.

Combine the flour, suet, onion and herbs, season with salt and pepper, mix well and add enough water to make a soft dough. Divide the dough into pieces roughly the size of a walnut and roll into balls on a floured board. Add the dumplings to the stew and continue cooking over a medium-high heat for a further 15–20 minutes, until the dumplings bob to the surface, and are light and fluffy.

Burgundy beef stew

Serves 4–5

150 gr (6 oz) streaky bacon
2 cloves garlic
150 gr (6 oz) firm button mushrooms
1 × 4 servings starter beef stew
25 gr (1 oz) butter
1 tablespoon flour
1·5 dl (¼ pint) red wine
bouquet garni
salt and freshly ground black pepper
2 tablespoons finely chopped parsley

Thaw the stew. Remove the rind and cut the rashers into 2·5-cm (1-in) pieces. Peel and finely chop the garlic. Thinly slice the mushrooms. Cook the bacon over a medium-low heat, without extra fat, for 4 minutes. Remove the bacon with a slotted spoon and add it to the stew. Add the garlic to the juices in the pan and cook over a low heat for 2–3 minutes or until soft but not browned. Remove the garlic with a slotted spoon and add it to the stew. Add the butter to the juices in the pan, heat until just melted, add the mushrooms and sauté over a medium-low heat for 3 minutes. Remove the mushrooms with a slotted spoon and add them to the stew. Blend the flour into the juices in the pan, add the red wine and bring to the boil, stirring all the time.

Heat the stew to boiling point, add the thickened wine and bouquet garni, season with salt and freshly ground black pepper and mix well. Cover and cook in a moderately hot oven (375°F, 190°C, regulo 5) for 45 minutes or until the meat is really tender.

Remove the bouquet garni, check seasoning and stir in the finely chopped parsley just before serving.

Beef stew with green peppers and kidney beans

Serves 4

1 × 4 servings starter beef stew
2 green peppers
1 clove garlic
2 tablespoons olive or vegetable oil
salt, pepper and ¼ teaspoon cayenne
1 tin red kidney beans
2 tablespoons finely chopped parsley

Thaw the stew. Remove the core and seeds of the peppers and cut the flesh into thin strips. Peel and finely chop the garlic clove. Heat the oil in a pan, add the peppers and garlic and cook over a low heat, without browning, for 5 minutes. Transfer the stew to a heavy pan and heat through until boiling. Add the peppers and garlic, season with salt, pepper and cayenne, cover tightly and simmer over a low heat – or cook in a moderate oven (350°F, 180°C, regulo 4) – for 30 minutes. Mix in the beans and the liquid from the tin and continue to cook for a further 15–20 minutes or until the dish is hot through and the meat is tender. Stir in the parsley just before serving.

Starter minced beef recipe

This minced meat recipe can be thawed in a saucepan and the basic dish can be transformed in a very short time into anything from a quick snack to a delicious shepherd's pie.

2 × 4 servings   Storage time: up to 3 months

4 onions
3 large carrots
75 gr (3 oz) dripping or 4 tablespoons olive oil
675 gr (1½ lb) raw minced beef
2 tablespoons flour
3–4·5 dl (½–¾ pint) rich stock or stock and leftover gravy

Peel and very finely chop the onion and carrots. Heat the dripping or oil in a frying pan, add the onions and carrots and cook over a low heat until the onion is soft and transparent. Remove the vegetables with a slotted spoon, add the meat to the juices in the pan, raise the heat and cook, stirring continuously, until the meat is nicely browned. Mix in the vegetables and stir in the flour. Cook for 2 minutes, stirring all the time. Blend in the stock, stirring until the mixture comes to the boil. Season with a little pepper and cook for 10 minutes.

To freeze: Cool, package in a suitable container, seal, label and freeze.

To serve: Thaw the starter recipe at room temperature or transfer it to a heavy saucepan and heat slowly until thawed. Add the second-stage ingredients and the herbs and seasoning, and continue cooking in the usual way.

Second-stage recipes

Again, these recipes are just to give you an idea of what can be achieved with the starter recipe. A host of other dishes can be produced on the same principle using ingredients you have to hand.

Quickies

Add some mushrooms, thinly sliced or finely chopped and lightly sautéed in butter, to the thawed and reheated basic recipe together with a generous sprinkling of finely chopped parsley and a tablespoon or two of double cream. Season with a little additional salt and pepper and a few drops of Tabasco, and serve on toast as a snack.

Add some tomato purée, a pinch of oregano and sage and one or two chopped, strained tinned tomatoes to the thawed and reheated basic recipe. Simmer over a low heat for 15 minutes and serve as a sauce for spaghetti.

Flavour the thawed and reheated basic recipe with a little Worcester sauce and some tomato ketchup, simmer for 5–10 minutes and serve the mince in a ring of mashed potatoes or fluffy boiled rice.

Chilli con carne

Serves 4

1 × 4 servings starter minced meat
1 × 225-gr (8-oz) tin tomatoes
2 cloves garlic
4 spring onions
1 tablespoon olive oil
1 tin red kidney beans
1 tablespoon tomato purée
2 bay leaves
1½ teaspoons chilli powder
¼ teaspoon paprika
pinch ground cumin
salt and freshly ground black pepper

Thaw and reheat the minced meat. Drain off the liquid from the tomatoes (this can be used in soups, stocks or gravy). Peel the garlic and press it through a garlic press. Trim the spring onions and cut them into thin strips, lengthwise. Heat the olive oil, add the garlic and onions and cook over a low heat for 2 minutes until the onions are soft – do not allow to brown. Strain off the liquid from the beans.

Add the garlic and onions to the minced meat together with the beans, tomatoes, tomato purée, bay leaves and spices. Season with salt and pepper. Cover and simmer for 20 minutes, adding some of the kidney-bean liquid if the mixture is too dry. Serve with rice and a green salad.

Curried minced meat

Serves 4

1 × 4 servings starter minced meat
1 × 225-gr (8-oz) tin tomatoes
1 green pepper
1 tablespoon olive oil
1½ tablespoons curry powder
¼ teaspoon ground ginger
1½ tablespoons finely chopped mango chutney
50 gr (2 oz) sultanas
salt and freshly ground black pepper

Thaw and reheat the minced meat. Drain off the liquid from the tomatoes and chop the tomatoes into small pieces with kitchen scissors. Add to the meat.

Discard the core and seeds of the green pepper and finely chop the flesh. Heat the oil in a saucepan, add the pepper and cook over a low heat for 3–5 minutes until the pepper is soft. Remove the pepper with a slotted spoon and add it to the meat. Add the curry powder to the juices in the pan and cook over a low heat, stirring, for 2 minutes. Add 2 tablespoons tomato juice, mix well, add the ginger and simmer for 4 minutes. Add the curry mixture, chutney and sultanas to the minced meat; season with salt and pepper, bring to the boil, cover and simmer for 20 minutes over a low heat.

Serve with fluffy boiled rice and the usual curry accompaniments.

Cheesey cottage pie

Serves 4

1 × 4 servings starter minced meat
675 gr (1½ lb) potatoes
12 gr (½ oz) butter
2 tablespoons double cream
50 gr (2 oz) finely grated Cheddar cheese
salt and freshly ground black pepper
1 tablespoon tomato purée
½ teaspoon Worcester sauce
1 tablespoon very finely chopped parsley

Thaw the minced meat in a saucepan. Cook the potatoes until tender in boiling, salted water; drain well, mash them until smooth and beat to a purée with the butter, cream and grated cheese. Season the potatoes with salt and pepper.

Add the tomato purée and Worcester sauce to the minced meat, mix well, bring to the boil and mix in the chopped parsley. Season with salt and pepper.

Spread half the meat mixture in a lightly greased pie dish. Cover with half the mashed potatoes, top with the remaining meat and spread the remaining potatoes over. Mark the top in a wavy pattern with a fork and bake in a moderately hot oven (375°F, 190°C, regulo 5) for 30 minutes or until the top is crisp and golden brown.

Serve with Italian mushrooms (see page 212) or some other exciting vegetable dish.

Meat balls

Serves 4

- 1 × 4 servings starter minced meat
- 1 clove garlic
- 50 gr (2 oz) fresh white breadcrumbs
- 2 tablespoons finely chopped parsley
- 1 large egg
- 25 gr (1 oz) grated Parmesan cheese
- salt and freshly ground black pepper
- flour
- 3 dl (½ pint) tomato sauce (see page 159)
- oil or dripping for deep-frying

Thaw the minced meat. Peel the garlic clove and crush through a garlic press. Drain off excess stock from the meat, using a sieve and pressing the meat gently with the back of a wooden spoon to drain it, reserving the stock. Combine the meat with the breadcrumbs, garlic, parsley, egg and cheese, season with salt and freshly ground black pepper and mix well until stiff and blended. On a well-floured board, divide the mixture into about 16 pieces and shape into balls.

Fry the meatballs in hot oil or dripping in a saucepan, shaking the pan, until they are crisp and well browned on all sides. Add the tomato sauce and the meat stock, bring to the boil, cover the pan and simmer gently for 20–30 minutes.

Serve the meatballs with spaghetti or noodles and some extra Parmesan cheese.

Beef olives with vegetables

Beef olives take time to prepare but they freeze well, so make this dish when you have plenty of time and freeze it to serve later.

Serves 4

4 thin slices beef cut from the topside or silverside, weighing about 175 gr (6 oz) each
225 gr (8 oz) sausage meat
1 beaten egg
100 gr (4 oz) minced ham
4 finely chopped pickled gherkins
1 tablespoon finely chopped parsley
small pinch sage and thyme
2 tablespoons flour
50 gr (2 oz) lard or dripping
1 medium onion
2 carrots
2 sticks celery
2 tablespoons tomato purée
300 ml (½ pint) pale ale
300 ml (½ pint) stock or water
salt and freshly ground black pepper
pinch mace and cinnamon

Beat the slices of beef between two pieces of greaseproof paper until very thin. Mix the gherkins with the ham, sausage meat, beaten egg and parsley. Season the mixture well with salt, pepper, sage and thyme. Coat one side of the beef slices with seasoned flour. Divide the stuffing between the meat slices, on the unfloured side, roll them up lightly so that the filling is not squeezed out, and secure with kitchen cotton or toothpicks.

Peel the onion, cut it into thin slices and divide into rings. Peel the carrots and cut them into thin *julienne* strips. Trim the celery stalks and cut them into thin *julienne* strips about 5 cm (2 in) long.

Heat the lard in a large heavy saucepan. Add the beef olives and brown them on all sides over a high heat. Remove the olives to a casserole dish with a slotted spoon. Add the vegetables to the juices in the pan and cook over a moderately high heat, stirring, until they have softened. Stir in the tomato purée, ale and stock or water and bring to the boil; season the sauce with salt, pepper, mace and cinnamon and simmer for 20 minutes. Pour the vegetables and sauce over the olives, cover tightly with foil and cook in a moderately hot oven (350°F, 180°C, regulo 4) for 1 hour.

To freeze: Cool, transfer to a suitable container, seal, label and freeze.

To finish
1 tablespoon cornflour
150 ml (¼ pint) double cream
1 tablespoon finely chopped parsley

To use: Defrost at room temperature for about six hours. Transfer to a large, heavy frying pan and heat through. Remove the olives and vegetables with a slotted spoon into a serving dish. Remove the string or toothpicks from the olives and keep warm. Mix the cornflour with a little of the sauce and stir over a medium heat until the sauce comes to the boil and is thick and glossy. Add cream, check seasoning, heat through without boiling and pour the sauce over the olives and vegetables. Sprinkle over the parsley just before serving.

Beef and macaroni pie

A good dish to serve when there are plenty of mouths to feed for a reasonable cost.

Serves 6–8
225 gr (8 oz) large macaroni
water
salt
225 gr (8 oz) good-quality minced beef
4 tablespoons sunflower oil
1 finely chopped large onion
1 medium-sized tin tomatoes
150 ml (¼ pint) red wine
1 tablespoon tomato purée
salt and freshly ground black pepper
½ teaspoon dried oregano
2 tomatoes
40 gr (1½ oz) butter
40 gr (1½ oz) flour
75 gr (3 oz) grated Parmesan cheese
125 gr (5 oz) grated Cheddar cheese
pinch cayenne
600 ml (1 pint) milk
2 egg yolks

Bring a large pan of salted water to a fast boil, add the macaroni and cook for about 15 minutes until tender. Rinse in cold water and drain well.

Heat the oil, add the meat and onion and cook over a high heat, stirring, until the meat is well browned. Add the tomatoes, tomato purée and red wine. Season with salt and pepper, mix in the oregano, bring to the boil and cook over a high heat, without a lid, stirring every now and then, until the sauce is thick (about 30 minutes).

Melt the butter in a saucepan, add the flour and mix well. Gradually blend in the milk, stirring continually over a medium-high heat until the sauce is thick and smooth. Add 75 gr (3 oz) of the Cheddar cheese, the Parmesan and cayenne pepper, and stir over a low heat until the cheese has melted. Remove half the sauce and add it to the macaroni, mixing well. Add the egg yolks to the remaining sauce, stirring over a low heat.

Layer the macaroni and meat sauce in a dish suitable for freezing and reheating. Add a top layer of thinly sliced tomatoes. Pour over the sauce with the egg yolks in it and top with the rest of the grated Cheddar cheese.

To freeze: Cool, pack in polythene bag, seal, label and freeze.

To use: Defrost at room temperature for about five hours. Reheat in a hot oven (400°F, 200°C, regulo 6) for about 30 minutes until the dish is heated through, the sauce is bubbling and the top is nicely browned.

Serve with a green vegetable or salad.

Starter lamb recipe (1)

2×4 servings Storage time: 3 months

1·35 kg (3 lb) stewing lamb off the bone
4 large onions
4 carrots
flour
salt and pepper
50 gr (2 oz) lard or dripping
6 dl (1 pint) stock

Cut the lamb into 1·25-cm ($\frac{1}{2}$-in) cubes. Peel and chop the onions. Peel the carrots and cut them into small dice. Roll the lamb in flour seasoned with salt and pepper. Heat the lard or dripping, add the onions and cook over a low heat until onions are soft and transparent. Remove the onions with a slotted spoon and add the meat to the juices in the pan. Raise the heat and cook the meat until browned on all sides. Remove the meat with a slotted spoon and combine it, in a casserole, with the onions and carrots. Mix the stock with the juices in the pan, scraping up all the sediment. Bring to the boil, stirring all the time, and simmer for 2 minutes.

Strain the stock over the meat and vegetables. Cover tightly and cook in a moderate oven (350°F, 180°C, regulo 4) for 1 hour.

To freeze: Cool quickly, transfer to a suitable container, seal, label and freeze.

To thaw: Thaw overnight in a refrigerator or transfer to a heavy pan and thaw over a low heat.

To use: Add second-stage ingredients to the thawed starter recipe and cook for a further hour or until the meat is tender and the ingredients all cooked.

Starter lamb recipe (2)

2×4 servings   Storage time: 3 months

1·8 kg (4 lb) stewing lamb on the bone (scrag, middle neck, etc)
4 large onions
4 carrots
flour
salt and pepper
50 gr (2 oz) lard or dripping
7·5 dl (1¼ pints) stock

Cut the lamb into pieces. Peel and chop the onion. Peel and dice the carrots. Roll the lamb pieces in flour seasoned with salt and pepper. Heat the dripping, add the onions and cook over a low heat until onions are soft and transparent. Remove the onions with a slotted spoon and add the meat to the juices in the pan. Raise the heat and cook the meat until browned on all sides. Remove the meat with a slotted spoon and combine it in a casserole with the onions and carrots. Mix the stock with the juices in the pan, scraping up all the sediment. Bring to the boil, stirring all the time, and simmer for 2 minutes.

Strain the stock over the meat and vegetables. Cover tightly and cook in a moderate oven (350°F, 180°C, regulo 4) for 1 hour.

To freeze: Cool quickly, transfer to a suitable container, seal, label and freeze.

To thaw: Thaw overnight in a refrigerator or transfer to a heavy pan and thaw over a low heat.

To use: Add second-stage ingredients to the thawed starter recipe and cook for a further hour or until the meat is tender and the ingredients all cooked.

Second-stage recipes

Lamb starter recipes are among the most useful standbys to have in the deep freeze, and can be made into a wide variety of dishes, traditional and exotic.

Cumberland lamb

Serves 4

1 × 4 servings starter lamb recipe 1
2 teaspoons Dijon mustard
3 tablespoons redcurrant jelly
thinly pared rind and juice ½ orange
1 teaspoon dried rosemary or 1 sprig fresh rosemary
½ glass port
pinch nutmeg
salt and freshly ground black pepper

Thaw the starter recipe and turn it into a flameproof casserole dish. Heat slowly, stirring to prevent sticking, until boiling. Add the mustard, redcurrant jelly, orange rind (cut into very thin *julienne* strips), rosemary and port. Season with salt, nutmeg and freshly ground black pepper, cover tightly after mixing well, and cook in a moderate oven (350°F, 180°C, regulo 4) for 45–60 minutes or until the meat is absolutely tender. If fresh rosemary has been used, remove it before serving.

Serve with stewed cucumbers (see page 212) when cucumbers are plentiful.

Cornish lamb pie with parsley

The unusually lavish use of parsley in this recipe makes a most subtle and flavoursome dish.

Serves 4

1 × 4 servings of starter lamb recipe 1
225 gr (8 oz) parsley
pinch sage and thyme
salt and freshly ground black pepper
150 gr (6 oz) shortcrust or flaky pastry
1 small beaten egg
1·5 dl (¼ pint) double cream

Thaw the starter recipe. Cut the stalks off the parsley (use these in the stockpot) and very finely chop the leaves. Place a third of the starter recipe in a pie dish, having first put a pie funnel in the centre. Cover the meat with a third of the finely chopped parsley; sprinkle with the tiniest touch of sage and thyme and season with salt and pepper. Repeat with 2 more layers of meat and parsley, and pour over any remaining juices. Roll out the pastry to 6-mm (¼-in) thickness. Cover the dish, damp the edges with water, press the pastry down firmly and crimp the edges neatly. Brush the pie with beaten egg seasoned with a pinch of salt and bake in a hot oven (450°F, 230°C, regulo 8) for 5 minutes and then in a moderate oven (350°F, 180°C, regulo 4) for a further 45 minutes. Make a small hole in the pastry topping, pour in the cream through a funnel and serve at once.

Note: If you want to make the dish go further, put in additional layers of very thinly sliced potatoes and a little extra stock.

Turkish lamb stew

Serves 4

1 × 4 servings starter lamb recipe 1
2 cloves garlic
2 green peppers
1 × 225-gr (8-oz) tin tomatoes
2 tablespoons olive oil
1 tablespoon tomato purée
¼ teaspoon ground coriander
2 bay leaves
1 tablespoon finely chopped fresh mint
salt and freshly ground black pepper

Thaw the starter recipe, turn it into a flameproof casserole and bring slowly to the boil. Peel the garlic and crush through a garlic press. Remove the core and seeds of the peppers and cut the flesh into thin strips. Chop the tomatoes. (I do this whilst they are still in the tin, using a pair of kitchen scissors.) Heat the olive oil in a frying pan, add the peppers and cook over a low heat for 5 minutes. Combine the peppers and tomatoes with the lamb, mix in the tomato purée, garlic, coriander and bay leaves, season with salt and pepper, cover and cook in a moderate oven (350°F, 180°C, regulo 4) for 45 minutes or until the meat is quite tender. (The dish can be cooked on top of the stove, over a low heat, but it will need stirring occasionally to prevent sticking.)

Remove the bay leaves, add the chopped mint, stir lightly and check seasoning. Serve at once.

Hot pot

Serves 4

1 × 4 servings starter lamb recipe 2
900 gr (2 lb) potatoes
100 gr (4 oz) frozen peas
salt and freshly ground black pepper
1·5 dl (¼ pint) water
½ teaspoon Worcester sauce
2 tablespoons finely chopped parsley

Thaw the starter recipe. Peel the potatoes and cut them into thick slices. Place one third of the starter recipe in a casserole dish, cover with one third of the potatoes and a scattering of peas and season with salt and pepper. Continue with these layers, finishing with potatoes. Pour over the water mixed with the Worcester sauce, cover and cook in a moderate oven (350°F, 180°C, regulo 4) for 45 minutes. Remove the cover and sprinkle with chopped parsley before serving.

Lamb stew with haricot beans

Serves 4

1 × 4 servings starter lamb recipe 2
100 gr (4 oz) haricot beans
1 small turnip
2 cloves garlic
1 tablespoon tomato purée
glass red wine
½ teaspoon dried rosemary
salt and freshly ground black pepper
1 tablespoon finely chopped parsley

Thaw the starter recipe. Soak the beans in cold water overnight. Cook the beans in boiling, salted water for 30 minutes, drain well. Peel the turnip and cut into small dice. Peel the garlic and crush through a garlic press. Mix the tomato purée with the red wine. Add the tomato purée and red wine to the starter recipe with the turnip, beans, garlic and rosemary. Season with salt and pepper, cover and cook in a moderate oven (350°F, 180°C, regulo 4) for 1 hour or until the beans are tender. Sprinkle with chopped parsley before serving.

Lamb stew with sour cream and herbs

Serves 4

- 1 × 4 servings starter lamb recipe 2
- 1·5 dl (¼ pint) white wine
- 1 sprig tarragon or 1 teaspoon dried tarragon
- 1 sprig thyme or 1 teaspoon dried thyme
- salt and freshly ground black pepper
- 1·5 dl (¼ pint) sour cream
- 2 tablespoons finely chopped capers
- 1 tablespoon finely chopped fresh mint

Thaw the starter recipe, transfer it into a casserole, add the white wine and herbs and season with salt and freshly ground black pepper. Bring slowly to the boil over a low heat, cover, and simmer for 1 hour or until the meat is absolutely tender. Check the seasoning, stir in the sour cream, capers and mint, and heat through without boiling.

Lamb pie

A delicious and aromatic lamb pie with an evocative flavour of Middle Eastern cooking.

Serves 6

- 1.1 kg (2½ lb) lamb from shoulder, middle neck or leg
- water
- 4 tablespoons sunflower oil
- 1 finely chopped onion
- 2 diced carrots
- 3 sticks celery
- 2 diced courgettes
- 1 teaspoon crushed coriander seeds
- 3 bay leaves
- salt and freshly ground black pepper
- 50 gr (2 oz) butter
- 3 tablespoons flour
- pinch grated nutmeg
- 3 beaten egg yolks
- juice and grated rind of 1½ lemons
- 225 gr (8 oz) cooked rice
- 225 gr (8 oz) shortcrust pastry
- beaten egg

Cut the meat into 1·5-cm (¾-in) cubes. Fairly thickly slice the celery including the leaves.

Heat the oil in a large pan. Add the meat and cook over a high heat until lightly browned. Add the onion, carrots and celery and toss lightly to mix. Cook over a low heat for five minutes. Cover with water, add the coriander seeds and bay leaves, and season with salt and pepper. Bring to the boil, skim off any scum from the surface and simmer gently for 1 hour. Add the courgettes and continue to simmer for a further 30 minutes. Strain off the stock.

Mix the egg yolks with the lemon juice and about ¼ pint of stock. Melt the butter in a clean saucepan. Add the flour and mix well. Gradually blend in the rest of the stock, stirring continually over a medium-high heat until the sauce comes to the boil and is thick and smooth. Reduce the heat, add the egg mixture and stir until the sauce is thick and glossy.

Mix in the rice, check seasoning and add a little nutmeg. Pour the sauce over the meat and vegetables and stir to mix. Transfer the ingredients to a pie dish and leave to cool.

Roll out the pastry until it is about ⅛ inch thick. Cover the pie with the pastry and cut an air vent in the top. Brush with beaten egg.

To freeze: Open-freeze until the pie is frozen through. Pack in a polythene bag, seal, label and return to the freezer.

To use: Defrost the pie overnight. Bake it in a hot oven (400°F, 200°C, regulo 6) for 10 minutes and then reduce the heat to moderately hot (350°F, 180°C, regulo 4). Continue to cook for a further 15–20 minutes until the pastry is golden-brown and the contents are heated through.

Starter pork recipe

2 × 4 servings Storage time: 2 months

1·35 kg (3 lb) lean pork	salt and pepper
4 large onions	37 gr (1½ oz) lard or dripping
flour	6 dl (1 pint) strong chicken stock

Remove any excess fat from the pork and cut the meat into neat 1·25-cm (½-in) cubes. Peel and thinly slice the onions and divide into rings. Season the flour with salt and pepper and roll the pork cubes in the seasoned flour until they are coated on all sides.

Heat the lard or dripping in a frying pan, add the onions and cook over a low heat until soft and transparent. Remove the onion with a slotted spoon, raise the heat and add the pork to the juices in the pan. Cook the meat until well browned on all sides. Remove the meat with a slotted spoon and combine it in a casserole with the onions. Add the stock to the pan juices and mix well, scraping up all the sediment from the sides of the pan. Bring to the boil, stirring all the time, and simmer for 2 minutes.

Pour the stock over the meat and vegetables. Cover tightly and cook in a moderate oven (350°F, 180°C, regulo 4) for 1 hour.

To freeze: Cool quickly, transfer to a suitable container, seal, label and freeze.

To thaw: Thaw overnight in a refrigerator or transfer to a heavy pan and thaw over a low heat.

To use: Add second-stage ingredients to the thawed starter recipe and cook for a further hour or until the meat is tender and all the ingredients are cooked through.

Second-stage recipes

Pork needs the addition of herbs and flavourings to complement its texture. The combinations are endless as pork goes well with both sweet and savoury ingredients, but care has to be taken not to make the dish too rich or heavy.

Porc à blanc

Serves 4

1 × 4 servings starter pork recipe
1 clove garlic
2 teaspoons marjoram
1 teaspoon caraway seeds
grated rind ½ lemon
2 red or green peppers
1 tablespoon olive oil
1 tablespoon paprika pepper

Thaw and reheat the starter recipe.

Peel the garlic and combine it with the herbs and lemon rind in a mortar. Mash the ingredients until almost smooth.

Remove the core and seeds of the peppers and cut the flesh into thin strips. Heat the oil in a frying pan, add the peppers and cook over a low heat for 5 minutes, stirring frequently.

Add the herb mixture and paprika pepper to the thawed pork and mix well. Bring to the boil. Cover tightly and simmer for 1 hour or until the pork is really tender.

Pork casserole creole

Serves 4

1 × 4 servings starter pork recipe
4 sticks celery
1 green pepper
1 small tin sweet-corn kernels
1 tablespoon olive oil
2 tablespoons tomato purée
½ teaspoon paprika pepper

Thaw and reheat the starter recipe.

Slice the celery. Remove the core and seeds of the pepper and finely chop the flesh. Drain off and reserve the liquid from the sweet corn.

Heat the oil in a frying pan. Add the celery and pepper and cook over a low heat for 3 minutes.

Blend the tomato purée with the pork, add the paprika and mix well. Mix in the celery, pepper and sweet corn and, if the sauce looks too thick, blend in a little extra liquid from the sweet corn. Bring to the boil, cover and simmer for about 1 hour or until the meat is thoroughly tender.

Check seasoning before serving.

Pork with apricots and sour cream

Serves 4

1 × 4 servings starter pork recipe
100 gr (4 oz) dried apricots
grated rind 1 lemon
pinch of sage and thyme
1·5 dl (¼ pint) dry cider
1 carton sour cream

Thaw and reheat the starter recipe.

Roughly chop the dried apricots and add them to the pork with the lemon rind, herbs and cider. Mix well. Bring to the boil, cover tightly and simmer gently for about 1 hour or until the meat is really tender. Check during the cooking time to see that there is enough liquid in the casserole, and if necessary add a little water.

Taste for seasoning and blend in the sour cream just before serving.

Belly of pork with red cabbage

An inexpensive but satisfying dish.

Serves 4–5

900 gr (2 lb) belly of pork
salt and freshly ground black pepper
pinch paprika
pinch ground ginger
1 finely chopped large onion
1 small red cabbage, shredded
pinch sage
1 teaspoon caraway seeds
150 ml (¼ pint) dry cider

Trim off the skin from the pork and cut the meat with the fat on it into 1-cm (½-in) wide strips. Rub the strips with a mixture of salt, pepper, paprika and ginger. Place the strips, fat side up, on a rack over a roasting dish and cook in a hot oven (425°F, 220°C, regulo 7) for 20 minutes. Drain off the fat into a large frying pan.

Add the onion to the pork-dripping and cook over a low heat, stirring until the onion is soft and transparent. Add the cabbage and cook for two minutes. Add the meat, sage and caraway seeds and transfer the ingredients to a casserole dish. Pour over the cider, cover tightly with foil and cook in a moderate oven (350°F, 180°C, regulo 4) for 40 minutes.

To freeze: Cool, pack into a suitable container, seal, label and freeze.

To use: Defrost the casserole for at least six hours. Turn into a casserole dish, cover tightly with foil and reheat in a moderately hot oven (350°F, 180°C, regulo 4) for about 30 minutes until heated through.

Serve with mashed or baked potatoes.

Sweet and sour pork

It is difficult in England to cook proper Chinese food, unless you happen to be near a shop that sells the right ingredients – so this makes no pretence of being the real thing. It is, on the other hand, a most delicious dinner-party dish. Serve it with noodles or rice mixed with small pieces of crisply fried bacon and thin strips of an omelette (made with 1 egg only) mixed with the rice. This can be made in advance and reheated.

Serves 6   Storage time: 1 month

900 gr (2 lb) lean pork
4 tablespoons cornflour
4 spring onions
1 green pepper
2 tablespoons caster sugar
2 tablespoons white wine vinegar
2 tablespoons orange juice
4½ tablespoons soy sauce
1½ tablespoons tomato purée
1½ tablespoons dry sherry
1·5 dl (¼ pint) chicken stock
1·5 dl (¼ pint) vegetable or olive oil

Cut the pork into small cubes and roll it in 2 tablespoons of cornflour. Trim the spring onions and cut them into thin strips lengthwise. Remove the core and seeds of the pepper and cut the flesh into thin strips. Combine the remaining cornflour with the sugar, vinegar, orange juice, 1½ tablespoons soy sauce, the tomato purée, sherry and stock, and mix until smooth.

Heat three-quarters of the oil in a saucepan, add the pork and cook over the highest heat possible for 5 minutes, turning all the time. Drain off all excess oil and add 3 tablespoons soy sauce. Cook for a further minute.

Heat the remaining oil in another saucepan and add the pepper and spring onions. Cook over a medium heat for 2 minutes. Add the sauce mixture and cook, stirring all the time until the sauce has thickened and is smooth and shiny. Add the pork and mix well.

To freeze: Cool, pack in a rigid container, seal, label and freeze.

To use: Thaw, wrapped, overnight in a refrigerator. Turn the thawed pork into a heavy pan and heat gently until thoroughly hot.

Country-style cassoulet

An excellent dish to have for a winter party. Although you will have to allow plenty of time for defrosting, this dish freezes well and needs little attention when you wish to serve it.

Serves 10–12

450 gr (1 lb) dried haricot beans
450 gr (1 lb) belly pork, with skin on
1 duck
675 gr (1½ lb) gammon
salt and freshly ground black pepper
pinch dried thyme and sage and 4 bay leaves
chicken stock (or water and stock cubes)

The finishing touches

100 g (4 oz) cubed salami or garlic sausage
6 cloves garlic
3 tablespoons dripping
3 tablespoons finely chopped parsley
50 gr (2 oz) fresh breadcrumbs

Cover the beans with cold water and leave them to soak overnight. Cut the belly of pork into small cubes. Remove the flesh from the duck and cut into cubes. Remove any rind from the gammon and cut the flesh into cubes. Combine the pork, duck, gammon and drained beans in a large flameproof casserole with the thyme and sage, season with salt and plenty of freshly ground black pepper, mix well and pour over enough stock to cover the ingredients.

Bring slowly to the boil, give the ingredients a good stir and place the bay leaves on top. Cover tightly with foil and cook in a slow oven (300°F, 150°C, regulo 2) for 2½ hours.

To freeze: Cool, remove the bay leaves, pack into a suitable container, seal, label and freeze.

To use: Thaw overnight, and transfer to a flameproof casserole. Heat the cassoulet slowly over a low heat, stirring gently to prevent sticking.

Peel the cloves of garlic and blanch them in boiling water for five minutes. Drain and mash them to a pulp and mix in the dripping and parsley. Add the salami or garlic sausage to the cassoulet with the garlic mixture, mix lightly and simmer gently for 20 minutes (if ingredients seem to be too dry add a little extra stock). Sprinkle over the breadcrumbs and brown under a hot grill before serving.

I like to serve this dish with some crisp French beans or *mange tout* peas.

Starter chicken recipes

Chicken still makes a relatively inexpensive dish for a family and by stewing or casseroling it with other ingredients, a medium-size bird can be made to stretch surprisingly far. By making a quantity of the basic recipe you can produce a considerable variety of different dishes in a short time – dishes that range from simple, country-style casseroles to very sophisticated recipes to serve for a dinner party. You can use older and less expensive birds for stewing and casseroling than for roasting, and these do, in fact, often have more flavour. If you live in the country it is often possible to buy these quite cheaply from a farmer who no longer has any use for them as laying birds.

1: Chicken on the bone

3 × 4 servings Storage time: 3 months

2 medium-size boiling fowl
flour
salt and freshly ground black pepper
3 large onions
4 carrots
bouquet garni
2 tomatoes
1·2 litres (2 pints) water
1 stock cube
37 gr ($1\frac{1}{2}$ oz) butter
2 tablespoons olive oil
1 teaspoon mixed herbs

Remove the legs of the chickens and cut each one in two at the joint. Cut off the wings as near to the joint as possible. Carefully cut off the breasts and cut each one into 2 pieces. Roll the chicken pieces in flour seasoned with salt and pepper. Peel the onions, reserving the skins. Peel the carrots, reserving the peel.

Break the chicken carcase into half and place it in a saucepan with the giblets, onion skins, carrot peelings, bouquet garni and the tomatoes, roughly chopped. Pour over the water, season with salt and pepper, add the stock cube and bring to the boil. Stir well, simmer for 2 hours, and then strain through a fine sieve. Remove the gizzards and hearts. (The carcase and vegetables can be boiled a second time to make a second lot of stock.)

Chop the onions and dice the carrots. Heat the butter and olive oil until the butter is melted. Add the onion and cook over a low heat until soft and transparent. Remove the onion with a slotted spoon, raise the heat and add the chicken pieces to the juices in the pan, a few at a time so that the pan does not become too overcrowded. Cook over a high heat until golden-brown on all sides. Remove the chicken pieces with a slotted spoon and put them into a casserole dish with the gizzards, hearts, onions and carrots. Add the stock to the juices in the pan, mix well and bring to the boil, stirring all the time and scraping the sediment off the sides of the pan. Strain the stock over the chicken. Add the herbs, cover tightly and cook in a moderate oven (350°F, 180°C, regulo 4) for 1 hour.

To freeze: Cool, pack in a suitable container; seal, label and freeze.

To use: Thaw overnight in a refrigerator, or in a heavy pan over a low heat. Add second-stage ingredients and continue cooking until chicken and other ingredients are tender.

2: Chicken off the bone

3×4 servings Storage time: 3 months

2 medium-size boiling fowl	1·2 litres (2 pints) water
bouquet garni	flour
4 large onions	25 gr (1 oz) butter
5 carrots	2 tablespoons olive oil
salt and freshly ground black pepper	1 teaspoon mixed herbs

Cut all the flesh off the chicken and cut it into neat 2·5-cm (1-in) pieces. Put the chicken carcase with the giblets and bouquet garni into a saucepan with one of the onions, peeled and roughly chopped, and one of the carrots, peeled and roughly chopped. Season with salt and pepper. Cover with the water, bring to the boil and simmer for 2 hours. Strain the stock through a fine sieve (the carcase can be boiled again to make a second lot of stock).

Roll the chicken pieces in flour seasoned with salt and pepper. Peel and finely chop the remaining onions. Peel the carrots and cut them into small dice. Heat the butter with the oil, add the onions and cook them over a medium heat until soft and transparent. Remove the onions with a slotted spoon, add the chicken to the juices in the pan and cook over a medium heat until the chicken is golden-brown on all sides. Remove the chicken and add the stock to the juices in the pan, stirring continuously over a medium heat until the stock comes to the boil. Place the chicken, onions, carrots and mixed herbs in a casserole dish, pour over the stock, cover and cook in a moderate oven (350°F, 180°C, regulo 4) for 45 minutes.

To freeze: Cool, pack into a suitable container; seal, label and freeze.

To use: Thaw in the refrigerator overnight, or turn into a heavy pan and thaw over a low heat. Add second-stage ingredients and continue to cook until chicken and other ingredients are tender.

Second-stage recipes

Once again, these are just some of the ways your basic starter recipes can be used to advantage. Almost any ingredients go with chicken, and with an exciting use of herbs and spices you can produce some really first-class dishes.

Country chicken casserole

Serves 4

1 × 4 servings starter chicken recipe 1
1 × 125-gr (5-oz) tin tomatoes
75 gr (3 oz) streaky bacon
100 gr (4 oz) firm button mushrooms
2 tablespoons finely chopped parsley
salt and freshly ground black pepper
150 gr (6 oz) frozen peas

Thaw the chicken recipe and turn it into a flameproof casserole. Heat the chicken gently until boiling.

Chop the tomatoes. Remove the rind from the bacon and chop the rashers. Very thinly slice the mushrooms. Fry the bacon, without extra fat, over a low heat for 5 minutes. Remove the bacon with a slotted spoon and add it to the chicken. Add the mushrooms to the bacon fat in the pan and cook them for 2 minutes over a low heat. Remove the mushrooms with a slotted spoon and add them to the chicken with the tomatoes and the parsley, season with salt and pepper, bring to the boil, cover and simmer for 30 minutes on the stove (or cook in a moderate oven, 350°F, 180°C, regulo 4, for a further 30 minutes or until the chicken is tender). Add peas 15 minutes before chicken is cooked, and mix well.

Eastern chicken

Serves 4

1 × 4 servings starter chicken recipe 1
1 × 225-gr (8-oz) tin tomatoes
2 green peppers
1 dried red chilli pepper
½ teaspoon turmeric
½ teaspoon ground coriander
salt and freshly ground black pepper
1 carton yogurt

Thaw the starter chicken recipe, transfer it to a flameproof casserole and bring gently to the boil over a low flame. Chop the tomatoes. Remove the core and seeds of the green peppers and cut the flesh into thin strips. Halve the red chilli, remove the seeds (these are very hot – take care to wash your hands after removing them) and very finely chop the flesh. Add the tomatoes, peppers and chilli to the chicken with the turmeric and coriander, season with salt and pepper, mix well, cover and simmer for 30 minutes. Stir in the yogurt just before serving.

Chicken with mushrooms

Serves 4

1 × 4 servings starter chicken recipe 2
1 teaspoon saffron
225 gr (8 oz) firm button mushrooms
37 gr (1½ oz) butter
1½ tablespoons flour
1 tablespoon fresh chervil (or 1 teaspoon dried chervil)
salt and freshly ground black pepper
2 tablespoons double cream
1 egg yolk

Thaw the starter recipe and turn it into a flameproof casserole. Bring to simmering point, strain off the stock and keep the chicken and vegetables warm in a low oven. Soak the saffron in 2 tablespoons hot water for 5 minutes and strain off and reserve the liquid. Thinly slice the mushrooms. Melt the butter in a heavy pan, blend in the flour and gradually add the stock, stirring continuously until the sauce comes to the boil and is thick and smooth. Add the chervil and the saffron juice and mix well.

Add the chicken and vegetables, season with salt and pepper and simmer for 30 minutes or until the chicken is really tender. Beat the cream with the egg yolk, add it to the chicken and heat through without boiling.

Serve the chicken with rice and sweet-sour red cabbage (see page 211).

Chicken Fellino

Serves 6 Storage time: 3 months

675 gr ($1\frac{1}{2}$ lb) boned chicken
1 large onion
1 clove garlic
325 gr (12 oz) grapes (preferably the small, seedless variety)
50 gr (2 oz) butter
1 tablespoon flour
1 teaspoon curry powder
$\frac{1}{4}$ teaspoon turmeric
6 dl (1 pint) milk
salt and freshly ground black pepper
1·5 dl ($\frac{1}{4}$ pint) single cream
6 slices thinly cut bread
2 tablespoons finely chopped parsley

Cut the chicken into thin slices. Peel and very finely chop the onion. Peel and very finely chop the garlic. Halve and de-seed the grapes unless they are the seedless variety.

Melt the butter in a saucepan, add the onion and garlic and cook over a low heat until the onion is soft and transparent. Add the flour, curry powder and turmeric and mix well. Gradually blend in the milk, stirring continuously over a high heat until the sauce is thick and smooth. Add the grapes and chicken, season with salt and freshly ground black pepper and simmer for 3 minutes.

To freeze: Cool, pack in a rigid container. Seal, label and freeze.

To use: Thaw the chicken, wrapped, overnight in the refrigerator. Turn it into a heavy saucepan, and place over a low heat until the chicken is really hot through – do not boil. Stir in the cream and check seasoning.

Cut the crusts off the bread and cut each slice into 2 triangles. Fry the triangles in hot fat until golden-brown and drain on kitchen paper. Transfer the chicken to a heated serving dish, surround with the fried bread, and sprinkle over the chopped parsley.

Chicken Chasseur

A classic chicken stew which freezes well.

Serves 6

1 chicken – about 1.5 kg (3 lb)
bouquet garni, 1 onion, 1 carrot – for the stock
salt, freshly ground black pepper and a little paprika
flour
300 ml (½ pint) dry white wine (a Médoc is ideal)
50 gr (2 oz) butter
4 tablespoons sunflower oil
300 ml (½ pint) chicken stock
3 tablespoons white wine vinegar
12 small onions or shallots
2 carrots
3 stalks celery
2 tablespoons flour
2 tablespoons tomato purée
¼ teaspoon dried tarragon
4 bay leaves

Joint the chicken. Cut the legs into two, remove the wingtips from the wings and cut the carcase into four pieces.

Brown the wingtips, neck, gizzard and heart in a saucepan in 2 tablespoons oil, add the bouquet garni, onion (washed, quartered but not peeled) and the carrot (cleaned and roughly chopped), season with salt and pepper and add enough water to cover. Bring to the boil, simmer for 30 minutes and then strain. Skim off any fat from the surface of the stock.

Peel the small onions or shallots. Peel and roughly chop the carrots. Cut the celery with the leaves on the stalks into 1-inch pieces.

Coat the chicken pieces in flour seasoned with salt, pepper and paprika.

Heat the butter with the rest of the oil in a large, heavy, frying pan. Add the legs and cook over a high heat for 5 minutes. Add the remaining chicken pieces and continue to cook for 10 minutes, turning every now and then, until thoroughly golden-brown. Remove the chicken with a slotted spoon into a casserole.

Add the onions, carrots and celery to the juices in the pan and stir over a medium heat until the onions are golden. Remove the vegetables to the casserole with a slotted spoon. Add 2 tablespoons flour to the juices in the pan and mix well. Add the tomato purée and gradually blend in the wine and half a pint of the chicken stock, stirring continually until the sauce is thick and smooth. Add the vinegar, tarragon and bay leaves and pour the sauce over the chicken and vegetables. The ingredients should be well-covered – add a little more stock if necessary. Cover tightly with a well-fitting lid or foil and cook in a moderately hot oven (350°F, 180°C, regulo 4) for 40 minutes.

To freeze: Cool, pack in a suitable container, seal, label and freeze.

To finish

175 gr (6 oz) firm button mushrooms
3 cloves garlic
150 ml (¼ pint) red wine
2 tablespoons finely chopped parsley

To use: Defrost at room temperature for about six hours. Transfer to a flameproof casserole or heavy pan and heat through gently. Remove the bay leaves. Peel and crush the garlic. Cook the button mushrooms in the red wine with the garlic for 5 minutes. Strain, add the mushrooms and garlic to the chicken and sprinkle over the parsley before serving.

Casserole of Normandy pheasant

An old classic but one that freezes well and makes good use of an older bird.

Serves 4

1 pheasant
flour
salt, freshly ground black pepper, and a pinch of cayenne
2 stalks celery
18 small pickling onions or shallots
2 rashers streaky bacon
1 large cooking apple
25 gr (1 oz) butter
1 tablespoon sunflower oil
bouquet garni

Joint the pheasant, cutting each leg in half, removing the wings and splitting the carcase in two pieces (or four if it is a large bird). Coat the pieces in flour seasoned with salt, pepper and cayenne. Trim and roughly chop the celery stalks. Peel the onions. Remove the rinds from the bacon and roughly chop the rashers. Peel, core and roughly chop the cooking apple. Heat the butter with 1 tablespoon sunflower oil in a large, heavy frying pan. Add the bacon and cook over a medium heat, stirring to prevent sticking, until the fat runs from the bacon. Remove the bacon to a casserole with a slotted spoon. Add the onions and celery to the juices in the pan and cook, stirring, over a medium heat for four minutes. Remove the celery and onions to the casserole with a slotted spoon, raise the heat under the pan, and add the floured pheasant pieces. Cook over a high heat, turning the pieces, until they are nicely browned. Remove the pheasant pieces to the casserole with a slotted spoon. Add the stock and cider to the juices in the pan and stir over a medium heat until the sauce has thickened and all the sediment has been amalgamated. Add the cooking apple and bouquet garni to the casserole, pour over the sauce (the ingredients should be covered), cover the casserole with foil and cook in a moderately hot oven (350°F, 180°C, regulo 4) for about 1½ hours until the pheasant is tender.

To freeze: Pack in a suitable container, seal, label and freeze.

The finishing touches

2 crisp eating-apples
2 slices white bread
40 gr (1½ oz) butter
2 tablespoons sunflower oil
150 ml (¼ pint) double cream
1 tablespoon finely chopped parsley

To use: Defrost at room temperature for about 8 hours or overnight. Turn into a heavy pan and reheat over a low heat so as not to destroy the texture of the pheasant. When the dish is heated through remove all the ingredients with a slotted spoon to a serving dish (discarding the bouquet garni). Add the cream to the sauce, check for seasoning, and reheat without boiling. Pour the sauce over the ingredients and keep warm.

Peel, core and slice the eating apples. Remove the crusts from the bread and cut the slices into small triangles. Heat the butter in a frying pan with the sunflower oil, add the apple slices and cook them over a low heat until they are just tender but not falling apart. Remove the slices with a slotted spoon and arrange them around the top edge of the casserole. Fry the bread triangles in the juices in the pan until they are crisp and golden, drain them on kitchen paper and lay them on the centre of the casserole. Sprinkle over the parsley and serve with mashed or baked potatoes and red or green cabbage.

Half-faggots

Real faggots require pig's caul and some other ingredients which are not always easy to find these days. This recipe is a short-cut variation on the real thing, providing a cheap, tasty meal for the family.

Serves 4–5 Storage time: 1 month

675 gr (1½ lb) pig's liver
2 onions
150 gr (6 oz) streaky bacon rashers
100 gr (4 oz) fresh white breadcrumbs
50 gr (2 oz) shredded suet
1 teaspoon finely chopped fresh sage (or ¼ teaspoon dried sage)
1 teaspoon finely chopped fresh thyme (or ¼ teaspoon dried thyme)
pinch freshly chopped fresh or dried marjoram
salt and freshly ground black pepper
flour
3 dl (½ pint) good rich stock

Mince the liver through the coarse blades of a mincing machine. Peel and *very* finely chop the onions. Remove the rinds from the bacon and mince the rashers.

Combine the liver, bacon, onions, breadcrumbs and suet with the herbs. Season with salt and pepper and mix well. Turn the mixture on to a floured board, and form into 8 even balls. Place the balls, side by side, in a shallow dish or foil case, pour over the stock and bake in a moderate oven (350°F, 180°C, regulo 4) for 30 minutes.

To freeze: Cool, pack in a foil or polythene container, pour over the stock; seal, label and freeze.

To use: Unwrap, cover the frozen faggots with foil, and bake in a moderately hot oven (375°F, 190°C, regulo 5) for 45 minutes. Check seasoning before serving.

Serve with mashed potatoes and a green vegetable.

Calves' liver Venezia

Calves' liver is expensive, but it is sometimes possible to get it more cheaply from a country butcher. The reason I include this recipe is that it is so well worth while grabbing the opportunity of getting calves' liver for this dish whenever you can. The secret is to cook the dish for only a very short time; so, as it is quick to prepare, I do not recommend cooking the finished dish and then freezing it, but rather preparing the liver for cooking and freezing that. Liver freezes well and thaws quickly.

Serves 6
Storage time: not longer than 2 months
675 gr (1½ lb) calves' liver

Wash and dry liver and cut into very, very thin slices 5 cm (2 in) long.

To freeze: Place the slices of liver on waxed paper or plastic film. Pack them in a polythene bag. Press out all the air; seal, label and freeze.

Second-stage ingredients

4 large onions
50 gr (2 oz) butter
2 tablespoons olive oil
1·5 dl (¼ pint) dry white wine
salt and freshly ground black pepper
1 teaspoon lemon juice
1 tablespoon finely chopped parsley

To use: Thaw liver, in its wrapping, in the refrigerator. Peel and very finely chop the onions. Combine the butter and oil in a frying pan, add the onions and cook over a low heat until soft and transparent. Add the wine and season with salt and pepper. Cook for 3 minutes. Raise the heat, add the liver and cook over a high heat for about 2 minutes until brown on both sides. Sprinkle with lemon juice and parsley and serve at once.

Vegetable dishes

Sweet-sour red cabbage

The perfect accompaniment to pork, bacon, ham and game dishes. Make it when red cabbages are in season and freeze to use at a later date.

Serves 6 Storage time: 3–4 months

1·35 kg (3 lb) red cabbage
37 gr (1½ oz) butter
1 tablespoon sugar
1½ tablespoons white wine vinegar
1·5 dl (¼ pint) water
2 cooking apples
4 tablespoons redcurrant jelly
½ teaspoon caraway seeds
salt and freshly ground black pepper

Remove the tough outer leaves of the cabbage and cut out the core. Finely shred the leaves. Melt the butter over a low flame in a heavy pan, add the sugar and stir until sugar is dissolved, without browning. Add the cabbage and cook for 3 minutes, stirring to prevent sticking. Add vinegar and water, bring to the boil and simmer for 1½ hours until the cabbage is very tender and almost transparent. Stir every now and then and add a little more water if necessary to prevent sticking.

Peel, core and finely chop the apples. Add the apples and redcurrant jelly to the cabbage with the caraway seeds. Season with salt and pepper and continue to simmer, still stirring occasionally, for a further 30 minutes.

To freeze: Cool, pack in a rigid container; seal, label and freeze.

To use: Turn frozen cabbage into a heavy pan with a little extra melted butter and cook over a very low heat until hot through.

Italian mushrooms

An unusual vegetable dish to serve with a rather plain main course.

Serves 4 Storage time: 1 month

450 gr (1 lb) firm button mushrooms
3 anchovy fillets
2 tablespoons olive oil
12 gr ($\frac{1}{2}$ oz) butter
1 tablespoon tomato purée

Very thinly slice the mushrooms. Drain and finely chop the anchovies. Heat the oil in a saucepan, add the mushrooms, and cook over a high heat for about 3 minutes until all the oil has been absorbed. Add the butter, tomato purée and anchovy fillets and cook just long enough for the butter to melt.

To freeze: Cool quickly, pack in a polythene container; seal, label and freeze.

Second-stage ingredients

2 cloves garlic
1 tablespoon olive oil
2 tablespoons finely chopped parsley
juice $\frac{1}{2}$ lemon
freshly ground black pepper

Peel the garlic cloves. Heat the olive oil in a saucepan, add the garlic and cook for 3 minutes, until browned. Remove the garlic with a slotted spoon and discard. Add the frozen mushrooms to the oil and cook over a low heat until the mushrooms have thawed and are hot through. Add parsley and lemon juice, season with freshly ground black pepper, and serve at once.

Stewed cucumbers

In a greenhouse all the cucumbers seem to be ready at the same time, and when they are in season they can often be extremely cheap to buy. They don't freeze when fresh because of their high water content, but they do make a delicious and unusual vegetable dish.

Serves 4 Storage time: 3 months

2 cucumbers
25 gr (1 oz) butter
2 tablespoons flour
scant 3 dl (½ pint) chicken stock
1 tablespoon finely chopped parsley
1 tablespoon finely chopped capers
salt and freshly ground black pepper

Peel the cucumbers and cut into 2·5-cm (1-in) dice. Cook the cucumbers in boiling salted water for 5 minutes until just tender but not mushy. Drain well.

Melt the butter, add the flour and mix well. Gradually blend in the chicken stock, stirring continuously over a medium-high heat until the mixture comes to the boil and is thick and smooth. Stir in the parsley and capers and season with salt and freshly ground black pepper. Fold in the cucumbers and remove from the heat.

To freeze: Cool. Pack in a polythene container; seal, label and freeze.

To use: Turn frozen mixture into a heavy pan and cook over a low heat until thawed and hot through. Check seasoning and serve at once.

Dandelions with bacon and almonds

A delicious vegetable to serve with roast chicken.

Serves 4 Storage time: 2 months

1 clove garlic
1 large onion
4 rashers streaky bacon
2 tablespoons olive oil
450 gr (1 lb) frozen dandelion leaves
salt and freshly ground black pepper
25 gr (1 oz) blanched nibbed or slivered almonds

Peel and very finely chop the garlic and the onion. Remove the rinds from the bacon and finely chop the rashers. Heat the oil in a saucepan, add the bacon and onion and cook over a low heat for 10 minutes. Add the frozen dandelions and cook over a medium heat, to break the dandelions up. Season with salt and freshly ground black pepper and cook for about 15 minutes or until the leaves are tender.

Pile on to a serving dish and top with almonds that have been lightly roasted in a hot oven until crunchy and golden-brown.

The Sultan's aubergines

Serves 6 Storage time: 3 months

3 large aubergines
4 tablespoons olive oil
3 large onions
3 ripe tomatoes
1 clove garlic
¼ teaspoon ground cinnamon
1 teaspoon caster sugar
1 tablespoon finely chopped parsley
salt and freshly ground black pepper
1 tablespoon finely chopped pistachio nuts

Put the aubergines in a saucepan, cover with water, bring to the boil and cook for 10 minutes. Drain at once and put the aubergines into cold water to which a few ice-cubes have been added to cool for 5 minutes. Drain well and wipe with a cloth. Cut the aubergines in half lengthwise and scoop out the flesh, taking care not to damage the shells. Place the shells in a lightly greased dish, brush them with 2 tablespoons olive oil, cover with foil and cook them in a moderately hot oven (350°F, 180°C, regulo 4) for 20 minutes or until they are quite soft. Leave to cool.

Finely chop the flesh of the aubergines. Peel and finely chop the onions. Peel the tomatoes by covering them with boiling water for 2 minutes and then slipping off the skins, and chop them finely. Peel and finely chop the garlic.

Heat 2 tablespoons olive oil in a saucepan, add the onion and garlic and cook over a low heat until the onion is soft and transparent. Add the tomatoes, cinnamon, sugar and parsley and season with salt and freshly ground black pepper. Simmer for 20 minutes and add the aubergine flesh. Cook for a further 10 minutes, drain off any excess juice if necessary and fill the aubergine shells.

To freeze: Pack the aubergines in a rigid container, fill in any spaces with crumpled kitchen paper; seal, label and freeze.

To use: Thaw overnight in the refrigerator. Sprinkle with the pistachio nuts and a little extra parsley, and serve well chilled; or place in a lightly greased baking dish, cover with foil and heat through in a moderately hot oven (350°F, 180°C, regulo 4) for about 15 minutes.

Ratatouille

Serves 6 Storage time: 1 week

4 courgettes
2 aubergines
4 large ripe tomatoes
1 red and 1 green pepper
1 onion
1 clove garlic
4 tablespoons olive oil
pinch sage, thyme and oregano
salt and freshly ground black pepper

Cut courgettes and aubergines into 6-mm (¼-in) slices. Peel tomatoes by covering them with boiling water for 2 minutes and then slipping off the skins; roughly chop the tomatoes. Remove the core and seeds of the peppers and cut the flesh into thin strips. Peel and thinly slice the onion and divide into rings. Peel and very finely chop the garlic.

Heat the olive oil in a heavy saucepan, add the onion and garlic and cook over a low heat for 5 minutes until the onion is soft and transparent. Add the peppers and cook for a further 10 minutes. Add the aubergines, courgettes, tomatoes and herbs. Season with salt and freshly ground black pepper, cover and cook over a low heat for 30 minutes, stirring every now and then.

To freeze: Cool, pack in a rigid container; seal, label and freeze.

To use: Leave to thaw at room temperature for about 3 hours. Turn into a saucepan and heat gently until hot through. Check seasoning.

Note: As there are already garlic and herbs in this dish before freezing, do not store for longer than 1 week.

Lunch or supper dishes

Marika's shepherd's pie

In order not to have to commit your pie dishes to the freezer, line the dish you plan to use with foil. Open-freeze the pie, and when it is solid, remove the pie in its foil casing and pack it in a polythene bag. When the pie is required, return the pie to the dish it was cooked in.

Instead of freezing one large pie, I often divide it between small individual dishes. These look attractive and you can produce exactly the right number of servings.

Serves 4 Storage time: 2 months

2 onions
25 gr (1 oz) dripping
300 gr (12 oz) minced cooked meat (beef or lamb)
1 tablespoon flour
1·5 dl (¼ pint) rich gravy or stock
1 tablespoon tomato purée
½ teaspoon Worcester sauce
salt and freshly ground black pepper
50 gr (2 oz) butter
450 gr (1 lb) cooked, mashed potatoes
3 tablespoons top of the milk

Peel and very finely chop the onions. Melt the dripping in a frying pan, add the onions and cook over a low heat until they are soft and transparent. Add the meat, increase the heat and cook, stirring continuously, until the meat is nicely browned. Add the flour and mix well. Blend in the gravy or stock, stirring until the mixture comes to the boil. Mix in the tomato purée and Worcester sauce and season with salt and freshly ground black pepper. Transfer to a pie dish.

Melt the butter and add two-thirds of it to the mashed

potatoes with the milk. Season with salt and pepper and beat until smooth and creamy. Spread the potato over the minced meat and dribble over the remaining melted butter. Pattern the top of the pie by running the back of a fork across it.

To freeze: Open-freeze until potato is solid. Pack in a polythene bag. Seal, label and freeze.

To use: Remove bag and heat through in a hot oven (425°F, 220°C, regulo 7) for 1 hour. Brown under a grill until the potato topping is crisp and golden.

Filled rolls

These make an exciting snack and can be made any time you have a few spare chicken livers available.

Storage time: 2 months

1 small French loaf (or some small crisp rolls)
100 gr (4 oz) butter
4 rashers lean bacon
225 gr (8 oz) chicken livers
100 gr (4 oz) mushrooms
1 onion
salt and freshly ground black pepper

Cut a slice across the top of the loaf and pull out all the soft bread from inside. Melt 75 gr (3 oz) butter in a large frying pan and fry the bread case and lid until it is golden-brown and crisp.

Remove the bacon rinds and finely chop the rashers. Finely chop the chicken livers and mushrooms. Peel and finely chop the onion.

Melt the remaining butter; add the bacon and cook until the fat oozes and the bacon is beginning to crisp. Add the onion and cook over a low heat until transparent. Mix in the chicken livers and mushrooms, season with salt and freshly ground black pepper, and cook for a further 2 minutes.

Fill the loaf with the cooked ingredients, press firmly together and leave to cool.

To freeze: Wrap the loaf in foil; pack in a polythene bag; seal, label and freeze.

To use: Leave on the foil wrapping and heat the frozen loaf in a moderately hot oven (400°F, 200°C, regulo 6) for 20 minutes until hot through. Unwrap during the last 5 minutes of cooking time to crisp the bread.

Savoury meat fritters

Serves 5–6   Storage time: 4–6 weeks

225 gr (8 oz) cooked beef, lamb or chicken
1 large onion
½ green pepper
2 rashers streaky bacon
2 large eggs
1 tablespoon olive oil
100 gr (4 oz) flour
1·5 dl (¼ pint) milk
1 tablespoon finely chopped parsley
salt, freshly ground black pepper and a pinch cayenne
fat for deep frying

Cut the meat into very small dice. Peel and finely chop the onion. Remove the core and seeds of the green pepper and finely chop the flesh. Remove the rinds and finely chop the bacon rashers. Separate the eggs.

Heat the oil in a frying pan. Add the bacon, onion and pepper and cook over a low heat until the onion is soft and transparent. Remove the bacon, onion and pepper with a slotted spoon and spread them on absorbent kitchen paper to remove excess fat.

Combine the egg yolks with the flour and milk, and beat with a rotary whisk until smooth. Add the meat, bacon, onion, pepper and parsley and season with salt, pepper and a pinch of cayenne pepper. Mix well.

Beat the egg whites until stiff and fold them lightly into the fritter mixture. Drop the fritters from a dessertspoon into very hot deep oil and cook, a few at a time, for 2 minutes each until well puffed and a light golden colour. Drain off all excess fat by placing the fritters on absorbent kitchen paper. Cool.

To freeze: Pack the fritters in rigid containers with cling-wrap or waxed paper between each layer, or open-freeze fritters before packing. Seal, label and freeze.

To use: Leave fritters to thaw in their containers for about 3 hours at room temperature. Drop the fritters into very hot deep oil for 1 minute to crisp and heat them. Or put the frozen fritters on a lightly greased baking tray and heat them through in a hot oven (425°F, 220°C, regulo 7) for about 10 minutes until crisp and hot.

Peperoni alla Giorgio

Serves 6 Storage time: 4–6 months

6 medium-size green peppers
75 gr (3 oz) long-grain rice
2 rashers streaky bacon
225 gr (8 oz) chicken livers
1 onion
100 gr (4 oz) mushrooms
2 tablespoons olive oil
1·5 dl (¼ pint) tomato sauce (see page 159)
salt and freshly ground black pepper
50 gr (2 oz) grated Parmesan cheese

Cut a slice off the stalk end of the peppers and scoop out all the seeds and membrane from the inside. Place the peppers in a bowl, pour boiling water over, and leave to stand for 5 minutes. Drain well and pat dry with kitchen paper.

Cook the rice in boiling salted water until tender. Remove the rinds of the bacon and finely chop the rashers. Trim and chop the chicken livers. Peel and finely chop the onion. Finely chop the mushrooms. Heat the olive oil in a frying pan, add the bacon and cook over a low heat for 5 minutes. Add the onion and cook for a further 3 minutes, stirring all the time until the onion is soft and transparent. Add the chicken livers and cook for another 5 minutes, stirring well over a medium heat, until brown on all sides. Add the rice and the tomato sauce, season with salt and pepper, and simmer for 5 minutes.

Fill the peppers with the mixture.

To freeze: Stand the filled peppers upright in a rigid container, filling any spaces with crumpled kitchen paper. Cover, seal, label and freeze.

To use: Leave peppers to thaw at room temperature for about 3 hours. Place in a lightly greased fireproof dish and pour a little hot water around them. Sprinkle over half the cheese and bake in a moderate oven (350°F, 180°C, regulo 4) for about 30 minutes. Remove on to a heated serving dish and sprinkle over the remaining cheese.

Bistro ham

Ham in a cheese sauce is a common enough dish – this is something rather more special, but you must use rather thick slices of really good ham off the bone.

Serves 6 Storage time: 4–6 months

450 gr (1 lb) ham cut into 12 slices
100 gr (4 oz) firm button mushrooms
1 large onion or, better still, 4 shallots
4 ripe tomatoes
1 tablespoon Dijon mustard
50 gr (2 oz) butter
1·5 dl (¼ pint) white wine
1 tablespoon flour
1·5 dl (¼ pint) milk
salt and freshly ground black pepper
1·5 dl (¼ pint) single cream
1 tablespoon finely chopped parsley
25 gr (1 oz) grated Parmesan cheese

Arrange the ham in a lightly buttered fireproof serving dish. Very thinly slice the mushrooms. Peel and very finely chop the onion or shallots. Peel the tomatoes by covering them with boiling water for about 2 minutes and slipping off the skins. Thinly slice the tomatoes.

Spread the mustard over the ham and cover with the slices of tomato. Melt 25 gr (1 oz) butter in a saucepan, add the mushrooms and the wine and cook for 3 minutes. Pour the mixture over the ham and let the juices soak in.

Melt the remaining butter in a saucepan, add the flour and mix well. Gradually blend in the milk, stirring continuously until the sauce comes to the boil and is thick and smooth. Season well with salt and pepper. Remove from the heat and mix in the parsley and the cream. Pour the sauce over the ham and sprinkle with the cheese.

To freeze: Cool the dish, cover it with foil, and pack it in a polythene bag. Seal, label and freeze.

To use: Leave the dish wrapped and thaw it at room temperature for 3 hours. Reheat in a moderately hot oven (350°F, 180°C, regulo 4) for about 20 minutes until hot through.

Crab mousse

Don't use frozen crab for this dish as it is not cooked before being frozen.

Serves 6 Storage time: 2 months

225 gr (8 oz) mixed white and brown crabmeat
1 tablespoon finely grated Parmesan cheese
1·5 dl (¼ pint) double cream
1½ teaspoons gelatine
1 tablespoon water
juice ½ lemon
1·5 dl (¼ pint) consommé
2 egg whites
salt and freshly ground black pepper
pinch cayenne pepper
slices of cucumber

Combine the crab with the seasoning and Parmesan cheese and pound in a mortar with a pestle until the mixture is smooth. Add the cream and mix well. Soften the gelatine in the water and lemon juice, heating it gently until the gelatine has melted. Add the gelatine mixture to the crab with the consommé. Beat the egg whites until stiff and fold them into the crab. Season with salt and freshly ground black pepper and cayenne. Turn the mixture into 6 ramekin dishes.

To freeze: Open-freeze the ramekins until solid. Pack flat in a polythene bag or in a rigid container with crumpled kitchen paper filling up any spaces. Seal, label and freeze.

To use: Thaw the ramekins, unwrapped, in a refrigerator overnight, and garnish with slices of peeled cucumber. Serve with hot toast.

Kedgeree

This dish was originally devised in India and was brought to England by those famous 'Indian colonels' when the British Empire was at its height. Provided you are prepared to titivate the dish before you serve it, kedgeree will freeze satisfactorily and is a good way to use up leftovers of salmon or smoked haddock.

Serves 4 Storage time: 1 month

100 gr (4 oz) rice
salt
300 gr (12 oz) cooked smoked haddock, finnan haddock or salmon
75 gr (3 oz) butter

Cook the rice in salted water until tender. Rinse in cold water and drain well.

Flake the fish, removing any skin or bones. Melt the butter, add the flaked fish and rice, and toss lightly until the butter is absorbed.

To freeze: Remove from the heat, cool quickly, pack in a rigid container or polythene bag. Seal, label and freeze.

Second-stage ingredients

25 gr (1 oz) butter
2 hard-boiled eggs
2 raw eggs
4 tablespoons double cream
salt and freshly ground black pepper
1 tablespoon finely chopped parsley

Thaw kedgeree overnight in a refrigerator, or at room temperature for 3 hours.

Melt the butter, add kedgeree and toss over a low heat until hot through. Quarter the hard-boiled eggs and beat the raw eggs with the cream.

Add beaten eggs and cream to kedgeree and mix over a low heat until the mixture is just beginning to thicken. Add the hard-boiled eggs and parsley, season with salt and plenty of freshly ground black pepper, mix lightly and serve at once.

Quiches

I find quiches the most admirable form of food to keep in the freezer (don't keep them for too long, though, or they will become flabby and tasteless). They are particularly useful for parties and can be served hot or cold with drinks, at picnics, supper and buffet parties; as a first or main course, as part of a packed lunch or even as an accompaniment to a plain soup as a starter. Here is a basic recipe for the classic Quiche Lorraine, with some alternative fillings. Uncooked quiche cases can be frozen for later use. Cooked quiches should be slightly underdone to allow for the reheating time and even quiches that are to be served cold should be reheated and cooled before serving to get rid of any moisture that may have built up during the freezing time.

I bake and freeze the quiches in inexpensive tin or foil cases. If you cannot afford to lose the use of the cases, open-freeze the quiches, wrap them carefully in polythene and store in a place in the freezer where they will not be damaged.

Basic Quiche Pastry Recipe

This is enough pastry to make 2 × 25-cm (10-in) quiche cases.

375 gr (12 oz) self-raising flour
pinch salt
150 gr (5 oz) butter or margarine
1 small egg
dry sherry or white wine

Sieve the flour and salt into a bowl. Add the butter or margarine cut into small pieces and rub it into the flour with your fingertips until the mixture resembles fine breadcrumbs. Make a well in the centre, break in the egg and gradually draw the egg into the flour with your fingers, mixing until the ingredients are all incorporated. Add about two tablespoons dry sherry or white wine and knead until the mixture forms a compact, elastic ball. Roll out at once, a third of the dough at a time, on a really well-floured board, making the pastry very thin, and line three flan cases.

Prick the bottom of the cases with a fork and open-freeze while you make the filling.

Classic Quiche Lorraine filling

Enough to fill 1 × 25-cm (10-in) quiche case.

4 thinly sliced leeks
1 thinly sliced medium onion
25 gr (1 oz) butter or margarine
175 gr (6 oz) minced ham
1 tablespoon finely chopped parsley

For the custard
3 eggs
100 gr (4 oz) cream cheese
150 ml (¼ pint) single cream
75 gr (3 oz) grated Cheddar cheese
salt, freshly ground black pepper, pinch cayenne and ground nutmeg

Topping
2 slices white bread
25 gr (1 oz) grated Cheddar cheese
25 gr (1 oz) grated Parmesan cheese

Melt the butter, add the leeks and onion and cook over a low heat until soft and transparent. Add the ham and parsley and mix well.

Beat the eggs well. Add the cream cheese and beat until smooth, mix in the cream, add the cheese and season with salt, pepper, cayenne and nutmeg.

Grate the bread (or reduce to fine crumbs in liquidizer). Grate the cheese for the topping. Add the Cheddar and Parmesan to the breadcrumbs and mix well.

Spread the filling in the quiche case, pour over the egg mixture, stirring it lightly with a fork so that some of the filling mixes with the custard. Top with the breadcrumb mixture. Bake in a moderately hot oven (350°F, 180°C, regulo 4) for about 40 minutes or until the quiche is a pale golden brown.

To freeze: Cool, open-freeze, pack in a suitable container, seal, label and freeze.

Alternative Quiche fillings

Smoked salmon or smoked haddock with spinach

Both delicious fillings. I buy smoked salmon trimmings when I can, freeze them and use them for a filling for special occasions. Smoked mackerel or haddock can be used as an alternative to the smoked salmon.

Serves 6–8
1 large finely chopped onion
50 gr (2 oz) butter
100 gr (4 oz) smoked salmon *or*
225 gr (8 oz) smoked haddock or mackerel
225 gr (8 oz) finely chopped cooked spinach
quiche case, custard and topping as basic recipe

Finely chop the smoked salmon (or steam the haddock until tender and flake the flesh; bone and flake the flesh of the smoked mackerel).

Melt the butter, add the onion and cook over a low heat until the onion is soft and transparent. Add the spinach and fish, mix well and remove from the heat.

Make the custard (see basic recipe page 223). Place the filling in the frozen case, pour over the custard, stirring it lightly with a fork so that the custard seeps through the filling, and top with the breadcrumb mixture. Bake in a moderately hot oven (350°F, 180°C, regulo 4) for about 30 minutes until light golden-brown. Cool, freeze and use as above.

Mixed Vegetable

This is the sort of quiche I make when I have to produce a meal in a hurry or have some vegetables in the refrigerator which need using up and which, made into this excellent quiche, can be successfully frozen. The quantities of vegetables can be interchanged, added to or subtracted from.

Serves 6–8
1 large onion, thinly sliced into rings
1 thinly sliced leek
2 tomatoes
2 coarsely grated courgettes
1 small coarsely grated aubergine
25 gr (1 oz) butter
pinch of oregano
2 tablespoons sunflower oil
quiche case, custard and topping as basic recipe

Cover the tomatoes with boiling water, leave for two minutes and slide off the skins. Halve the tomatoes, remove the seeds and core and roughly chop the flesh.

Heat the butter and oil, add the onion and leek and cook over a medium heat until they are soft and transparent. Add the aubergine and cook for four minutes over a medium heat. Add the courgettes, tomatoes and oregano, mix well and simmer for five minutes.

Place the filling in the frozen case, pour over the custard, stirring it lightly with a fork so that the custard seeps through the filling, and top with the breadcrumb mixture. Bake in a moderately hot oven (350°F, 180°C, regulo 4) for about 40 minutes until light golden-brown. Cool, freeze and use as above.

Other alternatives

Try combining ham and spinach, spinach and mushrooms with chicken, sliced courgette with ham and tomato and any other fillings of your choice, proceeding with the same method as laid out above.

Pastry

Raw or cooked, pastry freezes very successfully. Freeze those leftover pastry pieces (wrapped in a polythene bag) instead of letting them get hard and unusable in the refrigerator. Make double quantities of pastry to save yourself time, or make 2 or 3 pastry cases at a time instead of just enough for one meal.

Storage time: 6 months

To freeze: Divide the pastry into usable quantities; weigh and wrap. Seal, label and freeze.

To use: Thaw at room temperature for 2–3 hours and use as normal.

Or: Roll out the pastry, line patty, quiche or flan cases, open-freeze and then unmould and pack in rigid containers or between cardboard plates in polythene bags.

Or: Use the pastry to line foil cases.

Or: Bake the pastry 'blind' and freeze as above.

Pastry quantities

Have you ever noticed how many recipes give quantities for pastry that often almost double the amount actually required for the specified size of flan case? This is not really the writer's fault, as the amount of pastry used and the thinness it is rolled to vary considerably from person to person. To help you cut down on any waste (remember, however, that leftover pastry freezes well), here is a guide to the average quantities of pastry required for dishes of varying sizes.

The weight includes the flour and fat.

size of flan case	approximate amount of pastry		
	lined flan cases	flans with lids	tops only*
15 cm/6 in	100 gr/4 oz	150 gr/6 oz	100 gr/4 oz
17 cm/7 in	125 gr/5 oz	175 gr/7 oz	125 gr/5 oz
20 cm/8 in	150 gr/6 oz	250 gr/9 oz	150 gr/6 oz
22 cm/9 in	225 gr/8 oz	325 gr/12 oz	175 gr/7 oz
25 cm/10 in	275 gr/10 oz	450 gr/1 lb	225 gr/8 oz
30 cm/12 in	450 gr/1 lb	600 gr/1 lb 6 oz	275 gr/10 oz

*The quantity given for the top should be enough to make a thin strip of pastry to put round the dish. Any trimmings can be used for decoration.

Shortcrust pastry

450 gr (1 lb) plain flour
1 tablespoon icing sugar (for sweet pies and tarts)
½ teaspoon salt
150 gr (6 oz) butter
50 gr (2 oz) lard
3–4 tablespoons ice-cold water

The amount of water you need to use depends on the temperature of the ingredients, the atmosphere and your hands. The amount above is only a rough guide and as little water as possible should be used to bind the mixture.

Sift flour, (sugar) and salt into a bowl. Add the fat, cut into small slivers, and rub it lightly into the flour, with fingertips, until the mixture resembles coarse breadcrumbs. Add just enough water to mix to a smooth dough.

Follow freezing directions on page 98.

Rich shortcrust pastry for fruit pies

225 gr (8 oz) flour
2 tablespoons icing sugar
75 gr (3 oz) butter
50 gr (2 oz) lard
1 medium egg, beaten

Sift the flour and sugar into a bowl, add the fat, cut into small slivers, and rub it into the flour, with the fingertips, until the mixture resembles coarse breadcrumbs. Add the egg and mix lightly with your hands to a smooth dough.

Follow freezing directions on page 98.

Onion and saffron quiche

An unusual and delicious first course.

Serves 6–8 Storage time: 2 months

275 gr (10 oz) shortcrust pastry (see page 210)
1 teaspoon saffron
4 eggs
3 dl (½ pint) double cream
salt and freshly ground black pepper
2 tablespoons sultanas
4 onions
50 gr (2 oz) butter

Roll out the pastry thinly on a floured board (the thinner the pastry, the lighter and crisper the quiche will be). Use the pastry to line a 25-cm (10-in) flan case or small individual cases. Soak the saffron in 2 tablespoons boiling water for 10 minutes to release the flavour.

Beat the eggs with the cream and season with salt and freshly ground black pepper. Pour 1·5 dl (¼ pint) boiling water over the sultanas and leave to plump up for 10 minutes. Drain.

Peel and thinly slice the onions and divide them into rings. Melt the butter in a large frying pan. Add the onions and cook over a low heat for about 15 minutes until the onions are really soft and transparent. Do not allow them to brown. Leave to cool.

Arrange the onions in the flan case. Add the strained saffron water to the eggs and cream. Scatter the sultanas over the onions and pour the custard mixture over. Bake in a moderate oven (375°F, 190°C, regulo 5) for 40 minutes.

To freeze: Cool, cover with a cardboard plate (or open-freeze until solid), and pack in a polythene bag. Seal, label and freeze.

To use: Thaw overnight (or for 5 hours at room temperature) in the wrapping. Unwrap, put into a moderate oven (350°F, 180°C, regulo 4) and heat through for about 20 minutes. Cover with foil or greaseproof paper if necessary to prevent the quiche becoming too brown.

Serve at once.

Smoked salmon quiche

A sophisticated first course that uses only a little smoked salmon.

Serves 6–8 Storage time: 1 month

275 gr (10 oz) shortcrust pastry (see page 210)
100 gr (4 oz) smoked salmon
2 eggs
2 egg yolks
3 dl (½ pint) single cream
salt, freshly ground black pepper and a pinch cayenne
2 tablespoons finely chopped parsley

Roll the pastry thinly on a floured board (the thinner the pastry, the crisper and lighter the quiche will be). Line a 25-cm (10-in) flan case or small individual cases with pastry and chill in the refrigerator until required.

Cut the salmon into very thin strips. Beat the whole eggs and egg yolks together until smooth. Blend in the cream and mix very well. Season with salt, pepper, and a little cayenne and mix in the parsley. Arrange the smoked salmon in the flan case, pour over the custard and bake in a moderate oven (375°F, 190°C, regulo 5) for 35 minutes.

To freeze: Cool, cover with a cardboard plate (or open-freeze until solid) and wrap in a polythene bag. Seal, label and freeze.

To use: Thaw, covered, in a refrigerator overnight, or at room temperature for 5 hours. Reheat in a moderate oven (350°F, 180°C, regulo 4) for about 20 minutes until hot through. Cover with foil or greaseproof paper if necessary to prevent browning.

Chicken and parsley pie

Serves 8 Storage time: 1 month

shortcrust pastry (see page 229) made with 225 gr (8 oz) flour
2 onions
2 medium roasting chickens
flour, salt and pepper
2 large bunches parsley
4 rashers bacon
75 gr (3 oz) butter
3 dl (½ pint) chicken stock
1 beaten egg

Make the pastry and leave to chill for 30 minutes. Peel and finely chop onions. Joint the chickens, divide the legs in 2 and cut the breasts off the carcase. Roll the chicken pieces in flour generously seasoned with salt and pepper. Remove the stalks from the parsley and chop the leaves. Remove the rinds from the rashers, roll up tightly and cut the rolls into thin slices.

Melt half the butter in a frying pan. Add the onions and cook over a low heat until soft and transparent. Remove the onions with a slotted spoon and place them in a large shallow pie dish. Add the remainder of the butter to the juices in the pan, heat until bubbling, add the floured chicken pieces and cook over a medium-high heat until lightly browned on both sides.

Place the chicken joints with the bacon slices on top of the onion.

Combine the parsley and chicken stock in a saucepan and simmer gently for 3 minutes. Season generously with salt and pepper and pour over the ingredients in the dish.

Roll out the pastry to 6-mm (¼-in) thickness. Cut off a strip to make a rim around the dish, moisten with a little water and press down firmly. Cover with remaining pastry, pinching the edges to make a good seal, and decorate with some pastry leaves (cut out leaf shapes and thin stalks, and mark veins on leaves with the back of a knife), stuck down with a little water.

Brush the pie with the egg beaten with a little salt. Cut a vent in the centre and bake in a hot oven (425°F, 220°C, regulo 7). Reduce heat to moderate (350°F, 180°C, regulo 4), cover the top with damp greaseproof paper and cook for 30 minutes.

To freeze: Cool, open-freeze until solid and pack in a polythene bag. Seal, label and freeze.

Second-stage ingredient
3 dl (½ pint) double cream

To use: Unwrap. Cover frozen pie with a piece of damp greaseproof paper and place in a moderately hot oven (350°F, 180°C, regulo 4). Bake for 1 hour. Pour the cream in through a funnel and bake for a further 5 minutes before serving.

Note: The pie can also be left to cool to serve cold.

Mini puff-puffs

These are small rounds of savoury puff pastry which make delicious additions to almost any soup. They can also be popped on top of a stew or casserole for the last 10 minutes of cooking to make an exciting topping. Use frozen puff pastry.

100 gr (4 oz) puff pastry
1 beaten egg
salt and pepper

Roll pastry to 3-mm (⅛-in) thickness and cut into very small circles (about 1·25 cm or ½ in). Mix the egg with a little salt and pepper and brush the pastry circles with the egg. Put the puffs on a lightly greased baking sheet and bake in a hot oven (425°F, 220°C, regulo 7) for 5 minutes until puffed and golden.

To freeze: Cool on a wire rack, pack in a rigid container with plastic film or waxed paper between each layer. Seal, label and freeze.

To serve: With soups: Put frozen puffs on a baking sheet in a moderate oven (350°F, 180°C, regulo 4) and heat through for 5 minutes until hot and crisp.

With stews and casseroles: Put frozen puffs on top of stews or casseroles for the last 10 minutes of cooking time.

Emergency snacks

If your family demands food in dribs and drabs on occasions, coming in at any time and begging for a quick meal, the deep freeze can be a great asset. A stock of individual pizzas, some sandwiches which can be crisply fried straight from the freezer, home-made fish-cakes and beefburgers which can be cooked from the frozen state are better value and have more nourishment than any you can buy.

Stock up on a range of quickly cooked emergency foods when you have the time so that you – or they – can produce an almost instant meal from the freezer.

Crisply fried sandwiches

These really are a great standby in the freezer. Prepare the sandwiches in bulk with a variety of different fillings. (This is also a good way of using up leftover sandwiches if the fillings are suitable.) When required, the frozen sandwiches can be fried in hot fat; the filling will thaw during the cooking time, and the end result will be delicious, crisp and succulent sandwiches for an easy snack meal.

To make the sandwiches

Butter slices of bread and cut off the crusts. Use any of the following fillings, press firmly together and cut each sandwich into three fingers.

Fillings

Avoid egg, tomato, cucumber and all salad ingredients; the

best fillings are those involving cheese or cooked meats. Here are some suggestions:

Thin slices roast beef spread with mustard.

Lightly cooked rashers of bacon with slices of Cheddar cheese and some chopped green mango chutney.

Slices of ham with a slight spreading of mustard and slices of Gruyère cheese.

Cream cheese with chopped pickled walnuts.

Thin slices of Cheddar cheese spread with tomato sauce (see page 165).

To freeze: Wrap the sandwiches in layers separated by plastic film or waxed paper. Pack in polythene bags, press out all air; seal, label and freeze.

To use: Unwrap frozen sandwiches. Melt some lard or dripping in a large pan until smoking, add the sandwiches and cook over a moderately high heat until golden-brown on both sides. Drain on kitchen paper to remove excess fat and serve at once. Serve each sandwich wrapped in a paper napkin for easy eating.

Pancakes savoury and sweet

Sweet and savoury pancakes are among the best things to deep freeze. They come out tasting exactly as they did when they went in and are extraordinarily versatile. Make a big batch at a time and freeze them to stuff later with sweet and savoury fillings.

Storage time for unfilled pancakes: 6 months

Storage time for filled pancakes: 1–4 months depending on the filling

Savoury pancakes

Serves 4

150 gr (6 oz) plain flour
2 large eggs
3 dl (½ pint) milk
scant 1·5 dl (¼ pint) water
salt and pepper
1 tablespoon brandy*
3 tablespoons melted butter

*The brandy is optional but it does make a lighter, crisper pancake

Combine the flour with the eggs, milk and water. Season with a little salt and pepper and whisk with a rotary whisk until smooth. Mix in the brandy and leave to stand for 1 hour. Add the melted butter, mix well and pour into a jug.

Brush an omelette pan with a little olive oil and heat over a high flame. When the oil is smoking, pour in a tablespoon of batter and swirl it round the pan until it forms a thin, even skin. Cook over a high heat for 2 minutes, turn over and cook the other side. Both sides of the pancake should be golden-brown. Repeat the process with the remaining batter, brushing with a little extra oil after 2 pancakes have been made.

Stack the pancakes with a sheet of plastic film or waxed paper between each one.

To freeze: Pack the pancakes in a polythene bag; seal, label and freeze.

To thaw: Thaw in the wrapping for about 2 hours at room temperature or put frozen pancakes into a warm oven (325°F, 170°C, regulo 3) for 10–15 minutes until thawed.

Sweet pancakes

Serves 4

Follow the above recipe, but replace salt and pepper with 1 dessertspoon caster sugar, and proceed as before.

Chicken or turkey pancakes

Serves 4 Storage time: 1 month

1 onion
100 gr (4 oz) firm button mushrooms
37 gr (1½ oz) butter
1½ tablespoons flour
3 dl (½ pint) milk
275–300 gr (10–12 oz) finely chopped cooked chicken or turkey
2 tablespoons finely chopped parsley
salt and freshly ground black pepper
4 tablespoons double cream
8–12 savoury pancakes (see page 217)
50 gr (2 oz) grated Gruyère cheese

Peel and finely chop the onion. Very thinly slice the mushrooms. Melt the butter in a saucepan, add the onion and cook over a low heat until the onion is soft and transparent. Add the mushrooms and cook for 3 minutes. Blend in the flour and gradually add the milk, stirring continuously until the sauce comes to the boil and is thick and smooth.

Mix in the chicken or turkey and the finely chopped parsley and season with salt and freshly ground black pepper. Blend in the cream and remove from the stove.

To freeze: Cool the filling and spread it on the pancakes. Roll pancakes up neatly and pack them in a rigid container. Seal, label and freeze.

To use: Transfer frozen pancakes to a fireproof serving dish and sprinkle the grated cheese over. Cover with foil to prevent drying and heat for 30–40 minutes in a moderately hot oven (350°F, 180°C, regulo 4) until the cheese has melted and the pancakes are hot through. Brown quickly under a hot grill until the cheese is bubbling and golden-brown.

Devilled crab pancakes

Serves 4 Storage time: 1 month

1 small onion
1 small green pepper
50 gr (2 oz) butter
450 gr (1 lb) crabmeat
50 gr (2 oz) fresh white breadcrumbs
2 teaspoons finely chopped parsley
salt, pepper and a pinch cayenne
few drops Tabasco sauce
few drops Worcester sauce
8–12 savoury pancakes (see page 217)
2 teaspoons dry English mustard
1·5 dl (¼ pint) double cream
50 gr (2 oz) grated Gruyère cheese

Peel and finely chop the onion. Remove the core and seeds of the pepper and finely chop the flesh. Heat the butter in a saucepan, add the onion and pepper and cook over a low heat until the onion is soft and transparent. Add the crab, breadcrumbs and parsley, season with salt, pepper and cayenne, and blend in the mustard, Tabasco and Worcester sauces. Cook for 2 minutes and stir in the cream.

Fill the pancakes with the crab mixture and roll up neatly.

To freeze: Pack filled pancakes in a rigid container; seal, label and freeze.

To use: Transfer frozen pancakes to a fireproof serving dish and top with grated cheese. Cover with foil to prevent drying and heat in a moderately hot oven (350°F, 180°C, regulo 4) for 30 minutes or until the cheese has melted and the pancakes are hot through. Brown quickly under a hot grill until the cheese is bubbling and golden-brown.

Alternative fillings for savoury pancakes

Thinly sliced button mushrooms, sautéed in butter and folded into a rich white sauce flavoured with sherry and finely chopped parsley. Top with grated Cheddar cheese.

Prawns in a rich white sauce, flavoured with a little French Vermouth and some finely chopped chives. Top with Gruyère cheese.

Chopped scallops and a little finely chopped onion, sautéed in butter and combined with a rich creamy sauce.

Mixed shellfish, lightly sautéed in a little butter and combined with finely chopped peeled tomatoes with the core and seeds removed. Flavour with a little chopped parsley and dill, and top with grated Gruyère cheese.

Meat sauce for spaghetti topped with Parmesan or Gruyère cheese.

Cooked spinach mixed with cottage cheese. Top with a little grated Parmesan.

Half cream cheese and half red caviar mixed with finely chopped chives. Top with Gruyère cheese.

Flamed banana pancakes

Serves 4

8 sweet pancakes (see page 218)
8 small bananas
75 gr (3 oz) unsalted butter
juice and finely grated rind 1 orange
75 gr (3 oz) icing sugar
2 tablespoons rum

Put the frozen pancakes in a warm oven (325°F, 160°C, regulo 3) until hot through. Peel the bananas. Melt the butter in a frying pan, add the orange juice, orange peel and icing sugar and cook over a low heat for 2–3 minutes. Add the bananas and cook, turning them frequently, for 10 minutes. Remove the bananas with a slotted spoon, place each one on a pancake and roll them up neatly. Arrange the pancakes in a serving dish and pour over the juices from the pan. Heat the rum until bubbling, pour it over the pancakes and set light to it immediately.

Jubilee pancakes

One of those dashing puddings which has to be made at the last minute and which has the excitement of being hot and cold at the same time. Make sure the ice-cream is frozen solid before you start.

Serves 4

1 block vanilla ice-cream
8 sweet pancakes (see page 237)
8 tablespoons black cherry jam
4 tablespoons caster sugar

Cut the ice-cream into 8 slices. Spread half each pancake with a spoonful of black cherry jam, place a slice of ice-cream on the other half and roll up neatly. Place the pancakes in a fireproof serving dish and sprinkle with sugar. Put under a very high grill until the sugar has melted and is bubbling and turning brown.

Alternative fillings for sweet pancakes

Apricot jam, topped with a little lemon juice and sprinkled with caster sugar.

Apple purée mixed with finely chopped almonds and raisins, topped with caster or icing sugar.

Cream cheese mixed with sugar, finely chopped almonds and raisins.

Strawberry jam flavoured with lemon juice, sprinkled with finely chopped almonds mixed with caster sugar.

Purée of apples and blackcurrants flavoured with lemon peel and topped with icing sugar.

Ice-creams and puddings

Ice-cream obviously freezes well. What else could it do? Nevertheless, there are problems in freezing ice-cream and I think people have a tendency to take too many liberties with this product, especially when the ice-cream is home-made. Commercially made ice-cream has preservatives in it which give it a longer freezer-life.

Freezing home-made ice-cream

Use any of your favourite recipes and make the ice-cream in the usual way, taking care not to stint on the mixing processes which break up the ice-crystals forming in the mixture as it freezes. The smoother the ice-cream, the better it will freeze. The larger the ice-crystals, the more they will grow in the freezer and the result will be disappointing in the end.

Pack the finished ice-cream down as firmly as you can in a polythene container, and fill up any air spaces in the top with crumpled foil or kitchen paper. This is important. If there is air in the top of the container, the surface of the ice-cream will harden and discolour, and the taste and texture will deteriorate.

Do not pack in too-large quantities; it is better to divide the finished ice-cream into fairly small servings and pack it in smaller containers.

Do not store the ice-cream for too long in the deep freeze or the results will be disappointing. I would not recommend storing home-made ice-cream or water ices for longer than two months, and preferably for not longer than one month.

If you want to take individual servings out of a container of ice-cream, fill up the air space with crumpled foil or kitchen paper and make sure the container is completely sealed once more. Snap-on lids are not enough; the lid should be sealed with tape.

Freezing commercial ice-cream bought in bulk

Gallon containers of ice-cream often seem like an irresistible bargain, but think carefully before you buy them. Is the ice-cream really good? Will you use it quickly once you have opened the container? Once opened, the ice-cream will begin to deteriorate a little week by week. Cut this deterioration down to a minimum by filling up the carton with crumpled kitchen paper or foil every time you take out some of the ice-cream, and always seal the container with tape after replacing the lid.

Ice-cream melts fast and it doesn't refreeze successfully, so make sure the ice-cream you buy from a retailer or wholesaler gets home fully frozen and is put into the freezer at once.

Strawberry and passion fruit ice-cream

Small tins of passion fruit can be bought from good delicatessen shops.

Serves 6   Storage time: 6 months

225 gr (8 oz) strawberries
1 small tin passion fruit
100 gr (4 oz) icing sugar
1·5 dl (¼ pint) double cream
1·5 dl (¼ pint) single cream

Hull the strawberries and reserve a few for decoration. Mash the strawberries to a pulp with a fork. Strain the passion fruit through a sieve to remove the pips and mix the juice with the strawberry pulp. Add the sugar and mix well.

Whisk the double cream until beginning to stiffen. Add the single cream and continue to whisk until stiff. Fold in the strawberry mixture and turn into an ice-making tray. Freeze for about 1 hour until beginning to ice up, then turn into a bowl, break up and beat until smooth. Return to the freezer and freeze for at least 6 hours until solid.

To use: Remove from the freezer about 30 minutes before use and leave in the refrigerator until required. Scoop into individual bowls and top with sliced strawberries.

Note: The strawberries for decoration can be open-frozen and packed in a polythene bag; they should be thawed in a refrigerator for 4 hours before use.

Tangerello

Choose large tangerines, not the very small seedless ones.

Serves 6 Storage time: 4 months

6 large tangerines
juice 1 orange
1 tablespoon concentrated frozen orange juice
150 gr (6 oz) caster sugar
3 dl (½ pint) water
juice ½ lemon
1 egg yolk
3 dl (½ pint) double cream

Cut caps off the tops of the tangerines and carefully scoop out all the insides. Rub the tangerine flesh through a food mill or a sieve and combine it with the orange juice and concentrated orange. Combine the sugar and water in a saucepan, bring to the boil and cook over a high heat for 10 minutes. Leave to cool. Mix the sugar syrup with the tangerine juice and add the lemon juice. Beat the egg yolk until smooth and blend it into the juices. Pour the mixture into a heavy pan and cook it over a very low heat for 8 minutes, stirring continually. Turn into an ice-making tray and freeze for about an hour or until the ice is crystallizing around the edges. Remove from the freezer and beat well. Whip the cream until stiff and fold it into the frozen mixture. Mix lightly and return to the freezer. Freeze for a further 2 hours, then beat again until the ice-cream is smooth and creamy.

Fill the tangerine skins with the ice-cream, piling it up over the top. Put on the caps and stand them in a rigid container with crumpled paper between to keep them upright. (This must be done very quickly, and you may have to return the ice-cream to the freezer while you fill one tangerine at a time.) Cover, seal, label and freeze.

To use: Remove the tangerellos from the freezer 10 minutes before serving. Place each one on a few vine leaves, or any dark, shiny leaves.

Raspberry sauce

A good sauce that makes use of those second-grade raspberries which are always around after it has been raining or when the fruit ripens too quickly. This sauce can, of course, be made from frozen raspberries. Serve with steamed puddings, iced soufflés and ice-cream.

Storage time: 6 months

225 gr (8 oz) raspberries
100 gr (4 oz) sugar
juice ½ orange
grated peel 1 orange

Combine the raspberries, sugar, orange juice and peel in a saucepan. Bring to the boil and simmer gently for 15 minutes. Purée through a sieve or a food mill, or in an electric liquidizer (the latter gives a thicker texture but is not quite such a good sauce).

To freeze: Cool, pack in a polythene container, leaving 1·25-cm (½-in) headspace for expansion. Seal, label and freeze.

Second-stage ingredient
4 tablespoons Kirsch

To use: Thaw overnight in a refrigerator, or put the frozen purée over a low heat until melted. Add the Kirsch, mix well, taste for sweetness and serve cold.

Blackberry fool

This pudding can be made from frozen blackberries.

Serves 4–6 Storage time: 2 months

900 gr (2 lb) blackberries
grated rind and juice 1 lemon
100–150 gr (4–6 oz) sugar
1 tablespoon (1 envelope) gelatine
1·5 dl (¼ pint) milk
1 tablespoon brandy
3 dl (½ pint) double cream

Combine the blackberries, lemon juice, lemon peel and sugar in a saucepan and cook over a very low heat until blackberries are soft (about 15–20 minutes). Rub through a sieve and leave to cool. Combine the gelatine and milk and heat, over hot water, until the gelatine has dissolved. Add the gelatine mixture to the blackberries and mix well. Stir in the brandy. Whip the cream until thick and fold it into the blackberry mixture, mixing only just enough to blend the ingredients.

Pour the mixture into a serving dish or individual ramekin dishes.

To freeze: Wrap serving dish in a polythene bag (or individual ramekins in small polythene bags). Seal, label and freeze.

To use: Thaw, wrapped, in the refrigerator overnight. Unwrap and serve well chilled.

Orange tri-fool

Serves 6 Storage time: 2 months

8 trifle sponges
2 tablespoons thick honey
juice 4 large oranges
juice 2 large lemons
finely grated peel 2 oranges
grated rind 1 lemon
6 dl (1 pint) double cream
2 tablespoons brandy

Cut sponges into small cubes.

Combine the honey and fruit juices and mix until well blended. Add the fruit peel and cream and whisk with a rotary whisk until thick and stiff.

Sprinkle the brandy over the sponges and fold them into the cream mixture. Turn into a serving dish.

To freeze: Wrap in a polythene bag; seal, label and freeze.

To use: Thaw in a refrigerator, in wrappings, overnight. Unwrap and serve well chilled. Some roasted split almonds can be sprinkled over the top of the puddings.

Blackcurrant and raspberry kisses

Serves 4 Storage time: 3 months

300 gr (12 oz) blackcurrants
300 gr (12 oz) raspberries
150 gr (6 oz) sugar
juice ½ lemon
cornflour
water

Combine the fruit, sugar and lemon juice in a saucepan. Add just enough water to cover, bring to the boil and simmer gently until the fruit is soft (about 15–20 minutes). Purée through a sieve or a food mill. Measure the purée.

For each 3 dl (½ pint) purée, combine 3 teaspoons cornflour with a little water and mix to a smooth paste. Mix the cornflour paste into the fruit purée and cook over a medium heat until the purée has thickened and is clear and shining. Cool and pour into a serving dish.

To freeze: Wrap in a polythene bag; seal, label and freeze.

To use: Thaw, in its wrapping, in a refrigerator overnight.

Strawberry and orange water ice

Serves 6 Storage time: 2 months

900 gr (2 lb) strawberries
grated peel 1 orange
1·5 dl (¼ pint) water
150 gr (6 oz) sugar
1·5 dl (¼ pint) orange juice
2 teaspoons lemon juice

Purée strawberries through a fine sieve or a food mill. Blanch orange peel in boiling water for 5 minutes and strain well.

Combine the water and sugar, bring to the boil and cook for 5 minutes. Mix in the orange juice and lemon juice and leave to cool. Combine the strawberry purée with the orange syrup and grated peel, mix well and pour into a freezing tray. Freeze in the deep freeze or ice-making compartment of the refrigerator for 1 hour. Turn into a bowl, beat until frothy with a rotary whisk, put back in the tray and continue to freeze until solid.

To freeze: Transfer quickly to a polythene container, leaving 1·25-cm (½-in) headspace for expansion. Seal, label and freeze.

To use: Take out of the freezer and leave in its wrapping for 10 minutes before required. Serve at once in scoops.

Orange and chocolate mousse

Serves 4–6 Storage time: 1 month

225 gr (8 oz) plain chocolate (Bournville or Meunière)
3 tablespoons strong black coffee
2 tablespoons orange juice
grated peel 1 orange
5 eggs, separated
1 tablespoon brandy

Break up the chocolate and combine it in a basin with the coffee and orange juice. Place the bowl over a saucepan of simmering water and leave until melted. Leave to cool for a few minutes.

Add the egg yolks, one at a time, to the melted chocolate, stirring each one so that the mixture is really well blended.

Beat the egg whites until stiff and fold them lightly into the chocolate mixture. Spoon into a serving dish or individual ramekins.

To freeze: Wrap in a polythene bag: seal, label and freeze; or wrap individual servings in small polythene bags and seal, label and freeze.

Second-stage ingredient

1·5 dl (¼ pint) double cream

To use: Thaw the mousse in a refrigerator overnight in its wrappings. Unwrap, pour the cream over the surface and serve well chilled. A little grated chocolate can be sprinkled over the top, but the essence of this pudding is its simplicity – so don't over-decorate.

Summer pudding

One of the best of classic British puddings. Fortunately it freezes well. My own touch is in masking it with cream and studding it with roasted almonds.

Serves 6   Storage time: 2 months

675 gr (1½ lb) mixed raspberries, redcurrants, blackcurrants and black cherries
150 gr (6 oz) caster sugar
6 slices of stale white bread
6 tablespoons double cream
50 gr (2 oz) slivered almonds

Combine the fruit and sugar in a saucepan and cook over a low heat for about 15 minutes until the fruit is just soft and the juices are running. Strain off some of the juice without pressing the fruit. Remove the crusts of the bread, dip slices in the juice, and line the bottom and sides of a 9-dl (1½-pint) pudding basin with the soaked bread. Cover with half the fruit and then put in another layer of soaked bread. Spoon in the remainder of the fruit and top with another close-fitting layer of soaked bread. Pour over the remaining juice, cover with a plate placed upside down, and top with a heavy weight (I use a large tin of fruit). Leave in the refrigerator for 10 hours.

To freeze: Remove the plate, cover with tin foil and place in a polythene bag; seal, label and freeze.

To use: Thaw, still wrapped, in a refrigerator overnight. Turn out by running a knife around the side of the pudding and inverting it on to a serving dish. Mask with whipped cream. Stud with almonds which have been roasted to a light golden-brown in a hot oven for a few minutes.

Serve well chilled.

Lemon pineapple soufflé

Serves 6 Storage time: 2 months

1 large tin pineapple chunks	2 eggs
1 tablespoon (1 envelope) gelatine	100 gr (4 oz) caster sugar
juice and grated rind 1 lemon	3 dl (½ pint) double cream

Drain off and reserve pineapple juice. Crush the pineapple with a fork. Combine the gelatine with the lemon juice and 2 tablespoons pineapple juice and heat over a low flame until the gelatine has melted. Leave the gelatine mixture to stand for 10 minutes to cool.

Separate the eggs. Beat the yolks with the sugar until light and fluffy and a pale yellow colour. Add 1·5 dl (¼ pint) pineapple juice and the gelatine mixture, mix well and leave to stand until thickening, but not set firm.

Beat the egg whites until stiff. Beat the cream until stiff (doing it this way round you won't have to wash off the whisk in between beating whites and cream). Mix the crushed pineapple into the soufflé base, fold in the cream and then lightly fold in the beaten egg whites. Spoon into a freezer-proof glass dish.

To freeze: Cover with a polythene bag; seal, label and freeze.

Second-stage ingredient

100 gr (4 oz) black grapes

To use: Leave the soufflé, wrapped, to thaw in a refrigerator overnight. Unwrap and decorate with the grapes which have been halved and had the pips removed. Serve chilled with cream on the side.

Adam and Eve pudding

Serves 4 Storage time: 1 month

100 gr (4 oz) butter	2 eggs
100 gr (4 oz) caster sugar	grated rind 1 lemon
100 gr (4 oz) blanched nibbed almonds	6 medium-large cooking apples
	small pinch cinnamon

Beat the butter with the sugar until the mixture is smooth. Mix in almonds, egg yolks and lemon peel, and beat well.

Peel, core and quarter apples and arrange in a lightly buttered ovenproof dish; sprinkle with a little ground cinnamon.

Whip egg whites until stiff and fold them into the egg-yolk mixture. Spread the mixture over the apples and bake in a moderately hot oven (375°F, 190°C, regulo 5) for 20 minutes until a pale golden-brown.

To freeze: Cool, open-freeze and pack in a polythene bag when solid. Seal, label and freeze

To use: Leave in its wrapping and thaw at room temperature for 4–6 hours. Return to a moderately hot oven (375°F, 190°C, regulo 5) and bake for 15 minutes, until golden-brown and hot through.

Crumbles

Fruit crumbles are easily made and freeze well. Make them when the fruit for the filling is cheap and plentiful.

Crumbles can, of course, be made with frozen fruit; in that case they should not be refrozen after the topping has been added and the crumble cooked.

I find that using half flour and half ground almonds for the topping gives a more exciting flavour.

The crumble should never be burnt. If it begins to get too brown, cover it with a sheet of greaseproof paper dipped in water.

Rhubarb crumble

Serves 4   Storage time: 3 months

450 gr (1 lb) young rhubarb
100 gr (4 oz) granulated sugar
juice and grated rind 1 orange
100 gr (4 oz) plain flour
100 gr (4 oz) ground almonds
75 gr (3 oz) caster sugar
150 gr (6 oz) butter

Cut the rhubarb into 2·5-cm (1-in) pieces and place it in a

lightly greased pie dish or a foil dish. Sprinkle over the granulated sugar, orange juice and rind.

Combine the flour, ground almonds and caster sugar and rub in the butter with the fingertips until the mixture is the consistency of coarse breadcrumbs. Spread the mixture over the rhubarb. Bake in a moderately hot oven (400°F, 200°C, regulo 6) for 20 minutes.

To freeze: Cool, pack in a polythene bag, seal, label and freeze.

To use: Put the unwrapped frozen crumble in a hot oven (425°F, 220°C, regulo 7) for 20 minutes, then lower the heat to moderate (375°F, 190°C, regulo 5) and continue to cook for a further 40 minutes until the crumble is hot through and crisply golden-brown on top.

Serve hot or warm with cream.

Apricot crumble

Fresh apricots have a short season, but they make delicious puddings and can be reasonably priced. For cooked puddings I think they have a better flavour than peaches.

Serves 4 Storage time: 3 months

675 gr (1½ lb) fresh ripe apricots
100 gr (4 oz) granulated sugar
juice and grated rind ½ lemon
100 gr (4 oz) flour
100 gr (4 oz) ground almonds
100 gr (4 oz) caster sugar
150 gr (6 oz) butter

Cover the apricots with boiling water and leave to stand for 3 minutes. Drain, and slide off the skins. Halve the apricots, remove the stones, crack them open and reserve the kernels.

Arrange the apricots in a lightly greased pie dish or foil dish, sprinkle over the apricot kernels, granulated sugar, lemon juice and rind.

Combine the flour, ground almonds and caster sugar and rub in the butter with the fingertips until the mixture resembles coarse breadcrumbs. Spread the mixture over the apricots and bake in a moderately hot oven (400°F, 200°C, regulo 6) for 20 minutes.

To freeze: Cool, pack in a polythene bag; seal, label and freeze.

To use: Put the unwrapped frozen crumble in a hot oven (425°F, 220°C, regulo 7) for 20 minutes, then lower the heat to moderate (375°F, 190°C, regulo 5) and continue to cook for a further 20 minutes until the crumble is hot through and crisply golden-brown.

Blackberry and apple crumble

Blackberries are not all that exciting by themselves but they do go well with apples, and since both are available at the same time it is as well to make the most of them.

Serves 4 Storage time: 3 months

450 gr (1 lb) cooking apples
225 gr (8 oz) blackberries
125 gr (5 oz) granulated sugar
grated rind and juice ½ lemon
100 gr (4 oz) plain flour
100 gr (4 oz) ground almonds
100 gr (4 oz) caster sugar
150 gr (6 oz) butter

Peel, core and slice the apples and arrange them with the blackberries in a lightly greased pie dish or foil dish. Sprinkle over the granulated sugar, lemon juice and peel.

Combine the flour, ground almonds and caster sugar and rub in the butter with the fingertips until the mixture resembles coarse breadcrumbs. Spread the mixture over the blackberries and apple and bake in a moderately hot oven (400°F, 200°C, regulo 6) for 20 minutes.

To freeze: Cool, pack in a polythene bag; seal, label and freeze.

To use: Put the unwrapped frozen crumble in a hot oven (425°F, 220°C, regulo 7) for 20 minutes, then lower the heat to moderate (375°F, 190°C, regulo 5) and continue to cook for a further 20 minutes until the crumble is hot through and crisply golden-brown.

Rich black and white crumble

This really is rich and perfectly grand enough to serve for a dinner party. A little goes a long way and this recipe is ample for 6 servings.

Serves 6 Storage time: 2 months

2 bananas
300 gr (12 oz) blackcurrants
150 gr (6 oz) granulated sugar
juice and rind 1 orange
100 gr (4 oz) flour
75 gr (3 oz) caster sugar
100 gr (4 oz) nibbed almonds
100 gr (4 oz) butter or margarine

Peel and slice the bananas. Combine the blackcurrants and bananas in a pie dish or foil dish and sprinkle over the granulated sugar, orange juice and rind.

Combine the flour, sugar and almonds and rub in the butter or margarine with the fingertips until the mixture resembles fine breadcrumbs. Spread the mixture over the fruit and bake in a moderate oven (350°F, 180°C, regulo 4) for 20 minutes.

To freeze: Cool, pack in a polythene bag; seal, label and freeze.

To use: Unwrap, place in a moderate oven (350°F, 180°C, regulo 4) and bake for a further 40 minutes or until the fruit is cooked and the top is golden-brown.

Serve hot or cold with cream.

Fruit cobblers

These are similar to crumbles, but have a more cake-like topping. They make popular and warming puddings.

Serves 4 Storage time: 3 months

450 gr (1 lb) stewed and sweetened fruit
225 gr (8 oz) self-raising flour
pinch salt
50 gr (2 oz) butter
50 gr (2 oz) sugar
1·5 dl (¼ pint) milk

Arrange the cooked fruit in a pie dish or foil dish.

Sift the flour with the salt and rub in the butter until the mixture resembles fine breadcrumbs. Mix in the sugar and make a well in the centre. Add enough milk to form a soft but workable dough. Turn on to a floured board and roll out the dough to 1·25-cm (½-in) thickness. Cut into rounds with a 4-cm (1½-in) pastry cutter. Arrange the rounds neatly, overlapping, on top of the fruit.

To freeze: Open-freeze until the pastry is solid; pack in a polythene bag; seal, label and freeze.

To use: Unwrap. Brush the frozen pastry with a little milk and bake in a moderately hot oven (400°F, 200°C, regulo 6) for 20 minutes. Reduce the heat to moderate (350°F, 180°C, regulo 4), sprinkle a little caster sugar over the topping, and continue to cook for a further 30 minutes or until the topping is nicely golden-brown and the fruit is hot through.

Fillings for cobblers

Apples and blackcurrants.

Tinned peaches with some slivered almonds and some of the juice from the fruit.

Apples and strawberries.

Apples and blackberries.

Gooseberries, plums, etc.

Rhubarb and ginger Betty

Fruit Bettys are yet another way to make good use of fruit that is in season; other fillings you can try are apples with raisins; apples with blackberries; raspberries; apricots or peaches.

Serves 4 Storage time: 2 months

675 gr (1½ lb) rhubarb
4 pieces preserved ginger in syrup
100 gr (4 oz) fresh white breadcrumbs
75 gr (3 oz) shredded suet
grated rind 1 lemon
75 gr (3 oz) demerara sugar
pinch ground cinnamon
12 gr (½ oz) butter

Cut the rhubarb into 2·5-cm (1-in) lengths, chop the ginger and arrange half of the rhubarb and ginger in a lightly greased pie dish or foil dish. Combine the breadcrumbs, suet, lemon rind, demerara sugar and cinnamon, and mix well. Cover the rhubarb with half the Betty mixture, top with the remaining rhubarb and then with the rest of the Betty mixture. Dot with butter and bake in a moderate oven (350°F, 180°C, regulo 4) for 30 minutes.

To freeze: Cool; pack in a polythene bag; seal, label and freeze.

To use: Put the unwrapped frozen Betty into a hot oven (425°F, 220°C, regulo 7) and bake for 10 minutes. Lower the heat to moderate (350°F, 180°C, regulo 4) and continue to cook for a further 30 minutes until the topping is crisp and the fruit is cooked through.

Pain perdu

Known as Poor Knight's Pudding, and a cheap and delicious ending to a meal. It freezes surprisingly well and can be quickly reheated.

Serves 4 Storage time: 1 month

150 gr (6 oz) butter
1 egg
2 tablespoons cream
4 slices white bread with the crusts removed

Heat the butter until foaming and strain through a piece of muslin to clarify. Beat the egg with the cream until smooth.

Cut each piece of bread into 3 fingers. Dip the bread into the egg and cream mixture.

Heat the butter in a frying pan, add the bread fingers and fry over a medium high heat until crisp and golden-brown. Drain well on kitchen paper.

To freeze: Cool; pack in a rigid container with plastic film or waxed paper between each layer. Seal, label and freeze.

Second-stage ingredients
1·5 dl (¼ pint) cream
75 gr (3 oz) icing sugar
225 gr (8 oz) raspberries
caster sugar and cinnamon

To use: Place the frozen bread fingers on a lightly greased baking sheet and put in a hot oven (450°F, 230°C, regulo 8) for about 5 minutes until the toast is crisp and hot through.

Whip the cream until stiff, flavour with the icing sugar and fold in the raspberries. Pile the cream in a serving dish and surround with the hot toast, sprinkled with a little caster sugar and cinnamon. Serve at once.

Or: Serve the toast by itself with a sprinkling of caster sugar and cinnamon and with cream on the side.

Kickshaws

Useful standbys to use when you need a pudding at short notice. They have been popular in England from the fifteenth century, and they freeze surprisingly well.

Serves 4–6 Storage time: 1 month

225 gr (8 oz) puff pastry
apricot jam
1 beaten egg
vegetable or cooking oil for deep frying
caster sugar

Roll the pastry on a floured board until it is as thin as possible but still easily handled. Cut into circles with a 7·5-cm (3-in) pastry cutter. Knead pastry trimmings together, roll out again and cut as many more circles as you can. Place a spoonful of apricot jam in the centre of the circles, brush the edges with beaten egg and pinch them together firmly with the fingers. Seal the edges by pressing them gently with the back of a fork. Heat the oil until smoking, add the kickshaws, a few at a time, and cook for a few minutes only until they are puffed up, crisp and a pale golden brown. Drain them on crumpled kitchen paper.

To freeze: Cool, pack in a rigid container with plastic film or waxed paper between each layer; seal, label and freeze.

To use: Place the frozen kickshaws on a lightly greased baking sheet and heat through in a hot oven (450°F, 230°C, regulo 8) until crisp, golden-brown and hot through. Or, better still, fry the kickshaws again (just a few at a time), in very hot, deep oil, for a few minutes until puffed, hot through and golden-brown.

Rich almond cheesecake

Serves 6–8 Storage time: 2 months

225 gr (8 oz) shortcrust pastry (see page 229)
225 gr (8 oz) full fat cream cheese
2 tablespoons double cream
4 egg yolks
50 gr (2 oz) butter
grated rind ½ lemon
100 gr (4 oz) crushed macaroons
75 gr (3 oz) ground almonds
75 gr (3 oz) caster sugar
grated nutmeg

Line a 22-cm (9-in) flan case with the pastry (rolled as thinly as possible).

Mix the cheese with the cream until smooth. Beat the egg yolks and mix them into the cheese and cream. Melt the butter and add that to the cheese with the lemon rind, macaroons, ground almonds and sugar. Spread the mixture in the case and bake in a moderate oven (350°F, 180°C, regulo 4) for 30 minutes.

To freeze: Cool, pack between cardboard plates in a polythene bag; seal, label and freeze.

To use: Thaw in its wrapping at room temperature for about 4 hours. Unwrap and bake in a moderate oven (350°F, 180°C, regulo 4) for 12–15 minutes until golden-brown and hot through. Sprinkle with a little grated nutmeg and serve hot or warm with cream.

Note: If the pie browns too quickly during the first cooking, cover it with a sheet of greaseproof paper dipped into cold water.

Iced biscuit pudding

Serves 6 Storage time: 1 month

3 dl (½ pint) double cream	75 gr (3 oz) icing sugar
1·5 dl (¼ pint) single cream	12 ginger biscuits
4 tablespoons medium dry sherry	50 gr (2 oz) nibbed almonds

Whip the double cream until stiffening, then gradually whip in the single cream (the creams should not be *too* stiff). Turn the cream into a loaf tin and freeze for about 30 minutes until it is nearly frozen through. Remove it from the freezer, turn into a bowl and break up with a wooden spoon. Whisk in the sherry and icing sugar, whipping until the mixture is light and fluffy. Crumble the ginger biscuits with a rolling pin and fold half of them into the cream mixture and return it to the loaf tin. Cover with foil, pack in a polythene bag and return to the freezer.

To use: Roast the almonds in a hot oven until golden-brown. Turn out the ice-cream by dipping the tin into very hot water for a minute. Cover on the top and sides with the remaining crumbs and the nuts and serve at once.

Note: While the ice-cream is in the freezer the biscuit crumbs for decoration can be kept fresh in a sealed polythene bag.

Bread and baking

Bread, buns and rolls are among the four-star freezers – the produce that freezes particularly well. Buy top-quality bread from a baker who makes his own, or bake bread yourself in batches, to freeze in bulk.

You can freeze uncooked dough, but, on the whole, I find it preferable to freeze the fully baked article.

Bread is easy to make (with practice), and you get swifter and more efficient at the process every time you make it.

Bake when you have the time. Use fresh yeast if you can get it (most shops that bake their own bread sell fresh yeast; if you have to use dried yeast, see the packet or tin for the equivalent quantity to use). Freeze in quantities to ensure that your family have a good stock of really delicious bread that is even nicer than Mother used to make.

Unless you make toast, the best bread and rolls are those that are as fresh as the day they were baked. A deep freeze makes it possible to have delicious fresh bread every day of the year.

Bread should be thawed in its wrapping for about 6 hours at room temperature. Bread or rolls that are to be served hot and crisp can be put straight from the freezer into a moderately hot oven for 10–25 minutes, depending on size. Frozen slices can be toasted, allowing a few more minutes than for unfrozen bread.

Note: Bread that has been frozen will not keep fresh for quite as long a time as unfrozen bread, so only take out what you will require for one serving at a time.

Wholemeal breakfast rolls

Enough for 16 rolls Storage time: 3 months

225 gr (8 oz) wholemeal flour	1·5 dl (¼ pint) milk
225 gr (8 oz) strong plain flour	1·5 dl (¼ pint) water
2 teaspoons salt	14 gr (½ oz) fresh yeast
2 teaspoons caster sugar	7 gr (¼ oz) lard

Sift the flours into a bowl and mix in the salt and sugar. Combine the milk and water and heat to just above blood temperature (100°F/ 38°C). Blend the liquid into the yeast until smooth and leave to stand in a warm place for 5 minutes. Rub the lard into the flour with fingertips until the mixture resembles coarse breadcrumbs.

Make a well in the centre of the flour mixture, pour in the yeast liquid and gradually draw in the flour, mixing until the dough is smooth and comes away cleanly from the sides of the bowl.

Place the dough in a lightly greased bowl, cover with a cloth and leave to stand in a warm, draught-free place until well risen and doubled in bulk. Turn the risen dough on to a floured board and knead until smooth. Divide into 16 rolls, shaping them on a floured board and flattening them lightly. Place the rolls on a greased baking sheet, dust with a little flour and cover with a light cloth. Leave to rise in a warm place until doubled in size.

Bake in a hot oven (450°F, 230°C, regulo 8) for about 20 minutes until the rolls sound hollow when tapped.

To freeze: Cool the rolls on a wire rack and pack in a polythene bag; seal, label and freeze.

To use: Place the frozen rolls on a baking tray and heat in a moderate oven (350°F, 180°C, regulo 4) for 20 minutes or until crisp and hot through.

Household white bread

Enough to fill 1 × 900-gr (2-lb) tin or 2 × 450-gr (1-lb) tins

Storage time: 3 months

50 gr (2 oz) fresh yeast
1 teaspoon sugar
9 dl (1½ pints) water
1·35 kg (3 lb) strong plain flour
2 teaspoons salt
50 gr (2 oz) lard

Cream together the yeast and sugar. Heat the water to just above blood temperature (100°F/38°C) and blend into the yeast. Leave the mixture in a warm place for about 10 minutes until fermented and spongy.

Combine together the flour and salt in a bowl. Rub in the lard with fingertips until the mixture resembles coarse breadcrumbs and make a well in the centre. Pour in the yeast mixture and draw it into the flour using a wooden spoon and beating until the mixture forms a stiff dough which comes cleanly away from the sides of the pan. Turn on to a floured board (use white flour for kneading) and knead the dough for 10 minutes with the knuckles until it is smooth and elastic.

Place the dough in a lightly greased bowl, cover with a floured cloth and leave to rise in a warm place for about 1 hour until doubled in bulk.

Turn the dough on to a floured board and knead again (for about 5 minutes) until smooth and elastic once more. Return to the greased bowl again and leave to rise once more for a further 30 minutes. Shape into loaves, place the dough in greased tins and punch down firmly. Cover with a floured cloth and leave to rise a third time until it is once more doubled in bulk (about 30 minutes).

Bake the bread in a hot oven (450°F, 230°C, regulo 8) for 45 minutes until golden-brown, shrinking from the sides of the pan and sounding hollow when turned out and tapped on the bottom.

To freeze: Turn out on to wire racks, leave to cool. Pack in polythene bags, seal, label and freeze.

To use: Thaw in wrapping for 4–5 hours at room temperature. In emergencies, remove wrapping and place the bread in a moderately hot oven (350°F, 180°C, regulo 4) for 20 minutes – this will produce instant crusty bread but will shorten its freezer after-life.

Baps

Fresh bread is far more delicious and often cheaper than bought bread. Baps can be used as a base for hamburgers or a pizza topping, or they can be split and spread with clotted cream and strawberry jam.

Makes 10 baps   Storage time: 3 months

450 gr (1 lb) strong plain flour
1 teaspoon salt
50 gr (2 oz) butter
12 gr (½ oz) fresh yeast
1·5 dl (¼ pint) water
1·5 dl (¼ pint) milk

Sieve the flour into a bowl with the salt. Add the butter cut into small pieces and rub it into the flour with your fingertips. Combine the yeast with a little warm water and cream with a wooden spoon until smooth. Heat remaining water and milk until they reach 100°F/38°C or just over blood temperature. Blend the warm liquid into the yeast.

Add the yeast mixture to the flour, and mix with a wooden spoon until the ingredients form a stiff dough. Turn the dough on to a well-floured board and knead for 10 minutes until smooth and elastic.

Put the dough into a greased polythene bag and leave in a warm place to rise for about 1 hour, until the dough has doubled in bulk. Return to a floured board and knead again until firm and elastic. Divide the dough into 10 balls and flatten each one lightly with the palm of your hand. Place them on a floured baking sheet and dust lightly with flour. Cover with greased polythene and leave in a warm place for 20 minutes or until doubled in size.

Bake in a hot oven (425°F, 220°C, regulo 7) for 10–15 minutes until lightly browned.

To freeze: Cool, pack in polythene bags; seal, label and freeze.

To use: Thaw unwrapped for 1 hour at room temperature or reheat baps in a medium-hot oven (350°F, 180°C, regulo 4) for 10 minutes.

Baps with pizza topping

Serves 4

4 baps
1 small tin tomatoes
1 onion
2 tablespoons olive or cooking oil
pinch thyme and oregano
salt and freshly ground black pepper
8 slices mozzarella cheese
4 anchovy fillets

Cut each bap in half. Roughly chop the tomatoes. Peel and finely chop the onion. Heat 1 tablespoon olive oil in a saucepan. Add the onion and cook over a low heat until soft and transparent. Add the tomatoes and herbs, season with salt and freshly ground black pepper, bring to the boil, cover and simmer for 20 minutes, stirring every now and then to prevent sticking.

Brush the cut side of the baps with oil and spread with the tomato mixture. Top with half an anchovy, sliced lengthwise, and with a slice of cheese. Grill under a high heat until the cheese has melted and is bubbling.

Serve with salad.

Traditional pizzas

There is all the difference in the world between good and bad pizzas. Bad ones are too heavy on the pastry and too light on the filling, stodgy things that swell in your mouth and taste of cotton wool. A true Italian pizza is succulent and juicy, rich in aroma and taste, and generous with its filling.

Pizzas freeze well and make excellent and quickly produced snacks, picnics or supper meals.

Serves 4–6
Storage time: 1 month if garlic is included; 3 months if it is not

225 gr (8 oz) plain flour
1 teaspoon salt
4 tablespoons milk
1 teaspoon sugar
18 gr (¾ oz) fresh yeast
1 beaten egg
37 gr (1½ oz) melted butter
2 onions
2 cloves garlic (optional)
1 × 225-gr (8-oz) tin tomatoes
1 tablespoon olive oil
salt and freshly ground black pepper
pinch marjoram
¼ teaspoon dried oregano
pinch dried sage
1 tablespoon tomato purée
225 gr (8 oz) mozzarella cheese
1 tin anchovy fillets
8 black olives, halved and stoned

Sieve the flour with 1 teaspoon of salt into a warmed mixing bowl. Heat the milk to 100°F/38°C (just above blood temperature). Add the sugar to the yeast in a warmed bowl and mix to a paste. Add the milk and leave to stand in a warm place until the yeast mixture is spongy. Pour the yeast mixture into the centre of the flour and add the beaten egg and melted butter. Mix to a firm dough with a wooden spoon and then turn on to a floured board and knead until well blended, smooth and elastic. Put the dough into a greased polythene bag and leave in a warm place until doubled in bulk (about 1 hour).

Peel and finely chop the onion. (Peel and finely chop the garlic if used.) Chop the tinned tomatoes. Heat the olive oil, add the onion (and garlic) and cook over a low heat until transparent. Add the tomatoes, season with salt and freshly ground black pepper and add the herbs. Mix in the tomato purée, bring to the boil, cover and simmer for 20 minutes. Cut the cheese into the thinnest possible slices.

Return the dough to a floured board and knead once more until smooth and elastic. Roll out lightly to an oblong about 6 mm (¼ in) thick and turn up the edges slightly to form a ridge.

Drain the anchovy fillets. Spread the tomato filling thickly on top of the pizza and top with the anchovy fillets and black olives arranged in a pattern. Cover with slices of cheese.

To freeze: Open-freeze, then pack in a polythene bag; seal, label and freeze.

To use: Place unwrapped frozen pizza on a lightly greased baking sheet. Bake in a preheated moderately hot oven, (375°F, 190°C, regulo 5) for 30–35 minutes or until the cheese topping is melted and the pizza is golden-brown around the edges. Serve hot, warm or cold.

Or: Cook the pizza for 20 minutes before freezing; cool, pack, seal, label and freeze. Thaw the half-cooked pizza for 2 hours at room temperature, then put into a moderately hot oven (350°F, 180°C, regulo 4) and cook for a further 15 minutes.

Variations

Replace anchovies with thinly sliced mushrooms lightly sautéed in butter.

Replace anchovies with 150 gr (6 oz) very thinly sliced streaky bacon with the rinds removed.

Instead of the tomatoes, make a filling of very thinly sliced onions, divided into rings, cooked until soft in butter and combined with thin fillets of anchovies.

Note: For extra-quick pizza substitutes, spread the above fillings on thick slices of white bread with the crusts removed. Bake in a moderately hot oven (375°F, 190°C, regulo 5) for 15 minutes or until the cheese has melted and the underneath of the bread is crisp.

Teacakes

Makes 6 large teacakes Storage time: 3 months

25 gr (1 oz) fresh yeast	1·5 dl (¼ pint) water
1 teaspoon caster sugar	1·5 dl (¼ pint) milk

450 gr (1 lb) strong plain flour	25 gr (1 oz) butter
1 teaspoon salt	50 gr (2 oz) currants
25 gr (1 oz) sugar	milk

Cream the yeast with 1 teaspoon caster sugar. Mix in the water and milk warmed to just above blood temperature (100°F/ 38°C). Leave in a warm place for 10–15 minutes until spongy and fermented.

Combine the flour, salt and 25 gr (1 oz) sugar in a bowl and rub in the butter with fingertips until the mixture resembles coarse breadcrumbs. Add the currants, mix well and shape a well in the centre. Add the yeast mixture and mix until the ingredients form a firm, pliable dough. Turn on to a floured board and knead until smooth and elastic. Place the dough in a greased bowl, cover with a floured cloth and leave to rise in a warm place until doubled in bulk (about 1 hour).

Knead the dough on a floured board again, divide into 6 pieces, roll into balls and roll out lightly to about 15 cm (6 in) in diameter. Place on a greased baking sheet, cover with a floured cloth and leave to rise again until doubled in size. Brush with milk. Bake in a preheated oven (400°F, 200°C, regulo 6) for 15 minutes or until golden-brown.

To freeze: Cool as quickly as possible, pack in polythene bags; seal, label and freeze.

To use: Remove from the bag, place in a moderately hot oven (375°, 190°C, regulo 5) for about 10 minutes until piping hot. Split and spread with butter, or split, toast on split side and then butter.

Pickling and preserving

Good bargains in food are often available just when you are at your busiest. Ingredients for making pickles and chutneys, (often second-quality produce or 'glut' material) usually have to be utilized quickly. Don't worry if you don't have the time to preserve at that very moment; freeze the basic ingredients and use them later when you have time, on a wet weekend or a quiet evening.

These often old-fashioned pickles and relishes may be bought ready-made, but the cheap ones bear no relation to the real thing and the better varieties are very expensive.

Here are some ideas for exciting home-made chutneys, sauces and relishes, with recipes for the product and instructions on freezing the basic ingredients.

Note: I have given quantities for small amounts of preserves: increase all the ingredients if you wish to make in bulk. Use an aluminium pan for making preserves.

Pickled damsons

Good with cold chicken, hot or cold game, meat and game pies, and with roast pork.

Freezing damsons

Pick over damsons and wash if necessary. Pack without sugar in polythene bags; seal, label and freeze.
Storage time: 6 months

Recipe

For each pound of damsons:
2 sticks cinnamon
8 cloves
4 pieces root ginger
225 gr (8 oz) granulated sugar
malt vinegar

Thaw fruit in a refrigerator overnight and place it in an earthenware dish. Add the spices, sprinkle over the sugar and pour over just enough vinegar to cover. Cook at the bottom of a very low oven (300°F, 150°C, regulo 2) for 20 minutes until the damsons are beginning to soften. Leave to cool. Pour off the cold juice from the damsons and pour it through a fine sieve into a saucepan. Bring the sauce to the boil, pour straight over the fruit and leave to get cold again. Repeat the straining and boiling process once a day for 10 days and then leave the damsons to stand for a further 7 days before bottling. On the last day, strain off the juice, remove the spices and pack the damsons in clean jars. Bring the juice to the boil, pour it over the fruit and seal the jar with a piece of waxed paper and a cover of cellophane tied on tightly.

Keep for 2 months before opening.

Note: This straining and boiling process for damsons is more complicated than most recipes and is necessary because of the extremely tough skins, and the bitterness of the fruit.

Green tomato chutney

Green tomatoes are always available at the end of the season and since there is really no other good use for them, this delicious chutney cries out to be made.

Freezing green tomatoes

Remove the stalks, wash and dry the tomatoes and remove the skins by plunging tomatoes in boiling water for 2 minutes and

then slipping off the skins. Chop the tomatoes roughly, pack them in polythene bags, seal, label and freeze.
Storage time: 3 months

Recipe

450 gr (1 lb) green tomatoes
100 gr (4 oz) cooking apples
100 gr (4 oz) onions
1·5 dl (¼ pint) malt vinegar
100 gr (4 oz) sugar
¼ teaspoon dry mustard
1 teaspoon cayenne pepper
½ teaspoon salt
50 gr (2 oz) sultanas

Put the frozen tomatoes in a heavy pan and heat over a gentle heat until thawed. Peel and finely chop the apples. Peel and finely chop the onions.

Add the apples and onions to the thawed tomatoes with half the vinegar. Cook over a low heat until the apples and tomatoes are soft, stirring well. Add the rest of the vinegar, the sugar, seasoning and sultanas and cook for a further 10 to 15 minutes, by which time the chutney should be thickish and rich-looking, but in no way dried out.

Transfer the chutney to pots; cover, cool and seal.

Apple and mint chutney

Freezing apples

Peel, core and finely chop apples and put them in a solution of water and 1 tablespoon salt to every quart of water; drain well, pack in polythene bags, seal, label and freeze.
Storage time: 6 months

Recipe

900 gr (2 lb) cooking apples or windfalls
2 large ripe tomatoes
3 large onions
2 sticks celery
1 teaspoon dry English mustard
1 teaspoon cayenne pepper
6 dl (1 pint) malt vinegar
100 gr (4 oz) stoned raisins
2 tablespoons finely chopped mint
225 gr (8 oz) soft brown sugar
1 teaspoon salt

Leave the apples to thaw in the refrigerator overnight. Skin the tomatoes by dipping them into boiling water for 2 minutes and then slipping off the skins. Chop the tomatoes; peel and finely chop the onions. Finely chop the celery. Make the mustard and cayenne pepper into a paste with 1 tablespoon of the vinegar.

Combine the apples with the other ingredients and the mustard mixture, but not the sugar or salt, in a preserving pan; add half the vinegar and cook over a low heat for about 20 minutes or until all the ingredients are soft.

Add the sugar, salt and remaining vinegar, mix well, bring to the boil and cook for a further 10–15 minutes until the chutney is thick, rich-looking and shiny.

Leave to cool for 10 minutes; pack into clean jars and cover and seal.

Leave for 6 months, if you can, before eating.

Three Musketeers tomato ketchup

So much better than the bottled variety, and easy to make. Keep empty ketchup and sauce bottles for your own home-made products.

Note: This is an exciting, spicy chutney. If you prefer a more straightforward variety, leave out the peppers, chillis and celery.

Freezing tomatoes

Skin the tomatoes by covering them with boiling water for about 2 minutes and then slipping off the skins. Chop the tomatoes finely and remove any tough core. Pack them in polythene containers; seal, label and freeze.
Storage time: 3 months

Recipe

1 onion
2 cloves garlic
2 green or red peppers
2 red chillis
4 sticks celery
1·35 kg (3 lb) tomatoes
½ teaspoon paprika pepper
1 teaspoon cayenne pepper
juice 1 orange and 1 lemon
1 teaspoon salt
225 gr (8 oz) granulated sugar
1 tablespoon finely chopped mint
3 dl (½ pint) white wine vinegar

Leave tomatoes to thaw at room temperature for about 3 hours.

Peel and finely chop the onion and garlic cloves. Remove the core and seeds of the peppers and chillis and finely chop the flesh. Very finely chop the celery, and put all the vegetables in a preserving pan with the tomatoes. Cook over a low heat for 20 minutes until onions and tomatoes are really mushy. Add remaining ingredients and continue to cook until the sauce is thick and smooth. Taste for seasoning.

Rub at once through a fairly fine sieve to remove the tomato seeds, and bottle while hot in clean bottles (the Heinz wide-necked tomato-ketchup bottles are ideal). If you use narrow-necked bottles, pour the ketchup from a jug or through a funnel.

Sterilize the filled bottles to prevent fermentation in the ketchup. Place the filled bottles with the tops lightly screwed on in a large pan, on a false bottom to prevent their cracking. Fill the pan with water to the height of the ketchup and bring slowly to the boil. Boil fast for 15 minutes and then remove the bottles using a cloth or gloves, and screw the tops as tightly as you possibly can.

Store the ketchup in a cool, dark place. Keep the ketchup in the refrigerator once it has been opened.

Mushroom ketchup

Although this is an old-fashioned ketchup and seldom seen these days, a little is almost magical for flavouring soups, casseroles and gravies and tastes so much nicer than commercial varieties.

It is best made with those lovely field mushrooms that are large, firm and black, picked when the weather is fine.

Freezing mushrooms for ketchup

Wipe the mushrooms clean and break them into pieces with the hands – do not cut with a knife. Place them in a bowl and sprinkle each layer with salt. Leave to stand overnight. Rinse the mushrooms in cold water, mash them with a fork and pack them in a polythene container. Seal, label and freeze.
Storage time: 2–3 months

Recipe

675 gr (1½ lb) mushrooms
37 gr (1½ oz) salt
¼ teaspoon ground mace
¼ teaspoon ground ginger
1 teaspoon ground black pepper
3 dl (½ pint) malt vinegar
2 tablespoons port

Leave the mushrooms to thaw at room temperature for about 4 hours.

Put the mushrooms in a preserving pan with the other ingredients, except the port. Cook over a low heat for 30 minutes. Strain through a fine sieve, stir in the port and bottle at once. Screw down the caps and sterilize in the same way as for tomato ketchup (see previous recipe), but simmering the bottles for a good 30 minutes.

Marmalade

Seville oranges are only available for a short period and it may not always be possible for you to make marmalade at just that time. The oranges for making marmalade, however, freeze satisfactorily and can be kept for up to six months in the deep freeze. If you are short of room in your freezer, you can part-cook the marmalade, to the pulp stage, then freeze the pulp and finish making the marmalade later.

Freezing whole Seville oranges

Wash and dry oranges, remove the stalk ends and pack them in polythene bags. Seal, label and freeze.

To thaw: Do not unwrap. Thaw oranges in a refrigerator allowing 7 hours' thawing time to each pound of fruit.
Storage time: 6 months

Recipe

1·35 kg (3 lb) Seville oranges
juice 3 lemons
3·5 litres (6 pints) water
2·7 kg (6 lb) preserving sugar

Halve the thawed oranges, squeeze out as much juice as possible, strain the orange and lemon juice, and remove and reserve the pips. Very thinly pare off the rind of the oranges and cut it into thin strips. Chop the white pith and membrane. Combine the pith and pips in a large muslin bag, allowing plenty of room for water to circulate through the bag. Tie the bag tightly.

Place the peel, fruit juice and muslin bag in a large, heavy pan and cover with the water. Bring to the boil and simmer very gently for 2 hours, by which time the peel should be quite soft. Leave to stand in a cool place for 24 hours. Remove the muslin bag and squeeze well to extract all the juices. Add the sugar to the ingredients in the pan and cook over a low heat, stirring continuously, until the sugar is dissolved. Bring to the boil and boil rapidly over a high heat for about 30 minutes or until a little of the jelly put on to a saucer will set.

Pour into clean, warmed jars whilst the marmalade is still hot, and cover and seal at once.

Makes about 3·5 kg (8 lb) marmalade.

Index